William Symington

Messiah the Prince

The Meditorial Dominion of Jesus Christ

William Symington

Messiah the Prince
The Meditorial Dominion of Jesus Christ

ISBN/EAN: 9783744660617

Printed in Europe, USA, Canada, Australia, Japan

Cover: Foto ©Lupo / pixelio.de

More available books at **www.hansebooks.com**

MESSIAH THE PRINCE:

OR,

The Mediatorial Dominion of

JESUS CHRIST.

BY

WILLIAM SYMINGTON, D.D.,

LATE PROFESSOR OF THEOLOGY IN THE REFORMED PRESBYTERIAN CHURCH.

WITH

A MEMOIR OF THE AUTHOR

By HIS SONS.

London:
T. NELSON AND SONS, PATERNOSTER ROW.
EDINBURGH; AND NEW YORK.

1881.

EDITOR'S PREFACE.

DR. SYMINGTON's reputation as an author rests chiefly on his treatises on the Atonement and Intercession, and on the Mediatorial Dominion, of Jesus Christ. The former was published at the beginning of 1834, the latter at the beginning of 1839. Both books were popular in their day, and still hold a good place in theological literature.

The Atonement met a felt want. in this country, and four editions of it were issued in the United States, where it was used for a text-book for students. But during these forty-five years several valuable books have been produced on the same subject and constructed on the same main lines of Scriptural Calvinism. The works of Dr. Candlish, Dr. Crawford, Dr. Hodge, Mr. Dale and others, treat of the Atonement with reference to phases of thought which had not become prominent when Dr. Symington wrote.

A similar remark cannot be made regarding his other treatise. Much has been written—more spoken—on practical questions relating to the reign of the Mediator; but what the author said in his preface in 1839 remains true in 1879. No book dealing with the subject systematically and comprehensively, as a matter of theology rather than of polemics, has appeared. It is on this account that *Messiah the Prince* has been selected to be issued afresh as a memorial of one whose name will long be fragrant.

And also because the matter is one of high importance, the interest of which increases with time and the developments of Providence. Several who to-day occupy foremost places in the Church of Christ have recently expressed to the Editor their obligations to this book at the time when their opinions were forming. Its publication during the Ten Years' Conflict was recognised as highly opportune; and it may a second time be of service in guiding some to apprehend the teaching of Scripture concerning the relation in which the reigning Saviour stands to the Church and the State and the World.

Dr. Symington went over the same ground which is gone over here in his lectures as Professor of Theology. These lectures have been carefully used in preparing this edition, so that it has the advantage of a revision by the author himself twenty years after the first publication. It must be understood that any changes which may be observed have been made in this way. In one or two places these are considerable, but they affect the order of thought rather than the thought itself.

A. M. S.

BIRKENHEAD, 1879.

CONTENTS.

MEMOIR . . xvii

CHAPTER I.

NECESSITY OF THE MEDIATORIAL DOMINION.

INTRODUCTORY REMARKS	1
Connexion of Christ's offices	3
Importance of the mediatorial dominion	3
Terms explained	6
Mediatorial dominion necessary	6
To fulfil the divine purposes	7
To complete the character of the Saviour	9
To reward his obedience to the death	10
To bear down his enemies	12
To meet the wants of his people	14

CHAPTER II.

REALITY OF THE MEDIATORIAL DOMINION.

Prefigurations	17
Prophecies	19
Titles	21
Personal claims	21
Acknowledgment of others	22
Regal appendages	23

CHAPTER III.

QUALIFICATIONS FOR THE MEDIATORIAL DOMINION.

Personal dignity	28
Near relationship	30

CONTENTS.

	PAGE
Knowledge and wisdom	32
Power	33
Moral worth	34
Compassion and bounty	37
Authority	38

CHAPTER IV.

APPOINTMENT OF CHRIST TO MEDIATORIAL DOMINION.

Formally appointed from eternity	40
Solemnly set apart in the fulness of time	41
Actually invested at resurrection	43
Attested by many witnesses	45
Difficulties removed	46
Gives validity to mediatorial acts in all ages	47
Confers a right to subjection	48
Secures the overthrow of enemies	49

CHAPTER V.

SPIRITUALITY OF THE MEDIATORIAL DOMINION.

Not that it has no sort of connexion with what is secular	51
Spiritual in its Origin	51
Ends	53
Administration	54
Principles	56
Concomitants	57
Neglect of Spirituality the error of Jews	64
Millennarians	65
Papists	66
Test for trying Protestant churches	67
Means of testing personal character	69

CHAPTER VI.

UNIVERSALITY OF THE MEDIATORIAL DOMINION.

Importance of this view	71
Scripture proof	73
Embraces Inanimate creation	77
Inferior animals	79
Holy angels	82
Fallen angels	89

Embraces The family of man	95
Human associations	97
Providential dispensations	98
Objections answered	100
That tends to exclude the Father and Spirit	100
That confounds essential and mediatorial rule	101
That lays foundation for divine honours	102
That supposes the wicked to be interested in Christ	103
That it is at variance with fact	106
Glorifying to Christ	106
Comforting to Saints	107
Appalling to Sinners	108

CHAPTER VII.

THE MEDIATORIAL DOMINION OVER THE CHURCH.

Term *church* explained	110
Visible church defined	111
Sect. I. Christ gives the visible church existence	115
In every period	115
Marks of the true church	117
Sect. II. Organises, incorporates, and purchases it	120
Organises	120
Incorporates by covenant	121
Purchases with blood	123
Sect. III. Confers on it interesting properties	126
Spirituality	126
Independence	127
Subjection to Christ	128
Unity	129
Universality	136
Perpetuity	137
Sect. IV. Accomplishes important ends by it	139
The glory of God	139
The display of truth	140
The celebration of worship	142
The salvation of souls	144
Sect. V. Institutes its ordinances	146
Laws	147
Worship	149
Government	150
Discipline	151
Sect. VI. Prescribes the qualifications of members	153
Intelligent orthodoxy	153
Submission to ordinances	155

CONTENTS.

	PAGE
Apparent experience	155
Consistent conduct	156
These must be united	157
Actual saintship not the term of admission	158
SECT. VII. Appoints, qualifies, and invests office-bearers	164
Office-bearers necessary	164
Presbyters permanent office-bearers	166
These appointed by ordination	169
Ordination what	170
To whom it belongs	171
What it confers	175
The powers of office-bearers	176
Their qualifications	177
SECT. VIII. Renders administration effectual	179
Subdues	180
Comforts	181
Rules in heart	181
Protects	182
Consummates grace	183
SECT. IX. Diffuses and perpetuates	184
Universal diffusion	184
Perpetual duration	187
Concluding reflections	188

CHAPTER VIII.

THE MEDIATORIAL DOMINION OVER THE NATIONS.

SECT. I. Proof of the fact	192
Scripture injunctions	194
Ps. ii. 10	194
Predictions	197
Ps. xlvii. 2–9	198
Ps. lxxii. 10, 11, 17	198
Isa. xlix. 22, 23	199
Isa. lx. 10, 12, 16	201
Ezek. xlv. 17	202
Dan. vii. 13, 14	203
Rev. xi. 15	203
Rev. xxi. 24, 26	204
Designations	205
Governor among the nations	206
Higher than kings of the earth	206
King of nations	207
Prince of the kings of the earth	207
King of kings	208
Objections considered	210

CONTENTS.

	PAGE
SECT. II. Administration over the nations	213
Gives them existence	213
Watches over them	216
Demands obedience	217
Overrules rebellion	219
Executes judgments	221
Opens a way for the gospel	224
Protects church from injury	227
Will effect an entire change	228
SECT. III. Duties of nations to Christ	230
To respect his glory	231
To take his law as their rule	234
To have respect to the qualifications of their rulers	241
To have regard to him in their subjection to rulers	249
To swear allegiance to him	256

CHAPTER IX.

THE MEDIATORIAL DOMINION OVER THE NATIONS, CONTINUED.

The duty of nations to have respect to religion	262
Importance of the subject	262
The question stated	263
The duty in question maintained	265
From Christ's dominion over the nations	265
From New Testament language	267
From approved examples	269
From the mutual connexion of church and state	269
What religion can do for a nation	279
Benefit its institutions	279
Promote its Liberty	280
Wealth	280
Peace	281
Morality	282
Security	282
What a nation can do for religion	285
Protect it	286
Profess it	286
Give sanction to the Sabbath	289
Restrain irreligion	291
Give pecuniary support	292
No confounding of things that differ	293
From the injurious effects of separating them	296
From the impossibility of an entire separation	297
The state of the primitive church no valid objection	311

	PAGE
Inattention to this subject deplored	313
The support of false religion censured	316
Appeal to several classes of persons	317

CHAPTER X.

PERPETUITY OF THE MEDIATORIAL DOMINION.

Mediatorial reign in glory explained	318
Diversity of sentiment on the subject	322
Explanation of 1 Cor. xv. 24–28	323
Perpetuity proved	333
From Scripture	333
From the reward of Christ	336
From the impossibility of its terminating	338
From the necessities of the redeemed	341
CONCLUSION	349

MEMOIR OF THE AUTHOR.

A CLAUSE in the will of Professor Symington directs that " the whole of my manuscripts shall be committed to the custody of my son William, to be disposed of as may be thought proper, with this express reservation, that no part of my manuscripts shall be printed excepting such as may be left by me in a fit state for the press, and with *explicit instructions* that they shall be disposed of in this way." No manuscripts were so left; but his son at once began to prepare a Memoir, and intended to have accompanied it with a re-issue of his principal works. The labour of love was interrupted by repeated and serious illnesses; and seasons of health were fully occupied in the exhausting toils of a city pastor.

Dr. William Symington, junior, died on the 9th of February 1879, having carried on the Memoir to the year 1823, on a plan which would have resulted in a large book. His being the oldest son, and therefore more our father's companion than any of us; his sharing with him the pastoral charge for three years; his fine taste and literary faculty, make it matter of very deep regret that he was not able to execute his plan. He clung to the hope of doing so to the very last.

The lapse of so many years, the very scanty leisure of a minister in a large town, and a sad heart, must be held to excuse a youngest child for having contracted the record of our father's life into the limits of a sketch. No father could ever have commanded more of the veneration and affection of his children; but this circumstance, creating a distressing sense of inadequacy, has made my task such that escape from it would have been eagerly welcomed, if any escape, consistent with filial duty, had appeared. That, of course, could not be.

Those who did not know William Symington will learn, in part, how excellent and good a man he was; and his character may be recommended to the study of those particularly who are entering on the ministry of the gospel. "Onward and Upward" was a motto chosen by himself long ago, and was true of his whole life.

Those who did know him will painfully feel how far this attempt to delineate Dr. Symington's admirable character has failed; but to such I may appeal, in the words of Tacitus about his life of Agricola, "aut laudatus erit aut excusatus." This sketch can scarcely be praised, but let it be excused.

ALEX. MACLEOD SYMINGTON.

BIRKENHEAD, *July* 1879.

MEMOIR OF THE AUTHOR.

CHAPTER I.

BIRTH AND TRAINING.   1795–1818.

ÆTATE 1-23.

WILLIAM SYMINGTON was born at Paisley on the 2d of June 1795. We are not able to gratify curiosity by tracing his genealogy far back into the past, or to supply notices of the remoter ancestors from whom he was sprung. The family of Symington seems to have had its origin in the upper ward of Lanarkshire, to one of the parishes of which, near the base of Tinto, it has given its name, as also to another parish in the district of Kyle in Ayrshire; and as early as the times of the haughty lords of Douglas, whose "coronet so often counterpoised the crown," it produced men of considerable note and influence. It is more to our purpose, however, to observe that this region of Scotland, where the name is still a common one, was the stronghold of that stricter section of the Presbyterian Church, who suffered so much during the twenty-eight years of faithful contending and fierce persecution preceding the Revolution, and who at that time—while deeply grateful for the deliverance brought to the land by the accession of William and Mary to the throne, and foremost to evince their loyalty by the raising of the famous "Cameronian Regiment"—still held out from the main body, contending for the preservation in all their integrity of the attainments of the second Reformation. To those representatives, as they held themselves, of the old free kirk of Scotland—known by the name of "the Society People" until the accession to their ranks in the year 1706 of the Rev. John M'Millan, and the constitution in 1743 of the "Reformed Presbytery"—belonged the more immediate progenitors of the subject of this memoir. His grandfather occupied the farm of Shields, in the parish of Douglas; and several of the neighbouring farms, Poniel, Place, Monkshead, Crowhill, &c., were tenanted by his grand-uncles. From the last-named place, when on a visit to his friends there, we find him dating a boyish letter to his father: "From the seat of the Symingtons for five hundred years." His grandfather's house was frequently the abode of the earlier ministers of the denomination, when preaching and dispensing ordinances in that locality, and here a large family was carefully and piously reared, among whom was William Symington, his father, who was accustomed to tell with much humour how grievously one of these old ministers (the elder Fairley, we believe) had put him to the blush, when a little boy, before the whole family, by the question, "What made you so loud at your prayers this morning, William?"—which instantly called forth the self-condemning vindication, "It couldna' be me, I prayed nane."

When but a young man, this William left the parental

home, and settled in the town of Paisley, where, in the first instance, he laboured at the loom (a very different occupation then from what it has now become), and afterwards, when regard for his health led him to abandon sedentary work, entered into business as a woollen and linen merchant. His previous habits of industry, his frugality and enterprise, enabled him, with the blessing of God, to earn for himself and his household, in this business, an honourable competency. Some yet surviving can remember with pleasure his shop at the cross at Paisley, and its genial occupant. His natural talents, which were of no mean order, were made the more marked and memorable in their development by his shrewd wit, and a strong vein of humour and keen relish for innocent jocularity, while all about him was pervaded by that genuine, consistent, Christian character, in virtue of which he left to children and children's children the best of all inheritances. Not long after his settlement in Paisley he was united in marriage to Marion Brown, a help-meet of strong natural good sense and sterling Christian worth, and the member of a family distinguished for godliness. These pious parents were blessed with a numerous offspring, whom they brought up, as they had themselves been trained, in intelligent attachment to the principles of the Scottish Covenanted Reformation, and in the love and practice of holiness. Three of their sons were early dedicated to the ministry of the Church,—Andrew, the eldest, to whose life and labours we shall have occasion frequently to refer,— James, the youngest, who after affording high promise of future usefulness, and having been just licensed to preach the gospel, was cut down in the flower of life in April 1830,—and WILLIAM, ten years the junior of Andrew, whose earthly career we would now attempt to sketch.

Of his childhood and early youth we have not much information over which to linger. When about six years of age he was sent to an elementary school, where he remained till he had acquired some knowledge of English reading, grammar, writing, and accounts. Four years afterwards he entered the Paisley Grammar School, in which he continued a pupil for upwards of four years, and where he appears to have devoted himself with assiduity to the proper business of the classes through which he passed, and was always distinguished by more than a respectable station among his schoolfellows. There is no reason to think that his early youth afforded any remarkable promise of future distinction. There was no extraordinary precocity of talent, nor marked devotedness to the service of Christ, perceptible at this time. He was not exempt, probably, from those faults and follies which commonly bring a healthy schoolboy, with exuberance of natural spirit, into "scrapes." There may have been only too good reason for the trenchant rebuke of a servant in the family who, indignant at some juvenile misdemeanour which seemed in her eyes flagrantly inconsistent with the sacred calling to which even then he was supposed to aspire, exclaimed: "They'll be scant o' wood for the tabernacle, if they take thee to make a pin o't." It is manifest, however, that the propensity to evil was powerfully held in check by the wholesome restraints of parental government; by the example and counsel of his brother Andrew, who was early distinguished for gravity of character, and to whom he was not only then but ever afterwards accustomed to look up; and, above all and through all, by the gracious influence of Him to whom he had been dedicated from the womb, and to whom his pious mother was wont in devout humility to trace every promise of goodness and greatness in her sons. "You may well be proud of two such sons" (as Andrew and William), once said an acquaintance to Mrs. Symington, after the younger had begun to share the fame of the elder as a preacher; "they are as great an honour to you as if they had been two emperors." "No, no," was the Christian matron's reply, "give the honour to whom it is due; many a mother has ta'en mair pains than I ha'e done wi' twa ne'er-do-weels."

Among his private papers, one of the earliest date is a fragment in the form of an autobiography written when he was a Student of Divinity, and not afterwards resumed. It is a deeply interesting document, in which his object is to trace the influences which had contributed to the formation of his own character, and to assist him in ascertaining whether or not his mind had been truly brought under the power of divine grace. We could not better fulfil this part of our task than by presenting the reader with extracts from this fragment. In the outset we find him deploring that, throughout his schoolboy days, he was "a stranger to religious principle or even to serious thought, and plunged into all the frivolities of thoughtless childhood." "The wicked practices of my associates, in which I too readily joined, shall always be remembered with pungent grief. Here (the

Grammar School) the bad example of all around was too powerful to be counteracted by the pious instruction and sober walk of the domestic circle in which I lived. I shewed myself a depraved sinner by choosing the path of wickedness and turning my back on the way of rectitude." His aversion to *public* schools in after life, and preference of *home* education for his own children, may perhaps be in some measure accounted for by his recollection of their injurious moral influence on himself.

But the same record from which these words are taken contains abundant evidence that even thus early the Spirit of all grace was striving with His child, that the life-long struggle in which he was to be more than conqueror had already begun.

"The only subject of a grave kind with which I was at an early period impressed, and upon which I remember to have ruminated till quite overwhelmed, was one calculated to arrest the attention and confound the comprehension of a mind greater than that of a frivolous child—*eternity of misery*. A slavish fear of condemnation was no doubt at the bottom of my early contemplations of this awfully sublime subject, as I well remember not to have been so deeply impressed with its opposite—*everlasting felicity*. But even the appalling consideration which seemed to arrest my early thoughts was soon forgotten." "I remember only once during this period to have experienced something like what may be called *a religious fit*. The frivolity and sinful amusements of my class-fellows were exchanged for prayer and reading the Scriptures and other pious books. My natural levity was, as it were, for a moment transformed into the utmost composure and gravity. I selected from the school-boys one the circumstances of whose education and manners induced me to reveal to him my thoughts. A proposal was made to engage mutually in the same exercises, and to stir one another up by our company and youthful epistles, which was readily complied with. But this confidential treaty being discovered by some of our fellows, it became the subject of much ridicule and taunt. Our share of fortitude was too scanty to oppose the scorn of those around, and in a short time our youthful resolutions and ardent hopes were as though they had not been."

Having completed the usual course of an elementary education, he was at his own desire sent to Glasgow College in the autumn of 1810, and entered the Latin and Greek classes under Professors Richardson and Young, applying himself at once to the business of both classes with assiduity and spirit. "You will, I hope, mind your duty," writes his anxious father to the young student who had just left his roof, "and consider that though you are from under my daily notice, yet God seeth you always, and God hateth all sin. Mind that you are in Glasgow for the improvement of your mind; see that you progress in that matter; above all things, fear God, and I may say, fear all that do not fear him, though in a different way. Fear God, to love and draw near him; fear the latter, to avoid them as much as possible. Farewell. Dear William, yours in all duty."

"Be industrious in your room," counsels his brother Andrew; "prudent, reserved, and humble before others; and, above all, remember God. You have greater objects before you than the temporary fuss of academic contention, and higher rewards than the often partial and perishing laurels of the first of May. Depend upon it, diligence, the fear of God, prudence, and even only moderate talents, will bring a young man forward. And I can assure you that the grasp of your mind will afterwards so enlarge that you will wonder at yourself."

Such wise and wholesome charges were not thrown away upon the young student. "I was now," he himself writes in the autobiography, "a thoughtless youth of fifteen in the heart of a great and licentious city, and exposed to the immediate influence of a class of society not the most favourable for cherishing the seeds of pious instruction,—not a parent's eye to watch over my youthful steps, or to awe into the external observance of moral and religious duty. But blessed be God that, through the influence of a natural conscience which a regular system of instruction had formed to the abhorrence of gross and open vice, and the providential care of the Almighty, I was deterred from yielding to the thousand fascinating temptations with which I was every day surrounded."

Greek, Logic, Moral Philosophy, Mathematics, and Natural Philosophy, formed the subjects of his study, according to the usual curriculum, during the three succeeding sessions of his attendance at college. In all the classes he applied himself with exemplary diligence, and in several distinguished himself. Logic and Moral Philosophy had special attractions for him. To the study of the latter his application was so ardent and intense as to threaten injury to his health, and to call forth the kindly expostulations of his brother Andrew.

But his mind was now beginning to put forth its powers, and he was determined to excel. "It was during this session," he says, "that *I began to study.* And though the grave metaphysical questions of moral science were too much for my untutored mind, nevertheless a relish for philosophical inquiry was begotten which, with the ardent pursuit and final success which attended my studies, combined to render my third year at college neither unpleasant nor unprofitable." In both the Moral Philosophy and Mathematical classes he carried off prizes at the close of the session. Having thus completed his four years' course at the university, he now began to turn his thoroughly awakened mind with all earnestness to the study of Theology. But we must not leave this period of college life without marking his religious progress, and the way in which he was led to make a public profession of his faith.

His early religious impressions appear to have been all more or less intimately connected with the services, continued over several days, which usually accompany the dispensation of our Lord's Supper in Scotland. At that time " the Sacrament," enjoyed generally but once in the year, if not seldomer, was more of a great and solemn occasion than it is now. It was looked forward to with deep interest for many weeks before, and careful preparation was made for the due observance of the holy rite. It was then customary for members of the Reformed Presbyterian Church to travel to great distances from their homes, that they might enjoy opportunities of communion with their Saviour and with one another; and it was not unusual for pious parents, yearning for the salvation of their children, to take with them on these occasions such members of their families as were fit for the journey, that they might profit by what they saw and heard. There can be no doubt that the novelty of the scene, the voice and venerable appearance of the stranger-ministers, the varied addresses and appeals from the tent, the solemn distribution of the tokens, the crowds of reverent worshippers assembled on the mount of ordinances, the filling and emptying of the successive tables spread on the green field under the open sky, the more private exercises of godly fathers on the evenings of the preaching days, and the deep-toned religious conversation with which they beguiled the way as they travelled in groups to and from the appointed place, all tended to produce hallowed and lasting impressions on the susceptible minds of youth. These were not only times of precious reviving and strengthening to maturer saints, but times when many of " the seed of the blessed of the Lord" were led to take hold of God's covenant with their fathers. In company with his father, who was a Ruling Elder in the Church, and well known and beloved throughout the community, or in the society of other esteemed Christian friends whose acquaintance he had formed during his residence in Glasgow, young William Symington often travelled in the summer season to communions at Wishaw, Douglas, Laurieston, near Falkirk, and even as far as to Lorn in the Western Highlands. It is deeply interesting to mark the effect produced on him by such excursions.

In the summer after his return from his first session at college (1811) he was laid low by a severe attack of scarlet fever, from which after long debility he gradually recovered. While in the state of weakness in which this illness left him, he had some thoughts about religion, but these he considered could not properly be called *serious* thoughts. They had no practical effect. He still remained a stranger to the true knowledge of Christ. Soon after his recovery, however, he went to

Wishawtown, where the Lord's Supper was to be dispensed by the Rev. Mr. Mason. On seeing some youthful acquaintances to whom he was attached approach the table of the Lord, he "felt as though he could have joined the honourable company, and was disposed to interrogate himself why he was not a member of the Church, and on returning home he was prompted to question his mother on the nature of the ordinance and the pre-requisites of those to whom it was dispensed." The good thoughts and purposes thus suggested were to be ripened into decision by attendance on another sacramental occasion in the following year, as appears by the following extract from the autobiography, which may be commended to the special attention of the young reader, and of elders of the Church.

"In the month of August (1812) I went to Laurieston, in the vicinity of Falkirk, with a Christian friend (Mr. D. Campbell, a worthy elder in the Glasgow congregation, and long after a member of his session) who waited upon the celebration of Christ's death. His conversation was suitable and his example instructive. From this time I think may date the commencement of my serious impressions about divine things. The circumstances were favourable for thought. I was hearing sermons every day; and when I returned to my chamber there was no companion but my good friend, whose mind was too much occupied about the solemn work in which he was engaged to entertain me with trifles; and in his absence, my Bible. . . . I meditated. I conversed. My mind was in some degree impressed, and circumstances which we are accustomed to call accidental served to heighten the impression. On Saturday evening, as I approached one of the ministers (Mr. Mason) with whom I was acquainted, he, supposing my object to be the reception of a token, instantly pulled one from his pocket and presented it. I shrank back involuntarily, in such a way as discovered to him his mistake. The circumstance, however, was not without its use. It affected my mind, and created a variety of feelings, and wishes, and resolutions which may better be supposed than delineated. I retired in the evening to an adjoining forest for the purpose of secret devotion. The impression was still lively. My meditations and reflections were overpowering. I fell upon my knees and poured forth to God a fervent prayer that he would open my eyes to see the spiritual import of the sacred ordinance I was soon to witness, give me a personal interest in the glories which it represents, and prepare me in due time for sitting down at his table. After returning to my lodging I talked of it to my friend, who expressed a hope that I would see it my duty soon to join myself to the church by an open and voluntary profession, to which I made some indistinct, evasive reply. Upon my return home, these feelings in some measure passed away, with the immediate cause by which they were excited. But they were keenly revived when, not long after, an elder of the church with which my parents are connected waited upon me and talked of the propriety of making a public accession to the church. I mentioned several things which had weight with me as motives to postpone so serious a step in life. In the course of several conferences which followed, these were overcome, and after carefully examining the history and testimony of the Reformed Presbyterian Church, and seriously considering the nature of the sacred ordinance to which actual church-membership gave me access, I gave myself away to the Lord in a solemn personal covenant, and thus became a public member of the visible church by openly participating of the Lord's Supper. This step of my life shall never be forgotten, and as I have hitherto had occasion to reflect upon it with feelings of satisfaction and delight, I earnestly hope they may continue through eternity. My feelings and enjoyments at this period cannot be described, and often since, when contemplating my lethargy and indifference and sinful departure from God, have I recurred to this joyful season with the exclamation of Job in my heart, Oh that I were as in months past, as in the days when God preserved me, when his candle shined upon my head, and when by his light I walked through darkness! I could dwell with rapturous delight on this part of my history did not the recollection of sinful back-slidings mingle bitter ingredients into the cup of reflection."

After completing his fourth session at college, instead

of returning home as usual during the summer months, he remained in Glasgow, with the view of acquiring some knowledge of the Hebrew and French languages. About this time he became tutor to a young boy, grandson of Mrs. Robert Tennent, a venerable Christian lady, in whose family he continued to reside, excepting the five weeks of his attendance on the Hall at Stirling, for a year, either at Glasgow or their summer quarters at Largs. An intimacy was thus formed with Christian friends moving in a higher circle of society, which was productive of much pleasure and advantage, and which was interrupted only by death. While letters from different members of that family testify their high respect for the young tutor, he was ever accustomed to look back with pleasure to the happy days spent in their society, and to speak with gratitude of the kind attentions he had received and the benefits he had derived from "the Tennents."

During the earlier part of the present century the Theological Hall of the Reformed Presbyterian Church was presided over by the Rev. John M'Millan of Stirling, a man of grave and venerable character and an able and accomplished divine. His method of instruction, though sufficiently simple,—consisting mainly of extemporaneous lectures on the doctrines of systematic theology in the order in which these are presented in the Confession of Faith,—was not behind the age. Such was the mode of tuition commonly followed at that time, not only in the humble seminaries of the then despised dissenting communities, but even in the theological faculties of the national universities. But whatever defects may be chargeable on the system of teaching then in vogue, and whatever improvements may have been effected in later times, there is evidence sufficient to show that the prelections of the Professor and the preparation of the prescribed exercises had a stimulating effect on the minds of the students; and from the humble class-room, the little session-house adjoining the Craigs' Church,—less at that time even than it is now,—there came forth not a few able and successful ministers of the New Testament.

In September of the year 1814 our student accordingly repaired to Stirling. The picturesque situation and environs of the ancient town, and its stirring associations, had many charms for him. For four successive sessions he here "sat at the feet of Gamaliel," and found, as so many have done, his Hall days to be among the happiest of his life. Not long after his arrival he writes to his brother Andrew, expressing great satisfaction with the instruction he was receiving and the congenial work to which his faculties were now bent.

"Your satisfaction will increase," replies his brother,—subscribing himself "Yours with fraternal concern,"—"as the sphere of your knowledge enlarges and your faculties expand. Divinity is unsearchable. The highest attainments of the most profound come infinitely short of the immense subject. This study, when practically improved, raises the powers of the human mind to their highest pitch, and fills the soul with refreshing consolations. It is pleasant to think of a profession in life, the labours of which have so kindred a relation to man's highest end, and advancement in which carries the person himself on to that which is most noble, and which is eternal. But there is danger of the mind familiarising with the study from the call of duty, so as to become rather indifferent. I have had some difficulties on this matter. The life of religion is the best incentive to the study of theology. Might I say, while it is sublime as a *Science* or a *Theory*, its excellence chiefly appears as an *Art?* In this study laborious reading, deliberate thinking, patient investigation, impartial judgment, are required. All these will be successful if sanctified with prayer. The miner must dig perseveringly, and he finds the hidden treasure in small portions, which, after much toil and care and patience, become an aggregate treasure. You must labour. Gold is not sprinkled like common clay upon the surface. Intellectual attainments are but a part of the divine. These can shine only when surrounded with piety. The days of youth stamp the character for life. Circumspection in every particular is eminently required of the student for the ministry. All eyes are upon him."

In the spirit thus inculcated, he entered upon and prosecuted his theological studies, not only during the few weeks of each autumn which were spent at Stirling, but in the intervening months which were passed either at home, or in the family of Mrs. Tennent, or in the house of his brother Andrew at Paisley, who invited him to stay with him during the winter months, for the convenience of readier access to his library, and more uninterrupted fraternal conference. These were years of close and earnest study, in which we find him recording his resolution never to be in bed after six, when it was light at that hour, and in winter to be up with the sun,—to devote the morning to the Scriptures and works on systematic theology; the forenoon to composition, and works connected with the subject of composition; the afternoon and evening to ecclesiastical history, general literature, and recreation. Witsius and Bell on the Covenants, Brown's System of Natural and Revealed Religion, Paley's Natural Theology, Newton on the Prophecies, Shuckford's, Prideaux's, and

Milner's Histories, were among the books thoroughly studied by him at this time.

For some years before he had been in the habit of keeping a diary, but, ashamed at the slovenly way in which it had been written, he now committed it to the flames, and commenced anew. The journal thus resumed in July 1816, was continued, with a few breaks, sometimes only of a month or two, again of a whole year, and in one instance of more than three years, down till near the close of life. In the earlier portion of it we have the record of much deep religious exercise, lamentations over seasons of spiritual declension, resolutions for the future, notices of sacramental occasions which he had attended, and of books he was engaged in reading.

"I am again at Stirling," he writes 19th September 1816, "attending on the instructions of the very learned and pious Professor M'Millan. I would look forward to my future prospects, and see in them an important stimulus to the diligent improvement of every moment of time and to a careful attention to the lectures which I am now privileged to hear. May God bless them as a means of preparation! Thus may I be fitted for a station of public usefulness in the Church of Christ. May I still be more and more distrustful of myself, and write upon all my acquirements and labours, in the sincerity of my heart, the unfeigned motto, μονῳ τῳ θεῳ δοξα."

Of the year 1816 he speaks as the busiest and perhaps happiest he had spent. "Never before did I enter with such spirit into the retirements of study, never with the same eagerness did I pursue the acquisitions of knowledge." While living in Glasgow, he availed himself of the privilege of attending, as private student, on the lectures of several of the professors in the University, with the view of keeping up and confirming former attainments in languages and philosophy. It was during this year also that he made his first attempts in the field of literature, sending contributions on various subjects which engaged his attention at the time to the pages of the "Christian Instructor" and "Christian Repository."

To the "Christian Instructor" of July 1816 he contributed a paper on "The application of the name *Sunday* to the first day of the week," and another on "The neglect of Christians with respect to the Holy Spirit." Other papers of the same date which we find in his scrap-book, on "The Study of Church History," on "The Use of Uninspired Songs in the Worship of God," &c., although they do not appear to have been sent to any periodical for publication, serve to shew the great activity of his mind at this period.

There is also a long elaborate and able letter addressed by him about this time to the editor of the "Christian Repository," but which was not inserted, in reply to certain strictures which had appeared in that magazine on Dr. Alexander Macleod's (of New York) Lectures on the Revelation. The perusal of this work seems to have produced a very deep impression on his mind, and awakened in him that sentiment of profound admiration for its gifted author, which he always cherished and long afterwards expressed by giving his name to his youngest son. He shared, as might be expected in one of so ardent temperament, in the political excitement which pervaded all classes of the community during that eventful period in the history of Europe, and appears to have laboured under a solemn impression of the national guilt resting upon Britain as an abettor of the antichristian system. He even seems to have had some thought of following the example of Dr. Macleod, and seeking a home for himself in the new world; but from such purpose, if it was ever seriously entertained, he was dissuaded by the advice of wise friends. His venerable friend, Mrs. Tennent, whose Christian counsel was in many ways beneficial to him as a youth, and to whom he had lent Dr. Macleod's volume; thus writes to him from Largs (14th March 1816) : " I see now, my good friend, more reasons than one for your wishing to cross the seas; you wish to get sheltered in the land that will be free of the blood of the witnesses. Whether the Doctor is or is not right respecting Britain having that awful judgment before her, I think I shall be sheltered from the calamity without going so far. But if I were as young as you, perhaps I should like to accompany you over the Atlantic Ocean. My prayer is that my great High Priest may divide to me the deeper waters through which I most certainly am soon to pass, and land me where there will be no more death. He will take care of all his own people whatever their time or situation may be : to him it is my desire to commit myself, and all I am to leave behind me."

But we may not dwell much longer upon that period of his life which was devoted to theological study in connexion with attendance on the Hall. The diary shews how steadily he kept in view, during all those years, the great work which he had in prospect, his deep sense of the magnitude and responsibility of the office to which he aspired, and the high standard of qualification which he had proposed to himself; and contains abundant evidence of the assiduity with which he laboured to prepare himself for entering with efficiency upon the functions of the Christian ministry. By means of copious yet wisely selected and careful reading; by availing himself of every opportunity afforded for improving conversation and correspondence with Christian friends; by active efforts for the establishment and efficient on-carrying of such associations as the "Paisley Youths' Society for Religious Purposes;" by occasional visits to the bedsides of the sick and dying; and by the vigilant cultivation of devotional habits, he was during this period gradually ripening and being furnished for the Master's service. It was at this time also that his acquaintance commenced with her who was to be the future partner of his life, and it is not difficult to see how great a share this circumstance had in consolidating his character and in stimulating and directing his energies.

The following sentences from his diary shew with what feelings he looked forward to becoming a preacher.

"*January* 1, 1818. May I have the influence and aid of the Holy Ghost in the studies to which my attention is presently directed, and in due time may I be prepared and strengthened for publishing the glad tidings of salvation to perishing sinners! By a growing acquaintance with my own heart, and habitual meditation on the matchless perfections, mediatorial fulness, and infinite love of the Redeemer, may I be fitted for discovering to others the plagues of their own hearts, and for recommending to their esteem and reception the Saviour of the world." And again (May 4, 1818). "To-morrow I make my third appearance as a candidate for license. I desire this evening to devote myself anew to God. May he purify my motives in looking forward to the work of preaching the Gospel. May every selfish and mercenary principle be completely eradicated, and my soul be absorbed in the magnificent prospect of being instrumental in gathering souls to Christ!"

On the 30th of June 1818, at the age of twenty-three, having successfully passed his preparatory trials, he was duly licensed by the Presbytery, in the name of the Church's Head, to preach the everlasting Gospel, his brother Andrew presiding on the occasion; and on the following Sabbath (July 5) he made his first public appearance in the pulpit at Paisley, preaching from Rom. i. 16: "I am not ashamed of the Gospel of Christ."

"My life, my soul, my body, my talents, my opportunities of usefulness, my all, I dedicate to the Redeemer of men. May he never leave me nor forsake me, but as my days so may my strength be!" (*Diary*, June 30, 1818).

CHAPTER II.

EARLY MINISTRY IN STRANRAER.   1819–1825.

ÆTATE 23-30.

A SHORT time after receiving license, the youthful preacher set out on his probationary tour of the churches, and for about a year was employed in itinerating among the vacancies. The life of the preacher then was considerably different from what it is now, in these days of rapid and easy travelling. The long journeys from place to place were accomplished on horseback, and the pony with his saddle-bags were an indispensable part of the preacher's equipment. A suitable steed having been procured for him, whom he always speaks of by the name of "the Irishman," he traversed in this way almost the entire bounds of the Church, from Perthshire to Galloway, and from Berwick to the Western Highlands, and evidently enjoyed with much zest the new scenes into the midst of which he was thus carried, gratefully appreciating the hospitable entertainment which he received in the different houses where he sojourned, amusing himself by close observation of the various characters whom he met with in his wanderings, and eagerly availing himself of every opportunity of visiting places of interest on his way or in the neighbourhood of the stations where he laboured.

Though "in journeyings oft" at this season, he was fully alive then, as he ever continued to be, to the necessity of careful preparation for pulpit work, and always studied so to arrange his movements as to secure a day or two of bodily rest and retirement in the end of the week, that he might be ready for the duties of the Sabbath. And no doubt it is due to this cause, as well as to natural talent and previous training, that from the very first he proved a popular preacher, and at the very outset of his ministry acquired that fame as an eloquent and powerful evangelist, which never afterwards waned. Not only were the congregations which he supplied, and which, for the most part, were but small, charmed by a style of oratory more cultivated and graceful than they had been accustomed to from the older ministers of the denomination, but many from other churches, particularly from the Establishment, were attracted to the humble meeting-house by the rich and forcible exhibition of gospel truth. Crowds seem to have attended his preaching in almost every place to which his appointments carried him; and if he remained over a few weeks in one place, the audience was sure to increase on each successive Sabbath. It is a proof, too, of the estimation in which he was held, and the confidence which was placed in him by fathers in the ministry, that even while a probationer he was repeatedly employed to assist on sacramental occasions, and had sometimes the principal parts of service, such as the Sabbath evening sermon, assigned to him.

Soon after the commencement of his itineracy, a most harmonious call came out in his favour from the congregation at Airdrie, requesting him to take the oversight of them. But nowhere were his services more appreciated than at Stranraer, where the congregation had recently been deprived by death of their faithful and beloved minister, Rev. John Cowan; and to no place does he seem to have felt his heart so much drawn. His first visit to Stranraer was in January 1819, when he spent a happy month under the roof of Mrs. Cowan, widow of the late pastor. He preached on four Sabbaths to the vacant congregation; the following jottings culled from his diary are very significant :—

"*Stranraer, January* 8.—In house all day except a few moments that I went out to see the meeting-house and get the pulpit adjusted to my height. The chapel is neat and compact, though rather small.

"*January* 10.—Preached to very respectable audience. The day was extremely stormy.

"*January* 17.—Had a large and respectable audience. House quite packed. Spoke too loud, and so did not feel quite so comfortable. . . . Intimated a meeting for instituting a Bible Society.

"*January* 27.—Attended the first meeting of the Stranraer and Rhinns of Galloway Auxiliary Bible Society.

"*January* 31.—House immensely crowded, the day being very fine. Spoke with more ease than sometimes. O blessed Jesus! send thy Holy Spirit to water with His divine influences the seed that has been sown!"

Before he left Stranraer, the congregation there had resolved to endeavour to secure him as their pastor, and some of its members were most anxious to obtain from him some indication of his mind as to acceptance of their call. This, however, he deemed premature, feeling it to be his duty carefully to weigh the claims of the other congregation which had called him, and desiring to be made willing to go wherever he might be of most service to the Church. In due course a cordial invitation from Stranraer was regularly issued; and at the meeting of Synod in May the two calls were presented, when he made choice of that from Stranraer, praying the Head of the Church to prepare him for entering upon the solemn work of the ministry.

During this summer, while regularly preaching with great acceptance wherever his services were required, we find him busily engaged in purchasing books, and making other necessary preparations for his settlement in Stranraer. Early on the morning of August 14th, having taken affectionate leave of many kind friends, he left Paisley, his "dear native town, his father's house, and the people that were his." In a letter a few days later to his dearest friend, who was soon to become his help-meet in Stranraer, he thus describes his voyage thither:—

"On the morning after I left you, I went on board the 'Rob Roy' at Renfrew. We came to Greenock about eleven o'clock, but had to wait nearly five hours on the mending of the boiler. We left Greenock about four, and were at sea all night. The wind blew what sailors call a *half gale*, and it was right ahead. Every passenger on board was sick. I occasionally left my place and scrambled up to deck, to gratify myself with whatever could be seen—the lights on different parts of the coast, the island of Arran, the rock Ailsa, &c. We got to Loch Ryan soon after break of day, and were landed at Stranraer about six o'clock on Sabbath morning. Andrew preached all day. Monday and Tuesday I spent mostly with him. Wednesday was the solemn day."

On that day, 18th August 1819, he was ordained to the office of the ministry, in the presence of an immense crowd, estimated at between four and five thousand assembled in the burying-ground adjoining the meeting-house. The Rev. John West of Colmonell preached from 2 Cor. v. 20; his brother Andrew presided in the act of ordination; and the solemnity was closed with a sermon by the Rev. Mr. Rowatt of Penpont, from Phil. ii. 29.

"In the afternoon I ascended with trembling limbs and beating heart to commence my public ministerial labours. I do not remember to have been so much appalled at any former time. I addressed the audience from Exodus iii. 11 : 'And Moses said unto God, Who am I that I should go unto Pharaoh, and that I should bring forth the children of Israel out of Egypt?' As I have put my hand to the plough, the Lord keep me from looking back!"

Those who had heard, only a month before, his *last* sermon, were thus addressed by one who could claim to be "very intimately acquainted with his earlier career, and to have felt and witnessed the great power of his influence throughout his whole course."

"I have a very lively recollection of his settlement in his former charge, now nearly forty-three years ago. The tall and elegant form of the youth who, on that solemn day, received his ordination vows, deeply impressed with the responsibility of the arduous office he was undertaking, is still vividly before me. A most warm and hearty welcome did he receive from the people, who were justly proud of their young minister. The name he bore was, even then, well known and honoured throughout the Church. The people expected much, and they were not disappointed. Well do I remember the remarks of the rural patriarchs of those days—men of godliness and integrity, familiar with their Bibles, well read in the olden divinity, and well instructed by their previous pastors— as on the evening of Sabbath after Sabbath they travelled on foot to their distant homes, recalling with grateful and admiring affection the rich and eloquent discourses to which they had just listened.

By refreshing each other's memories with the precious truths they had been hearing, they easily beguiled the length of the journey."

On 27th June 1820 he was united in marriage to her to whom for about two years he had been tenderly attached, Agnes Speirs, eldest daughter of Mr. Robert Speirs, farmer at Inch, near Paisley, who was to be the faithful companion of his pilgrimage to the end, the sharer of all his joys and sorrows. Having been thus happily settled in the place where he believed God had appointed him to labour, he immediately threw himself with characteristic ardour into his proper work, and the record of the earlier years of his ministry in Stranraer affords ample evidence of great pastoral diligence and devotedness. While a large part of his time was given to study and careful preparation of the discourses which Sabbath after Sabbath he delivered with so much acceptance and effect to the audiences which thronged the church to overflowing, until larger accommodation had to be provided, no other part of pastoral duty was neglected or discharged in a perfunctory manner. In visiting the sick, holding diets of visitation and examination, often at a considerable distance from his home, for the congregation was scattered over many parishes, and in instituting and conducting classes for the instruction of the young, it may be truly said that he was instant in season and out of season. From the first, in performing all such duties, he proceeded on a regular plan, duly considered, determined on and adhered to, which enabled him to get through a far greater amount of work than could have been accomplished by one less accustomed to act upon system.

It was not long till the effects of such an earnest ministry began to appear, not only in the growth and prosperity of the congregation, but in the influence for good diffused throughout the general community. Evangelical religion was at a low ebb then in that locality. The preachers were but few and far between who testified the Gospel of the grace of God; and the truths so eloquently and forcibly propounded by the young minister sounded strange and startling to many ears. He early found admission into the best society of the place, and instead of conforming himself to the frivolous worldly customs which he found prevailing, sought to elevate and Christianise the tone of that society. Many were induced to study their Bibles who had seldom before thought of looking into such a book. A party of strolling players, who had been well patronised on their former visits to Stranraer, commenced operations on the evening of a day observed as a thanksgiving in his congregation, but complained sadly of the small attendance, the manager of the company assigning as the reason of their failure, that *some new minister* had condemned theatrical entertainments and dissuaded the people from giving them countenance. "I wish," he adds, "I could as effectually persuade them to give up card playing and parties on Sabbath." The influence exerted by his ministry at this period, beyond the bounds of the congregation and church, will be seen from the following letter from a very dear friend of our father, a Christian lady then living in Stranraer, but now and for many years resident in England :—

"When my father entered upon a government situation at Stranraer, obtained for him by the widow of his maternal uncle, Sir John Dalrymple Hay, the darkness of spiritual ignorance which prevailed in Wigtonshire and in parts of Kirkcudbrightshire and Dumfriesshire, was a darkness that might be felt. With a few bright and blessed exceptions, vital religion was rare, and principally existed amongst the humbler classes of society. From these sounded forth the varied excellences of the young minister. At that time he stood almost alone in his views, aims, and efforts, and curiosity was excited. One person after another went to hear for themselves the eloquent and promising young man. Numerous objections were brought forward to deter people; these kept back many, and caused others to delay for a little while going to hear the fearless, faithful preacher. But his bold, uncompromising, and lucid statements of Gospel truths were proclaimed in such attractive language, with so much earnestness, good feeling, and refinement of mind and manners, that few, I may say none, that went once, could resist the desire and opportunity to go again. Prejudice gave way, and objections were dealt with as chaff. Early in April 1820 I was brought home ill from school. As an invalid, I was an object of solicitude to my parents, and more constantly in their company and present in the society of visitors than is usual for girls; and heard the conversations and remarks current at that period. It was interesting to observe that the topics were generally politics, the landlord's past and present rent-rolls, the best and wisest plan to adopt to meet the farmer's difficulties, the danger of the coast, the Portpatrick harbour, and *Mr. Symington*. All admitted his pulpit abilities (either from hearsay or personal knowledge), his store of information, his refined taste, his intelligent eye, his beaming countenance, his power to attract, instruct, and win; and yet with all this, it was the glorious subject in hand, not himself, that was prominently before the mind and powerfully fixed in it. From my father's public post he mingled amongst all classes of the community, and heard alike the comments of the county families, town residents, and naval officers, as well as those of farmers, labourers, sailors and fishermen. Their remarks shewed the depth and extent to which Scripture truths had penetrated. It was not deemed right that a government officer should attend elsewhere than at the parish church, but one or more of our household were allowed in turns to go occasionally to hear Mr. Symington, and were charged to treasure up, so as to retail to others, what could be remembered of the instruction received. This was communicated from one to another, if not with fulness and accuracy, at least with zest and pleasure, and much religious knowledge was thus diffused. His sermons were like a nail fastened in a sure place, but it was his lectures and expositions that were remembered best, and conveyed the most light and benefit. The words of the passage expounded, when re-read, helped to recall what had been stated, and the mind and heart were stored and fed by the Divine Word. I was not often able to have the privilege enjoyed by those in stronger health, and can only remember being present on a few occasions, and at one Bible class as a listener. I sat in a pew at right angles to the catechumens, who were placed in front of the desk. Their undivided attention, gravity, and intelligence bespoke the interest they felt, the solemnity of the theme under consideration, and the vigour and depth of their apprehension of it. I had one dear listener to any scraps which I could gather together and convey to her, either directly or at second hand; and that was Mrs. Captain R——, then in deep consumption. She used to greet me with 'Well I——,' or 'Now I——, tell me what you heard last Sunday at Mr. Symington's, or have heard from those who were present;' and in her eager desire to listen, would forget the tray before her with the food she so greatly needed. After we left Stranraer in 1822, our information regarding your father's ministrations were mainly received from General M'Dowell, Sir Andrew and Lady Agnew, the late Lady Hay and Mrs. Berger. In 1825, during a round of visits, we renewed our personal intercourse with our esteemed friend, heard him preach in his enlarged church, and met him at breakfast at Mr. A. M'Dowell's. He had then a band of attached friends around him, who appreciated him as he deserved, and aided him in many ways in his works of faith and love."—I.M.

Another member of the same esteemed family thus vividly describes her recollections of these early days at Stranraer:—

"In my thirteenth year I first saw in company, and occasionally heard Dr. Symington, and heard my mother and your mother converse. As one of us three sisters was permitted a seat in a pew, we brought home *Truth* as we best could to the home circle on the Sabbath evening, for the Gospel was precious in those days at Stranraer.

The morning lectures, from the eighth of Matthew, taught many concerning Christ. The first sermon I recall was on ' What is his name?' (Exod. iii. 13), followed evidently with design, on the Perfections of God—Power, Wisdom, Goodness, &c. At a later date, those of particular use to myself were on these texts: ' Cursed is every one which continueth not in all things written in the law to do them;' 'Christ hath redeemed us from the curse of the law, being made a curse for us;' 'Where sin abounded, grace hath much more abounded.' After this I was in a different position—interested and decided. Visiting at G——, I found a governess in mental distress. She was tempted and sorrowful. Too young to advise or teach, I offered to send to her that which I might gather from your father's services. She asked me to read her details to himself. The reply you have, of spring 1822. So *immediate*, so frank a reply made me feel Dr. Symington will be my friend. This clause in that letter has comforted many: 'When I place myself on a seat on which I have never before sat, I trust or *believe* that it will support me; it is not till after I have sat on it that I become *assured* that it does support me.' During 1819 to 1822, *many* whom we knew in circles all around believed, for the Gospel was powerfully sent home to the hearers of your dear father by the power of the Holy Ghost. Thus permanent friendships began—new societies were formed—*new lives began.*"

The letter alluded to above is a specimen of wise ministerial fidelity. We give extracts calculated to be useful to some reader who may be disquieted with similar doubts and difficulties.

"The thing at which your young friend seems to have stumbled is the doctrine of *Election*—a doctrine not only recognised by both the national churches in our land, but one which I firmly believe to be sanctioned by him 'who cannot lie.' Were I therefore conversing with your friend, I should try to persuade her that, while she freely acknowledged the doctrine as one of 'the true sayings of God,' and derived from it ground at once of adoration and of praise—adoration at the sovereignty with which the choice is made, and praise that ever any of our fallen family should have been made the objects of God's eternal love—it should at the same time give her no uneasiness in inquiring into the state of her soul. If on examination she finds that she is a subject of grace, she has every reason to conclude that she is elected —she is among those who are denominated *the election of grace*—she has *made her calling and election sure*. If she has not the comfort of arriving at this conclusion, if she still finds herself to be in a state of nature, she has *no reason* to consider that she is among the non-elect, and her duty is to improve with diligence those means of grace and salvation in the use of which God is pleased to communicate the blessings of His love; she must look to Him in the Gospel, convinced that they that look shall be saved; she must seek Him daily, in the confidence that He never bade any seek His face in vain; she must betake herself to prayer and make her voice be heard in the morning, in the full persuasion that He will incline His ear, hear, and her soul shall live.

"There is one subject more on which I feel inclined to subjoin a few sentences. It is the distinction betwixt *doubting* and *unbelief*. These are apt to be confounded; and the young Christian in particular is ready to conceive that the former is at least presumptive, if not decisive, evidence of the latter. But it is one thing to believe— it is quite another thing to be assured of our being believers or in a state of salvation. Whenever a sinner trusts in Christ for salvation, he believes; whenever he puts dependence on the righteousness of the Redeemer for the eternal welfare of his soul, he is a believer: but his assurance that he is in a state of grace, that is to say, that he has believed, must follow at some distance of time the previous act. When I place myself on a seat on which I have never before sat, I trust or *believe* that it will support me—it is not till after I have sat on it that I become *assured* that it does support me.

"These observations are made if possible to ease the mind of your young friend. But it must not be inferred from them that *assurance* is neither a necessary nor a possible attainment. Assurance is attainable. An apostle could say, ' Hereby *we know* that we are of the truth and shall assure our hearts before Him ' (1 John iii. 19). This is implied in the promises made to particular characters, by which all who possess these characters are assured of their enjoying the blessings annexed. (Matthew v. 1, &c.) The saints have often reached this most desirable attainment,—as Jabez, David, and Job, who could say, ' I *know* that my Redeemer liveth,' &c. And that it is the duty, no less than the privilege, of all to seek the assurance of which we are speaking appears from the exhortation, 'Brethren, give diligence to make your calling and election sure' (2 Peter i. 10, 11). While it is our duty to seek the comfort of assurance, it is also our duty to be on our guard against *occasions* of doubting. Upon these I find I cannot enlarge. I may simply observe that doubts are occasioned either by *erroneous notions*, as in the case of Asaph (Psalm lxxvii.); or by *indolence*, as in the case of the Spouse (Song v.); or by *sinful passions* which war against the soul (1 Peter ii. 11); or by *Satan*, of whose devices the people of God are not ignorant. By guarding against these we shall best preserve ourselves from all that uneasiness and torture which necessarily attend a state of dubiety with respect to our eternal interest, and it should be our daily prayer that grace may be given us so to do, for without the aid of the Holy Spirit we can *do nothing*.

"With best wishes for the spiritual welfare of yourself and friend, I remain, my dear Miss G——, yours very sincerely,

"WILLIAM SYMINGTON.

"STRANRAER, *January* 4, 1822."

The ministry begun with such assiduity and ardour was continued in the same earnest and devoted spirit which marked its commencement during the whole course of his twenty years' residence and labour in Stranraer. Of this part of his life it would be in vain to attempt any detailed narrative, exhibiting in consecutive order the events of each passing year. We must content ourselves with a general survey of the whole, merely attempting to record some of the more prominent features of a comparatively quiet and uneventful history.

The stream of his domestic life flowed on for years smoothly and happily, uninterrupted by any great bereavement or trial. In his character and habits he was eminently *domestic*. What Wordsworth says of the lark, "True to the kindred points of Heaven and *Home*," was a quotation often on his lips, and might be said to be to a large extent exemplified in his own life. When absent, as he frequently was, for short intervals from his family on public duty, he always wearied till the time arrived when he could return to them; and his letters to his wife and children when away ever breathed a spirit of the warmest affection and solicitude. At Stranraer all his seven children were born to him. Each, as his diary testifies, was received at birth as a gift from God, and dedicated in the most solemn manner to his service. Their birthdays were noted year by year in his pocket-book, that he might specially remember and dedicate them anew. And now that he is gone, many affecting proofs appear of how his heart yearned for their highest good, with an intensity of affection far beyond what they could have imagined while he was yet alive. He had, at this time, a very decided preference for the system of *home education* over that of the public school, which might be owing partly to a cause already adverted to, viz., his recollections of the injurious influences to which he himself had been exposed when a schoolboy, and partly to the inferior character of the local schools at that time. Until his children were pretty well advanced in the rudiments of education, the father and mother were their sole instructors. In a letter to his brother James, we find him saying: "The evenings are devoted to family reading. Besides, I give the children a part of every forenoon and afternoon, and they are already somewhat acquainted with the first principles of English grammar, geography, natural history, and arithmetic. Besides

English reading and religious knowledge, they also write a little every day. Now that I have got into it, I do not dislike teaching them. This will be interesting to mother." The aid of a private tutor was afterwards called in; but it was not till after the removal of the family to Glasgow that any of them were sent to a public school.*

About two years after his settlement at Stranraer, our father began a course of systematic sermons, covering the breadth and length of Calvinistic theology. For these he read elaborately; and the matter thus accumulated, was of considerable service when, thirty years later, he was called to prepare a course of lectures as Professor of Systematic Theology. These sermons were not fully written out: the time that could be found for their preparation was rather given to thorough study, logical arrangement of topics, and such filling of the heart with the practical bearings of the doctrines discussed as effectually secured a delivery anything but uninteresting. These sermons formed a basis on which much future reading was laid.

Alongside of a pulpit ministry sustained with unflagging vigour, there went careful pastoral work. A record remains in his own handwriting of successive visitations of the congregation extending from 1819 to the end of March 1839, that is, till within two months of his leaving Stranraer. These visits were in addition to those constantly required by baptisms, marriages, sicknesses, and deaths. Classes for the young were kept up with spirit

---

* Here ends the manuscript left by my brother, the late William Symington, D.D.—A. M. S.

season after season, and were attended, especially an afternoon class for young ladies in the middle of the week, by many who were not connected with the congregation.

The sphere of our father's ministry was not confined to Stranraer. He preached often in the villages around—Cairnryan, Kirkcolm, Portpatrick, Glenluce, New Luce, Carnweel, Kirkmaiden—sometimes on weekdays, sometimes on Sabbath evenings; and the audiences always grew larger and more interested so long as he remained in Galloway. And in these days the dispensation of the Lord's Supper was an occasion of great public interest in the less populous parts of Scotland. At Newton Stewart and Whithorn; at Springholm and Castle Douglas; at Quarrelwood and Dumfries; at Colmonell and Kilmalcolm, he was eagerly listened to by open-air audiences often numbering thousands. Martyrs' sermons; sermons in behalf of the great Catholic societies, the beginning of home auxiliary branches formed in the south of Scotland; and sermons in aid of the Sabbath-school and the Temperance cause, were preached during these years in many places. The generation among which all this seed was scattered has nearly quite passed away, but there were many fruits; and unexpected wafts of fragrance from the mown grass sometimes meet us still when an old man or woman, hearing our name, will say, "Aye, you're a son of William Symington, are ye? I heard him at such a place in such a year, and it seems but yesterday. Eh! he was a grand preacher, your father."

A reference has been made to his attending the first

meeting of the Stranraer and Rhinns of Galloway Auxiliary to the British and Foreign Bible Society, in January of 1819, when he first visited the town which was to be the scene of twenty years' earnest labour. A few notes may here be gathered from his diary shewing the remarkably early dates at which he began to take lively interest in this and other great societies for the spread of Christ's kingdom.

"*March 8th*, 1821.—Attended meeting of Bible Society Committee, which is always conducted in the most heartless manner."

"*September 9th* (*Kirkcudbright*).—Preached in the flat of a large mill. Immense concourse; but small collection for the Bible Society."

"*April 11th*, 1821.—Preached a sermon for the Sabbath Schools. Few people in church. Great coldness here about every scheme of public benevolence."

The sermon, that on *The Evil of Ignorance,* was published; and more cheerful entries occur before long.

The Conversion of the Jews had begun to engage his heart so early as 1822, in June of which year we find him preaching in behalf of the London Society at Gatehouse, and saying, "Very poor audience and collection." But he was not discouraged. In 1825 he preached, at Annan, the sermon which was afterwards published on *The Salvation of Israel;* and we shall find many later proofs of deep and intelligent interest in a cause which even to-day is far from receiving the sympathy due to it. How long will it be before the Christian Church, longing for more power and blessing at home and among the heathen, shall awake to see the hindrance in its own neglect of the Master's direction to begin at Jerusalem?

At the close of 1825 a Society for Religious Purposes was formed in Stranraer, in which our father took zealous interest from the first. It seems to have had for its object the diffusing of information about whatever was being done anywhere for the spread of Christianity, and the collection of funds which the Committee distributed annually among the various societies. He used often to say that his own birthday and that of the London Missionary Society were the same, and that each of his children were contributors from their infancy. A stronger impulse, however, in the matter of missions to the heathen was to come twelve years later.

While thus originating some parts of the machinery which the evangelical revival called for, and heartily helping to work other parts already originated, our father's chief care was his own congregation. It grew apace in membership, and the desire of the public to hear occasionally continued unabated. Sir Andrew and Lady Agnew of Lochnaw, and Lady Hay of Dunraggat, were sometimes to be seen in the "Cameronian Meeting-house," glad to find seats among the crowd. In June of 1824 the old building was taken down, preaching being kept up on the green while summer lasted, and in the Relief or the Antiburgher Meeting-house when autumn came; and on the 2d day of January 1825 he entered the pulpit of a new and handsome church, adapted to the size of the audience. But while he was profoundly grateful for this measure of prosperity, it was very far from satisfying his heart. We find him at one time earnestly pleading with his hearers to pray for the revival of vital religion among them, and at another time bewailing in secret the *vis inertiæ* of prevailing apathy and indifference to spiritual things against which he had to struggle. He was much too deeply in earnest to let the applause of crowds take the place of saving results. His brother Andrew seems to have found the young minister in a mood of despondency when he visited Stranraer in the summer of 1825, for the first letter after his return closes thus :—

"PAISLEY, *July* 7, 1825.

"MY DEAR BROTHER,— . . . Every situation in which a minister can be placed has its difficulties. I cannot refrain from expressing my increased conviction that yours is one of great interest and usefulness. You are in part entered on the labours of others, but you are also breaking up fallow ground. The cause of evangelical truth and of the Reformation is finding a way to a class of society who formerly were ignorant of it, or were blind with unfavourable prejudices. The little opposition you receive is a favourable sign. Be strong in the Lord and in the power of his might. Your circle is much wider than that of the obscure occupant of Oakshaw Street conventicle. And I hope, through the divine blessing, your labour will not be in vain. Some success you may be permitted to see to encourage you, while there may be much to see hereafter, when you rest from your labours and your works follow you. But it cannot be all success now. We must have something to exercise faith. Without the enemy, where were the soldiers? Let us endure hardness as good soldiers of Jesus Christ."

These words are a very slight specimen of a correspondence, rich in all good things and extending over many years, which the Christian world would, we think, receive with pleasure and profit. Only scanty extracts, and these only on one side, can be given here.

CHAPTER III.

LATER MINISTRY AT STRANRAER—AUTHORSHIP.
1826–1839.

ÆTATE 31-44.

THE reader of the two previous chapters will have formed some conception for himself of the character of William Symington, and of the sphere in which his ministry was exercised. No attempt will be made to follow his life year by year, giving details of its principal events. Embracing fully thirteen years in this chapter, we shall arrest attention on some indications of growth and fruit-bearing.

The spring of all our father's success and usefulness lay in watchful, secret piety. Extracts from his diary have already indicated this. We do not wish to multiply these, and shall, therefore, here present two, nine years apart, which the reader may regard as faithfully indicating the habitual frame and temper of the inner man.

"*April* 17*th*, 1826.—For some time back attention directed to subject of secret prayer, in performance of which I charge myself with remissness as regards frequency, length, and spirit. With divine aid I would wish to amend; and for this purpose to act on some such plan as the following :—

"MORNING. Adoration, praise, thanksgiving, petition for personal blessings, &c., &c.

"MID-DAY, say two o'clock. Petitions and thanksgivings for wife, children, inmates, servants. For *relatives*,—mother, brothers, sisters and their families. *Acquaintances* and personal friends. *Enemies*, or such as act towards me in that character.

"AFTERNOON, say five o'clock. *Congregation*, — young, aged, sick, troublesome, occasional hearers, &c. *R. Church* in general. Church *at large*, — extension, knowledge, purity, peace, unity. Pagans, Mohammedans, Jews, &c., &c.

"EVENING. Personal confession, dedication, petition, &c., &c.

"I would wish to observe something of this plan daily, and when so situated as not to have opportunity of retirement, to retire as much as possible in my own thoughts at the given time, and employ myself in ejaculations on the subject.

"*June 2d*, 1835.—I am this day forty years of age, and feel solemnised at the thought of having reached such a period, while at the same time so deficient in many things, I may say in everything that is good. The good Lord pardon all my many shortcomings, and make the remainder of my days more useful to others and profitable to myself. Alas! how little advancement have I made in the divine life, if I have made even a commencement; and how little if anything have I done for God during my past existence. Truly may I say, 'I am a worm and no man.' Blessed Jesus! send thy Spirit to enlighten, sanctify, comfort, and seal to the day of redemption. And to thee be glory for ever. Amen."

These words were never intended to meet any eye except his own; they are printed that those who knew our father as the busy, genial man he was, may understand the hidden secret of his strength. And for those who did not know him, it may be as well to say that no one more loathed than he did the spiritual gushing which it seems so difficult to reconcile with sincerity toward him who seeth in secret.

The living in the sight of God and earnest simple faith, the unfeigned humility and profound sense of the seriousness of life, which are indicated by these extracts, were accompanied by early rising, careful arrangement of his time, and plans of study. Order and method became with him almost a passion; and any who wonder at the amount and variety of work he accomplished will find the explanation there rather than in his vigour of mind or any favouring circumstances.

The happy tenor of domestic life in the manse was twice interrupted during this period by afflictions which left behind them peaceable fruits of righteousness.

The fourth child and second son of the family, Robert, was born on the 22d of August 1827, and that day solemnly "committed to the grace and care of a covenant God." Just six years later, on the 29th of August 1833, when playing with two of the older children in the manse garden, the stone pillar supporting a sun-dial was upset and fell on his body, causing some internal injury which resulted fatally in less than thirty-six hours. It is very characteristic of our father that there should be found among his papers a carefully written "Memorial of a severe domestic bereavement" extending to sixteen pages, in which every circumstance of the overwhelming calamity is recorded,—the names of friends who were present, the means used by three surgeons, the prayers offered; and in which the special marks of the heavenly Father's hand are detailed, with the spiritual lessons he sought to learn. There is reason to think that this memorial was read by him many times in later years. Our mother—who on such occasions revealed the firmness which comes from high principle, a quality commonly veiled by her great gentleness and never-to-be-forgotten love—asked Robert, "Who redeems you, my sweet dear?" "Christ." "Would you like to go to Christ?" "Yes." "Where do the righteous go at death, my dear?" "To heaven." "Who are the righteous that go to heaven at death?" "Such as believe in Christ, love God, and hate evil." "Would you like to go to heaven?" "Yes." Nearly thirty years later, during the few months of her widowhood, she recalled how the little sufferer had answered the next question—"Would you not be sorry to leave us all?"—by clasping his arms round her neck and bidding her not cry because he was going to be with Jesus. At the same time (the summer of 1862) the mother, who drew to herself almost more, if possible, of her children's revering love than our father did, charged her youngest child never to forget a certain friend. "You were an infant six weeks old when Robert died. Mr. M'G—— had baptized you, and was on his way home when the tidings overtook him. He turned his horse and came back on the Saturday evening (Robert had died in the morning) and preached on the Sabbath; and I crept into the vestry with you at my breast, and heard him preach on 'Jesus wept.' Never forget Mr. M'G—— as long as you live."

At the close of 1836 the home of Professor Andrew Symington was desolated by fever. A son and a daughter in the prime of youth were laid in the same grave; and within a very few weeks the grave was re-opened to receive the mother and one of her twin-children newly-born. Sympathising deeply with the brother whom he loved and honoured as a second father, William Symington had gone to Paisley to attend the funeral, and purposed to remain and occupy the pulpit in Oakshaw Street; but tidings reached him that the scourge had entered his own manse. He hastened home to find three of his children under typhus. On New Year's day, 1837, he made the last entry in his diary for fully three months. Day and night till the 22d he watched assiduously over sick beds on which the cloud deepened daily, all the six children being visited with the same alarming disease; then he came from the pulpit to bed, and did not rise for eight weeks. The plague had fastened on himself; and during the remainder of the winter the manse was turned into a hospital.

On the 2d of April we find him making the first use of his restored pen in fixing for his own spiritual profit the memorable features of the dispensation, under regular heads eight in number. The hand of his heavenly Father is recognised in sending help through five women in humble station, four of them strangers, when friends stood aloof in fear of contagion: in sparing his life while his brother Walter was taken away; in remarkably sustaining our mother, so that, although getting only snatches of rest for five weeks, "the supports of religion never forsook her—her calm trust in the promises served to bear her through;" in the provision made for his pulpit, and in special answers to prayer. On the 7th of May he was allowed to return to his pulpit after more than three months' silence, and preached on Lam. iii. 22. He records with thankfulness the marked attention of a large audience, and the "freedom and much earnestness" he enjoyed " in calling on sinners to betake themselves to a God of mercies." The family being now either wholly or nearly restored to health, the 1st of June was set apart as a day of domestic thanksgiving; and the entries in his diary for that day and the following—his forty-second birthday—shew him prayerfully anxious "that some saving impressions may be left on the hearts of the dear young persons who have been plucked as brands from the fire," and that "the Husbandman, who has been pruning me much of late, may cause His pruning to issue in my bringing forth more fruit."

We shall see how his prayer was answered; but meanwhile we must look back to observe the steady growth of his public influence. One of the very few of our father's early friends who still survive very kindly supplies the following recollections.[*] The Rev. Thomas Liddell, D.D., minister of the parish of Lochmaben, writing in 1862, says—

"My acquaintance with my beloved friend Dr. Symington commenced in the spring of 1826, when I had the great privilege of entering the family of the late Sir Andrew Agnew of Lochnaw, as tutor to his two eldest sons. When I arrived at Lochnaw I had not yet received license, or orders, to preach. I felt myself thus more at liberty on Sundays to exercise my freedom of hearing and worshipping. I was thus not long in finding out the place of meeting of the *Cameronians* in Stranraer, six miles distant from Lochnaw. After a few Sabbaths of interrupted attendance, being very much struck with the learned, profound, and systematic style in which the minister delivered his messages from the inspired book of the Lord, I introduced myself, and soon found that he was the polite, affable gentleman out of the pulpit, as I had previously found him to be the diligent and ripe student, the sagacious and judicious expositor of Scripture, and the earnest and fearless ambassador of Christ, in his place of accredited teacher in the congregation.

"From the time now described our acquaintance ripened into

---

[*] Dr. Liddell has recently passed away.

intimacy, and the most devoted friendship and Christian attachment, increasing in warmth and intensity to the very last of his stay on earth. My visits to him in Stranraer, as a Christian friend, were frequent, and, on my part, most edifying and profitable. Most ready did I find him to open to me his rich and varied stores of knowledge and experience, as a student and a pastor. His exchange visits to me at Lochnaw Castle were as frequent as his pastoral duties would allow. His visits were very highly valued and appreciated by Sir Andrew and Lady Agnew. In both of them he found warm admirers of his talents as a preacher, and of his devotedness to the cause of Christian truth in his advocacy of it, not only in eloquent words, but in holy and consistent practice. . . . In consequence of his not being restricted, by the nature and terms of his commission within *parochial* limits, he not unfrequently—nay, he very often—volunteered to preach for the attainment of Christian missionary objects; and on such occasions his fame as an eloquent orator for Christian ends attracted large congregations, formed of all grades of society, and of all ecclesiastical denominations, assured as they all came to be, that nothing merely sectarian in church government would be the theme dwelt on, but chiefly 'Jesus Christ and him crucified' as the ground and object of the Christian's faith, and the aim of the Christian's exertions. . . .

"I must now record my much cherished remembrance of him in his domestic relationships. His unquenchable affection, in the highest sense, for his wife and children was very striking and remarkable. In the year 1833 I happened to pay a visit to my very kind friends at Lochnaw. [Dr. Liddell was then minister of Lady Yester's, Edinburgh.] While there I received a sudden message from Dr. Symington, intimating that his son Robert had been deprived of life in a moment. . . . I can never forget the beautiful mingling of natural sorrow and Christian acquiescence in the mysterious and sovereign will of their heavenly Father, as manifested by both the suffering parents, on the occasion of this the first and only loss they were called as parents to sustain."

The ministry thus described was kept fresh by unwearied and conscientious study. Whatever was new and valuable in theological literature was got, so far as his means allowed, and read with care. Elaborate digests of the contents are often to be found on the fly-leaves at beginning and end of his books. He kept up also his acquaintance with Hebrew and Greek. And the devotional habits already mentioned quickened all with fresh spiritual life.

Another friend whom our father made about this time was Dr. Welsh, then minister of Crossmichael. Between him and the future moderator of the Disruption Assembly there was a fulness of intelligent sympathy, on questions affecting the Church of Christ in Scotland, which led each to embrace whatever opportunities—not very frequent—they found of meeting. He formed also the acquaintance of Dr. Chalmers, when more than once he came into the neighbourhood on his great errand of church extension; and speaks with warmth of the pleasure he had in spending a day with the greatest man of his generation at Lochryan House in 1838. There will be occasion to mention these distinguished friends again.

It is with very peculiar pleasure that we insert here the recollections of one, less distinguished, who was far more than any other the friend of our parents' hearts, a saintly man and greatly beloved by all who have the privilege of knowing him. The Rev. James M'Gill of Bournemouth, speaking of this period, says—

"An impulse was given to the cause of religion in the whole district. A relish for evangelical preaching was widely and rapidly diffused, which not only caused his own church to be densely crowded, but which led to the erection of new churches and the settlement of additional ministers, in other denominations as well as our own. Bible, and missionary, and educational societies, libraries and Sabbath-schools, sprang up in the town and neighbourhood. A mighty power was felt to be at work. In short, what in these days Dr. Chalmers was to Glasgow, and Dr. Andrew Thomson to the west end of Edinburgh, that, in many respects, was William Symington in Wigtonshire and Galloway."

The same intimate and cherished friend thus gathers together our father's "lofty endowments and qualities":—

"His singularly well-balanced mind; his clear perception of truth; his marvellous power of presenting it in the most luminous and impressive form; the extraordinary degree in which he combined great powers of observation, piercing discernment of character, and sound practical judgment, with metaphysical acumen and abstract thought; . . . his love of order, the perfect regularity of all his habits; his accuracy and diligence; his careful and conscientious improvement of time, never in haste, never forgetting anything; his ceaseless activity, always performing a vast amount of labour. These qualities were continually operating on those around him. His very appearance was enough to shame away from his presence everything like sloth, or idleness, or disorder, or the slovenly performance of any kind of duty.

"As a preacher he had no equal in our own church, and very few equals in any other, in the beautiful arrangement of his discourses, the transparent clearness of his statements, the elegance and force of his language, the warmth and earnestness of his appeals, accompanied by that complete command of his subject which arose from habits of perfect preparation."

To this period belongs our father's work as an author. Although he wrote much and published a little after going to Glasgow, it was in the prime and vigour of his early manhood at Stranraer that the greater part of his literary work was accomplished. There the demands for pastoral, pulpit, and public labour, although great, were not so exacting and exhausting as in the great city: at any rate, having the will, he made the time. Besides the elaborate sermons which were gathered by the author into a volume in 1850, he published a little work on the profane use of the Lot in 1827, and in the same year a Life of John Williamson, a lad in Dumfries who died at the age of sixteen after giving unusual promise of talent and grace. This little work he was induced to undertake by his friend Mr. M'Diarmid, the distinguished editor of the "Dumfries Courier," who furnished him with the facts. A life-long friendship, helpful to our father's literary culture and of which the fragrance is not yet quite spent, subsisted between the man of letters and the earnest minister.

In 1829, when the Catholic Emancipation agitation was at its height, he published a little treatise called "Popery the Mystery of Iniquity," being the substance of sermons preached five years before, on the occasion of a Roman Catholic Chapel being erected in the town. In the same year the Charge to minister and people, delivered at the ordination of Mr. M'Gill as minister of Hightae, was printed,—an utterance full of suggestive things, faithfully and racily put. About the same time he elaborated the plan of a work on "The State and Prospect of the Jews," in ten chapters. A MS. remains, written in 1828, which contains a very full skeleton, with references to sources of information astonishingly minute and full. And there is another MS. of at least twelve years' later date, going carefully over the same ground, which proves how long the hope of writing on this great theme had kept hold of his heart. One handles this outline with a wistful sadness that the author was not permitted to perform the service he so longed to perform; but doubtless it was said to him, "Thou didst well that it was in thine heart."

We ventured to speak of the severe afflictions which marked the years 1833 and 1837 as resulting in fruit. In each case one of his two principal works followed the affliction at the distance of about twelve months. The treatise on the "Atonement and Intercession of Jesus Christ" had been begun in 1831, but laid aside in consequence of uncertain health and much other work. The death of his son probably moved him to fresh labour as both the best medicine for sorrow and the most fit response to the Master's chastening; and the work was issued in May of 1834. The treatise on the "Mediatorial Dominion of Jesus Christ" had been begun before the affliction in 1837, but not much more than begun: as soon, however, as his health was restored, and the long arrears of pastoral work were faithfully overtaken, he gave all the leisure he could command to writing for the press; and the goodly octavo which appeared in December 1838 was the result. Of this latter work we need not say anything, seeing that the reader has it in his hands; but a pleasing story may be told. Our father's diary, under date 14th November, says: "This day finished MS. of 'Messiah the Prince,' and on Monday (12th) corrected first proof-sheet;" and just eight days later comes the following: "Was surprised this morning by a letter from Dr. Chalmers, announcing that the Senatus Academicus of the University of Edinburgh had, on the 20th, unanimously conferred upon me the degree of Doctor in Divinity. This is a most unexpected honour from man, which will require new grace to keep me humble and to enable me to act consistently. The Lord grant the needed grace, and make me more desirous of the honour that cometh from God only." The degree, given with reference to his former book and to his public usefulness, was just in time to appear on the title-page of the forthcoming volume. Every circumstance about it was gratifying. Moved by Chalmers and seconded by Welsh, the degree was heartily conferred by the Senatus. Edinburgh, it was found, had by a few days anticipated his own Alma Mater, Glasgow, which had a diploma filled up and waiting the signatures of some members of its Senatus. And the country minister and his wife, whose frugal care had struggled hard to make the ends of a very scanty stipend meet, after waiting some weeks in fear that a demand would come for considerable fees, found that it never came! The explanation was given some time afterwards, when Sir Andrew Agnew, presiding at a public dinner at Stranraer in honour of Dr. Symington, took the opportunity to mention that, being in Edinburgh at the time when the degree was gazetted, and knowing how seriously the usual fees would affect his friend's purse, he had taken the liberty of going to the University that he might have the pleasure of discharging them; and had been told that in this case they were entirely dispensed with.

The origin of another considerable fruit is deeply interesting, in more than one way. In October of 1837 Dr. Duff visited Stranraer, in the course of his splendid missionary progress through Scotland; and our father seems to have received a remarkable impulse from the great apostle of modern missions. He speaks of the meeting thus: "Dr. Duff's statements are clear, his reasoning sound, and his eloquence surpassing anything I ever heard. Notwithstanding a weak frame and a bad voice, his appeals are most impassioned and thrilling. He touches the springs of emotion, lays down the path of duty with unceremonious fidelity, and rebukes the apathy and indifference of professing Christians with fearless independence." Missionary zeal was, as we have seen, no new thing for Dr. Symington; but the deep impression made now led to its taking a new direction. After speaking of the "inexpressible satisfaction and delight of hearing Duff, and the great privilege of meeting with that great and good man," our father adds: "May it be blessed for increasing my zeal for the conversion of the heathen." These were not words, of course, soon to be forgotten. On the 12th of January 1838, observed as old New Year's day in Stranraer, he gathered the youth of his congregation, read missionary intelligence, delivered an address on the obligation of Christians to diffuse the Gospel among the heathen, and formed a juvenile missionary society on the spot. Nearly sixty names were put down and about £10 subscribed; but not content with this very gratifying result, he reaches forth in faith and prayer to much greater things: "May this be the commencement of a mission to the heathen from the Reformed Presbyterian Church!" We by no means wish to claim for Dr. Symington the honour of altogether originating the New Hebrides Mission which four years later received the sanction of the Synod; but this is the earliest historical trace of that mission, and he did his utmost to help it from the first.

In the year before their death our parents had the great satisfaction of receiving under their roof two honoured missionaries, Mr. and Mrs. Inglis, through whom largely the Lord of the harvest had changed Aneityum into a Southern Iona, and with them a native elder whose baptismal name, *Williamu*, linked the former savage with the earnest Scottish minister.

The success of the New Hebrides Mission has been remarkable; and it stirs many a thought which it would not be easy to express, to reflect that Alexander Duff unconsciously received in old age the fruit of his address at Stranraer. The happy union of the Free and Reformed Presbyterian Churches in 1876, brought the thriving mission in Polynesia under his care as convener: he mastered the facts of its growth, and gave it a warm place in his noble heart; but it is scarcely possible that he could know of the interesting link between 1877 and 1837. Those who accomplish most for the Lord Christ are those whose faith is the least dependent on knowing about fruits here. "He that reapeth receiveth wages and gathereth fruit unto life eternal, that both he that soweth and he that reapeth may rejoice together" (John iv. 36).

Before passing from the years covered by this chapter, it is right, while omitting much else that might have been of interest to some, to mention two things briefly. Our father helped his revered brother, Dr. Andrew Symington, in freeing the Church of our fathers from that narrowness in matters of occasional hearing and the like which would have obscured its testimony for great truths by surrounding it with a chill and misty atmosphere, far from being Christ-like. Both brothers did much in this direction, by their personal influence and in the courts of the Church.

Indications of a loosening from Stranraer appear in occasional references to the size and scatteredness of the congregation, and in repeated invitations to preach in the West. In 1836 a call came from the congregation of West Campbell Street, Glasgow, and his diary contains a very remarkable proof of his conscientiousness in an elaborate weighing of the *pros* and *cons*. To print this could serve no good purpose, but we would not be doing justice to our father's memory if we did not mention the fact with emphasis. In those days the translation of a minister was almost, or quite, a new thing; and, by the Synod refusing to present the call, he was saved the pain of a public statement. A decision then would probably have been in favour of Stranraer; at least, when the West Campbell Street congregation renewed their call in the beginning of 1838 he promptly declined it. The publication of "Messiah the Prince," and the recognition of his public worth by the University of Edinburgh, were soon followed by a unanimous call from the Great Hamilton Street congregation, Glasgow. He seems to have been saved from much anxiety as to his decision, first, by referring back to the exceedingly elaborate calculation of reasons for and against made three years before; and secondly, by the supreme court deciding on the 16th of May to present the call. This was regarded as so far *vox ecclesiæ, vox Dei:* and from that date a distinct epoch of his life began.

CHAPTER IV.

EARLIER YEARS IN GLASGOW. 1839–1853.

ÆTATE 45–58.

THE perusal of our father's private records during those years, and of a mass of materials which would suffice for a complete biography, leaves an impression of immense diligence, of large success, and of a hidden life, growing in godly simplicity and humility, by which all the visible strength and success are explained.

In the spring of 1839 Dr. Symington was permitted to accomplish a long-cherished wish in a visit to London. He was the guest of the family mentioned at the beginning of this sketch, some of the members of which were among the earliest seals of his ministry. The whole month of April was thus spent; and most interesting records remain in his journal and letters of how each day of the great holiday was occupied. The principal sights of the great city were explored; many meetings of the religious and missionary societies were attended, in some of which he took part; the services of different churches were keenly observed; and a considerable amount of intercourse was enjoyed with persons eminent in the Christian world.*

---
* Dining at the house of the late Earl of Galloway, with whom he had

The holiday was well-timed, as it was certainly well-earned. It was a break in his career, dividing it at mid-time; and the impulse to mind and heart from witnessing fresh scenes and mingling with men and enterprises hitherto known chiefly by report, was the most suitable under which to enter on an enlarged sphere. On the wide field of Christian labour in the second city of the empire he entered two months after his return.

The leaving Stranraer was full of distressing heart-strain, and it was a relief when the farewell was at length spoken. On his forty-fifth birthday (June 2d) he preached to a sorrowing crowd on the words: "With me it is a very small thing that I should be judged of you, or of man's judgment: yea, I judge not mine own self. For I know nothing by myself; yet am I not hereby justified: but he that judgeth me is the Lord" (1 Cor. iv. 3, 4); and again on the 23d, from Paul's farewell words at Miletus. He thus speaks of the parting in a letter, dated July 8th, to one of the friends whose guest he had recently been in London:—

"So we are fairly moved from Stranraer and settled in this great city. The parting with my flock was the most trying event I have ever met with. The affection of my poor people was

---

met as President of the Galloway Auxiliary to the Bible Society, the household was assembled about midnight for family worship. The Bishop of Vermont, another of the guests, had read the Scriptures, when Dr. Symington was unexpectedly called on to pray. He thought the occasion a fit one on which to use the Lord's prayer; but scarcely had the first words been uttered when they were taken up and repeated by more than sixty voices! For this he had not reckoned, and used to say that he feared some of the petitions had been missed.

extraordinary. I never witnessed such expressions of genuine grief. The last Sabbath I was at Stranraer was an awful day to me. The forenoon service was from Acts xx. 20-27; that in the afternoon from ver. 32. Many lingered about the church door to get a last look and shake of my hand; and on Tuesday hundreds followed me to the ship with tears and audible weeping. It was more than I could stand, and I was obliged to keep below till the vessel began to move, and then I went on deck and received and returned their salutations as long as we were in sight."

On the 14th of July William Symington was introduced to the congregation in Great Hamilton Street, Glasgow, by his brother and second father, Professor Andrew Symington of Paisley; and his text for four Sabbaths was: " By manifestation of the truth commending ourselves to every man's conscience in the sight of God. But if our Gospel be hid, it is hid to them who are lost" (2 Cor. iv. 2, 3).

That portion of the old historical Church of Scotland which bore the brunt of the Stuart tyranny and regarded the Revolution Settlement of 1688-90 as a compromise unworthy of the Church's attainment from 1560 to 1638, remained long without a ministry, keeping up its spiritual life by means of the societies which Cameron and Renwick had organised. The Reformed Presbyterians in and around Glasgow continued thus until 1765, when the Rev. John Macmillan (son of the first minister of the Church, Macmillan of Balmaghie) became their pastor. He preached to large audiences in the fields till 1777, when a small place of worship was built at Sandhills, about three miles east of the city. In 1791 another meeting-house was erected in the Calton of Glasgow, and for some years the preaching alternated between the two places. At length Sandhills was given up. In 1794 the Rev. John Fairley became the colleague of Mr. Macmillan, and continued in the pastoral charge until 1807. The congregation remained for seven or eight years without a minister, when the Rev. David Armstrong, "a good man, and a substantial and able preacher," was ordained (February 23, 1815). In 1819 the present church in Great Hamilton Street—large, and, for these days, handsome—was built. Mr. Armstrong died on the 30th of March 1838, leaving a congregation of about three hundred members, over which our father was set, many of whom came in to worship from places three, five, and even eight miles distant.

We shall not be charged with partiality if, looking back over forty years, we say that his influence and success kept pace with the rapid growth of the city, and that his ministry of twenty-three years was a distinguished blessing both to the Reformed Presbyterian Church and to the community at large. His pulpit work told at once in Glasgow, as it had done in Stranraer. The Communion-roll had fifty or sixty names added to it at each half-yearly dispensation of the Lord's Supper, and the church, seated for a thousand persons, was soon quite filled by a stated congregation. And side by side with preaching there went faithful and very exhausting pastoral work. There were systematic visitations from house to house; the sick felt the support of his sympathetic counsels and prayers; the young were gathered into weekly classes; Sabbath-schools and mission work were organised;

ordinary prayer-meetings, missionary prayer-meetings, and district fellowship meetings were established or strengthened: by every means his own vigorous Christian spirit was diffused into the large and growing congregation.

Courses of monthly lectures on Sabbath evenings became a remarkable feature of his ministry. The first was on the Book of Daniel, and began in November 1839. So great was the popularity of the new preacher that, after the first six lectures had been given, it became necessary to deliver the remainder in the afternoon as well as the evening, a second audience waiting on the street eager to secure the places vacated by the first. The course on Daniel was concluded in July 1842; another course on the life of Joseph was begun in August, and extended to March 1845; the same unprecedented demand for a repeated delivery lasting for five years. A course of lectures on the Apocalypse, begun on the 4th of May 1845,—marked as the day on which "my son William preached his first sermon,"— was not finished until October of 1850, being interrupted more than once by prolonged afflictions. The audiences were as large as ever, but the repeated delivery was not continued for want of strength. These discourses, like all his public utterances, were the fruit of much careful preparation,—not fully written, much less read—but thoroughly studied and digested, the beginning of each sentence and references to texts being put down in neat and orderly form. Not read, certainly; for no one understood more thoroughly the true theory of preaching as a *concio ad populum*, an address in which the speaker is in full, electric communication with his hearers. The larger writing was reduced to notes on a thin slip; these he went over again and again until his mind was familiar with the whole process of thought; by prayer his soul was brought up to the level of the divine message he was charged to utter; and thus were secured the pellucid clearness, the obvious mastery, the unaffected unction, which made his preaching so attractive and useful. Not a few who are now ministers of various churches in different places, still speak with pleasure and gratitude of the opportunity enjoyed by them of hearing these courses of lectures while pursuing their studies at the University.

Professor Binnie, now of the Free College, Aberdeen, was intimately associated with Dr. Symington from the time of his going to Glasgow as a member of his congregation, and a greatly valued friend. He very kindly writes thus—

"How much your father excelled as a preacher there is no need to tell: the crowds who constantly resorted to his ministry, from first to last, sufficiently attest that. Other testimonies could easily be given. A venerable friend of mine in Stirling, who was an elder of the Established Church long before the Disruption of 1843, told me that, having occasion to pay an annual visit to an estate belonging to him in Galloway, it was his unfailing custom to arrange his visit so that he might spend a Sabbath day in Stranraer; and this he did for the sole purpose of hearing Dr. Symington preach.

"Some of the causes of his popularity were obvious to every hearer. He had all the natural parts of an orator,—a commanding and winsome presence; a good voice; singular lucidity of thought and expression. He never lost himself in misty attempts at thinking, or failed to convey clearly what was in his mind. But other and deeper causes were at work. For one thing, he was a most diligent student, giving himself continually to reading and meditation. Besides having always in hand some course of systematic reading in divinity, he kept himself well abreast of the best literature of the day. . . . What is of still greater importance, he knew and loved the Gospel of the grace of God: his preaching, therefore, whatever the topic might be, was always perfumed with a certain unction which commended it to the hearts of Christian hearers. And this again was connected with the fact that he was a man of prayer. From himself, indeed, one did not hear much regarding his private feelings and habits. He was reticent about himself, perhaps to a fault. But secret emotion cannot be quite hidden. If, when he entered the pulpit, his garments often smelled of myrrh, the reason, I do not doubt, was that he had just come forth from the palace of the King."

The records of his inner life now before us abundantly confirm what Dr. Binnie has so finely expressed.

The services of such a man were sure to be claimed by the city charities, by the large religious societies, and in behalf of the evangelical side in great public questions, such as Sabbath observance, Non-intrusion, resistance to Papal aggression, and the like. These services were cheerfully rendered to the utmost measure of his strength. For many years he was Secretary, in conjunction with Dr. A. N. Somerville (who still survives in a singularly world-wide fruitfulness), of the Glasgow branch of the National Bible Society of Scotland. To the Old Men's Charity, the Boy's House of Refuge, and other similar institutions, he gave practical help year after year, by preaching to the inmates and serving on the committees. And for all his frequent platform appearances in the City Hall and elsewhere, in which he was hailed by large audiences, he made the same careful preparation as for his sermons.

When these manifold labours were beginning, he undertook another literary task, the editing of Scott's Commentary. The brief leisure which he was able to command among the noble scenery of Loch Long and Loch Lomond during June of 1841, was spent in writing the introductory essay to that work; and for a long time thereafter no week passed without the preparation of notes, or the irksome correction of proof-sheets.

The year 1843 must meanwhile be regarded as the highest mountain peak in the history of the Church of Scotland this side of 1638: another and loftier is yet to be reached when, the relations of the reigning Mediator to both Church and State being more adequately apprehended, the Church shall be one again, more thoroughly reformed, more perfectly united and free than she has yet been, "and the Highest himself shall establish her." The book "*Messiah the Prince*" had been well known these four years among those who were struggling for the crown rights of the Redeemer against Erastianism; and its author had now, besides meeting more frequently with Chalmers and Welsh, added to the list of his friends such men as Dr. Brown of St. John's, Dr. Smyth of St. George's, Dr. Henderson of St. Enoch's, and Dr. Buchanan of the Tron. He had watched the Ten Years' Conflict with eager sympathy; and when the middle of May came, every preparation was made to admit of his being in Edinburgh to witness the event in which he so heartily rejoiced.

"*May* 18*th*, 1843.—Witnessed the Disruption in the

Church of Scotland. A splendid sight, worth living a century to behold! The meeting at Canonmills immense, and proceedings full of deepest interest." He walked with the great procession from St. Andrew's Church to Canonmills; attended the Free Assembly the next day; and on the Monday following gave an account of the magnificent event to his congregation. When sometimes asked why he, who sympathised with it so enthusiastically, did not join the Free Church, he would say, "With a great sum you have purchased this freedom, but we were free-born," thus pleasantly expressing what is better understood to-day than it was then, that the church he represented had long anticipated the Disruption, although with smaller numbers and no public *eclat*, by standing aloof from what has proved the root of so much mischief, the Revolution compromise.

The Reformed Presbyterian Church met the public excitement in the way for her most appropriate. The Synod was convened in the first week of July to commemorate the Bi-Centenary of the Westminster Assembly by sermons and speeches; and sent a cordial message of goodwill to the new Assembly. On that occasion Dr. Symington read a Historical Sketch of the Westminster Assembly which, together with other papers of considerable value by other ministers, is now to be found in a little volume published at the time. In the conclusion of that paper he put emphasis on his longing after union thus—

"May the Lord the Spirit give the ministers and members of the divided churches of the Reformation one heart and one way, that they may fear him for ever, for the good of them and their children after them! Then—and not till then—shall be fulfilled the great, the bright, the glorious conceptions of the Solemn League and of the Westminster Assembly; it being the explicit design of the latter 'to bring the church at home into *nearer agreement with other reformed churches abroad,*' and of the former 'to bring the churches of God in the three kingdoms TO THE NEAREST CONJUNCTION AND UNIFORMITY, AND TO ENCOURAGE OTHER CHRISTIAN CHURCHES TO JOIN IN THE SAME OR LIKE ASSOCIATION AND COVENANT, TO THE ENLARGEMENT OF THE KINGDOM OF CHRIST, AND THE PEACE AND TRANQUILLITY OF CHRIST'S KINGDOMS AND COMMONWEALTHS."

A more extended celebration took place in Edinburgh during the following week, in which ministers of various denominations took part. Dr. Symington was asked to open the meetings with a sermon, and preached in Canonmills Hall on "Love one another" (John xiii. 34). It is due to his revered memory, since he did not live to take part in the happy union consummated in June 1876, to give the concluding paragraphs of that sermon. He took part in the subsequent proceedings; and exclaims: "Two days of high delight. Felt great satisfaction in meeting so many of different denominations who harmonise on the grand doctrines of Christ. May blessed fruits result from these meetings."

In the beginning of this year Dr. Wardlaw published a volume of "Discourses on the Nature and Extent of the Atonement," in which he traversed the views expounded by Dr. Symington in his book ten years before. Judging Dr. Wardlaw's opinions fitted to do harm, he wrote an elaborate review in the "Scottish Presbyterian" for November 1843. Dr. Wardlaw replied in a pamphlet entitled "The Reviewers Reviewed;" and the controversy was closed, in so far as these two theologians were concerned, by a second paper in the same journal for May 1844. These papers commanded by their vigour and acumen the high respect even of those whom they did not fully convince. They are in our judgment of permanent value and the best of our father's writings. It is delightful to know that the controversy only for a little time estranged the two faithful servants of Christ: before long we shall find them together on the platform of Christian union.

A few years later he interested himself in the republication of Dr. Charles Hodge's "Essay on the Extent of the Atonement" (Review of Beman) from the "Princeton Review." The pamphlet was introduced to the British public by a preface, written by him, and to which the names of Thomas M'Crie, Robert Candlish, and William Cunningham, as well as his own name, were attached.

While enjoying vigorous health and in the midst of the fullest activities, our father resolved to set his house in order. Two sentences from his will, which is dated 21st March 1845, may be given as shewing the spirit in which this duty was discharged.

"*First*, That my wife and children shall continue to walk in the ways of truth and godliness, resting their hopes of eternal salvation on the finished righteousness of Jesus Christ the Son of God and the alone Saviour of sinners, adhering to the visible fellowship of that church which shall appear to them, on diligent, conscientious examination, to possess the firmest basis of scriptural authority, and choosing as their companions, whether permanent or occasional, only such as give evidence that they fear God and keep his commandments."

Then, after bequeathing to each child by name a piece of household furniture, he concludes thus :—

"These individual bequests I make that my children may possess a memorial of the love and esteem of their affectionate father, who, having dedicated them often to the Lord in prayer, and recorded many supplications on their behalf at the throne of grace, through the merit and grace of the blessed Jesus cherishes the good hope of meeting them all in the FATHER'S HOUSE, in which are many mansions, there to resume social intercourse and to enjoy throughout eternal ages the blessings of an inheritance that is incorruptible, undefiled, and that fadeth not away."

The knowledge that this most precious document was signed and ready must have been a source of comfort to our beloved father when, six months later, he was very suddenly brought down to the gates of death. Early in October an inflammatory attack, occurring between Saturday night and Sabbath morning, exhausted his strength in a few hours; and eight weeks passed in silence. Another illness, of nearly equal duration but less alarming, occurred in the winter of 1848-49. Let it be enough to say that both of these led to exercises of personal piety as deep as those already recorded.

In 1846 Dr. Symington was permitted to see the desires he had long cherished in behalf of the house of Israel in some measure realised. On 14th May the Rev. John Cunningham, a man of colossal learning and the most single-hearted devotedness, was ordained missionary from the Reformed Presbyterian Church to the Jews in London. Dr. Symington, who had eighteen months before written a Pastoral Address on the Conversion of the Jews, was appointed to give the customary charge,—an address full of scriptural wisdom and spirit; and for many years afterwards, acting as the Synod's missionary secretary, he formed the link between the missionary and the Church.

Our father was urged to attend the conference in Liverpool out of which the Evangelical Alliance sprang; but while that conference was meeting he was stretched on a bed of sickness. When he recovered, he took part heartily in the work of the committees by which preparation was made for the constitution of the Alliance in August 1846; and particularly interested himself in securing that the intercession and reign of Christ should be recognised in the Basis, for this purpose moving the addition of certain words to the fourth (afterwards made the fifth) article. Mr. Bickersteth, in proposing the adoption of the Basis, alluded to the change thus made in the following terms :—

"After having come together in so large a conference on the former footing, I felt at first some hesitation in making the addition: but in this I soon found I was short-sighted. I did not look at the largeness of our work—at the wide field which was gradually opening before us. My Scotch brethren and my American brethren have helped me here. When my beloved brother Dr. Symington proposed, and Dr. Wardlaw seconded, the addition to the fourth article, my whole mind concurred with it: but I was afraid to consent till I saw how the other brethren came forward and concurred in the alteration. And it was singular enough that, at the next meeting, my friend and beloved brother Dr. Keith, when I stated to him that the aggregate committee had made that alteration, gave me permission to propose his name to the nomination committee. He is going on an important mission to Germany: may the Lord bless him in it! I may add that he told me he felt comfort and assurance in going as a member of the Evangelical Alliance to the brethren on the continent with that amendment subjoined." *

Before the time came for the great meetings in London he had studied the subject of Christian union and made himself master of all its bearings. The part he took in the conferences, his journals, and letters, bear witness to the lively delight he felt in the inauguration of this great means for promoting and turning to good account the visible unity of Christians. On the 23d of August he preached in the pulpit of Dr. James Hamilton, Regent Square; and on the 25th moved the following resolution : " That in this Alliance it is distinctly understood, that no compromise of the views of any member, or sanction of those of others, is either required or expected; but that all are held as free as before to maintain and advocate their religious convictions, with due forbearance and brotherly love." The following sentences from his speech will be read with interest in the light of those efforts after incorporating union in Scotland which began two years after his death :—

"There is no danger, I think, from a cordial acquiescence in the sentiments of the resolution: but there may be some danger of individuals going away with the impression that they are to keep up their differences of opinion for ever. Now, one of the things which from the very commencement has commended this movement to my mind has been that it holds out to me a prospect—I grant, but a very distant one—that our differences of opinion will be got over. It is one of the means, and it appears to me one of the most likely means, of bringing us to be of one mind. There is, indeed, a mode of speaking on this subject which, I confess, I do not like. There is a talking of *forgetting* our differences, and *banishing* our differences;

---

* Official Report of Evangelical Alliance, p. 79.

and as some express it, *merging* our differences. I go further than all these: I want the differences to be done away with altogether. I am afraid that, if we merely agree to *forget* them, it will not be long before something forcibly reminds us of them. I am afraid, if we merely *banish* them, like some old culprits they will find their way back before the time of punishment has expired. I am afraid, if we only *merge* them, there will be some sectarian antiquary who will invent a diving-bell to bring them up from the bottom of the ocean. I think the best way, therefore, is to get rid of them altogether; and I have very great confidence in the moral influence of this Alliance, in finally disposing of our differences. I think there is, in the moral influence exerted on the minds of the members by our devotional exercises and by combined action, that which may give rise to another element which will bind us together and bring us to agreement, that is, communication of ideas, which has always been an element in the union of individuals formerly strangers. In these things there is much that is calculated to unite us. It is not the inability to place our distinct opinions in a clear light, that keeps us from seeing eye to eye; but there is a worldly feeling, a prejudice, in our breasts that prevents us from doing justice to our own intellects and judgments: and until such an influence as that I have adverted to is exercised, we should never be able to see these things alike. This is not theory. If I may refer to my own experience, I would say, I realised this at the Bi-centenary Commemoration of the Westminster Assembly, three years ago. We met there under peculiar circumstances; it was immediately after the heat of the Voluntary Controversy in which we had been pitted together for years. We read the Scriptures of truth—we sang the praises of God—we joined in prayer—we read essays in one another's hearing. And the result was, although I had taken part in the controversy and though I did not feel that I had compromised my principles, that I could not for my life have said a bitter thing of any one member with whom I had been associated there."[*]

It was a favourite phrase of our father, in speaking of anyone whose course of life he had occasion to observe from year to year, "He's a growing man;" and he

[*] Authorised Report, pp. 196–198.

rejoiced whenever he could say this with truth. The handling of his private records reminds us of the phrase, and brings to the children who were accustomed to look on him as perfect the feeling how true the phrase was of himself. There was a pretty thick octavo book, in strong boards and closed with a stout lock, which used to lie on his study table, an object of some curiosity and awe. Only now (1879) is that book open before us, and we make the discovery that it was begun on the 10th of January 1848, under a "long continued and growing and painful sense of defectiveness in experimental piety. . . . I find it difficult, amid the turmoil of incessant occupation, to keep alive the flame of inward devotion. It is not the secular business of the world only, but the more sacred business of a minister's life, which is apt to trample down, or trample out, the fire of personal religion." Page after page, on to the end of his life, reveals how earnestly and prayerfully he strove to counteract these influences by courses of devotional reading, by noting the hand of God in providence, and by a solemn exercise of personal consecration once a month. The contents are far too sacred for publication; but we may venture to give a portion of the entry on 2d June 1853.

"This day I complete the fifty-eighth year of my life and enter on the fifty-ninth, coming near to what Dr. Chalmers calls happily 'the Sabbath of our earthly existence,' the seventh decade of life. The year has been one of great health, calling for gratitude ; and of much activity, calling for prayer to God to bless it to his glory. I have not for long done so much work in my study as during the past year; and through God's grace I am enabled to continue this kind of cherished labour.

"From the point of time which I now occupy I feel favourably situated to contemplate 'the funeral procession of centuries, the hand's-breadth of man's earthly existence, and the vast gulf of duration beyond.' Let me hear the summons, 'Behold the Bridegroom cometh, go *thou* out to meet him!' Let me diligently inquire whether I am receding from or approximating to the source of all light and life—whether I am nearing 'the blackness of darkness for ever' or the blaze of celestial brightness. In the year on which I am about to enter, and during the brief remainder of my earthly pilgrimage, may I have grace to put forth the energies of my soul more vigorously in the service of God in the Gospel of his Son; and, in order to this, may I be studious to secure for myself as much time as possible for exercises of sacred devotion—'those golden hours to fit me for the skies.' Thou divine Spirit! work in me according to thy mighty power! Μονῳ Θεῳ τιμη και δοξα."

These words reveal the secret of the past part of our father's life and of the fruitful years that remain.

CHAPTER V.

PROFESSORSHIP AND LAST DAYS.   1853–1861.

ÆTATE 58-67.

THROUGHOUT the whole of his ministry William Symington took hearty interest in young men. The dignity of his character, although felt by everyone, did not prevent his intercourse with the young being genial and helpful: it was soon forgotten in the consciousness of sincere goodwill and sympathy. At Stranraer the opportunity of intercourse with those preparing for the ministry was limited; but when he came to Glasgow he put himself into contact with the students of the Reformed Presbyterian Church attending the University, formed classes for them, and invited them to his house.

The following letter, the date of which very nearly marks the writer's jubilee as a minister, shews the kind of influence Dr. Symington exerted in this direction. Every reader will, we are sure, share our feeling of very sincere gratitude that this memoir is enriched by such a communication.

"5 WESTOVER VILLAS, BOURNEMOUTH, HANTS,
12*th June* 1879.

"MY DEAR MR. SYMINGTON,—I am glad that you have undertaken to write a memoir of your lamented father. He was a very distinguished man: many who have now passed away would have read with the deepest interest the record of one whom they so much admired and loved.

"Beyond the immediate circle of his own family, I do not think there was anyone that was more indebted to him than myself. When he was ordained at Stranraer I was thirteen years of age, just the time of life when the mind begins to open; and his sermons were to me the chief source of mental stimulus and spiritual instruction. When, a few years later, I became a student of divinity, he treated me with every possible kindness, admitting me to his study, showing me whatever work he was engaged with, conversing freely on every subject which he thought would interest me, and, without seeming to exercise the least authority, really guiding my thoughts and directing my studies. When I was ordained in July 1829, he preached the ordination sermon, and delivered the charges to the minister and people which were at the time published. Looking over some of the numerous letters which I received from him then and afterwards, although saddened by the memory of the many desolating changes which fifty years have wrought, it is refreshing to recall, not only his talent and eloquence, which were known to all, but his sound judgment, his wise counsels, his great and considerate kindness, and his powerful personal influence. He constantly told me of the books he was reading, giving me his opinion of them, and directing my attention to whatever he thought specially worthy of notice. This I felt at the time, and still more I feel now at the distance of so many years, was intended for my benefit. . . . Your father made frequent mention of the essays of John Foster, the sermons of Robert Hall, the works of Isaac Taylor, Tytler's 'History of Scotland,' and the biographies and histories of the first Dr. M'Crie. Foster's 'Essay on Decision of Character' he read many times, and I always thought that celebrated essay had a considerable share in moulding his own character. Hall's sermons he always delighted in, saying they were the finest specimens of pulpit eloquence in the English language. Isaac Taylor was a special favourite, and his successive volumes were eagerly perused and warmly recommended." *

---

* The names may here be given of some of the authors whose works he read in later years. He kept a book in which some remark on each volume read was inserted. Hare; Trench; Dr. Arnold; Alford; Stanley; Birks; Henry Rogers; Jeffrey; Macaulay; Stephen; Arthur; Rigg; Vaughan; M'Crie; Chalmers; Hanna; Guthrie; Arnot; Candlish; Whately; Masson; Livingstone; Lord Dufferin; George Wilson; Hugh Miller, and many others.

"For myself, I can only say, with all sincerity, that if I have been of any use in the world, if my ministry has been of any service to those among whom I have laboured, this is, under God, greatly due to his character, his instructions, and his example. And I am not the only one who might have made a similar confession. His influence had the happiest effect upon the whole church of which he was a member: the intelligence, the mental culture, and the efficiency of her ministers were perceptibly improved; and their worth and excellence were better known and acknowledged than they had previously been, after he became one of their number.—Believe me to remain, my dear Mr. Symington, yours very truly,

JAMES M'GILL."

In the communication from which an extract has been already given, Professor Binnie mentions a significant fact.

"I can never forget a parting visit I paid him in his study one day in the autumn of 1845. I was going off to spend a winter on the continent. He made me kneel along with him, and commended me to God in a prayer which affected me far more than any public prayer of his had ever done: it was so simple, so warm, so wise, so clearly an outpouring of the heart."

It was our father's custom thus to pray with his children at turning-points in the journey of life, and on other special occasions.

The theological training of the students of the Reformed Presbyterian Church had been, since 1820, under the care of Dr. Andrew Symington of Paisley. In the middle of September 1853, while the Hall was in session, his health gave way suddenly, in consequence of an injury received in leaving a railway carriage. Still the noble old man toiled on in his much-loved work, meeting with us in his dining-room during the last week, when unable to cross the road to the Hall. The last of these meetings was on the morning of the 20th; on the evening of the 22d he fell asleep,—a ripe saint, tender, prayerful, fervent, eloquent, "full of faith and of the Holy Spirit," a man to whom the rare privilege was granted of having trained nearly all the ministers of his church who survived him, besides many others in Ireland and America, and who lives in the grateful love of every one who knew him.

When he returned from his deathbed, the bereaved brother wrote in his diary: "The scene was a solemn and affecting one. May I have grace to improve it by following the dear departed in his faith, holiness, humility and devotedness, by occupying till Christ come, and by standing ready for the call of my divine Master." Many similar references, written at much later dates, shew how keenly the loss was felt which closed a singularly warm and fruitful brotherhood; and among our father's papers there is the full plan of a memoir of the man whom he revered and loved more than any other.

The Synod met early in January 1854, and unanimously appointed Dr. William Symington to the vacant Chair of Systematic Theology, the efficiency of the Hall being at the same time greatly increased by the appointment of Dr. Goold to a new Chair of Biblical Literature and Church History. The office was accepted with undisguised pleasure, for the work was his delight; but at the same time with some hesitation and many fears, for he was now in his fifty-ninth year. The record of secret devotions, to which reference has been made, bears witness to the profound sense of responsibility and the many prayers with which he entered on the task.

Those about him, however, even those in the family, were not permitted to see much of these feelings. What we saw was an increase of diligence, where there seemed no room for increase; earlier rising so as to secure more than the one hour hitherto spent in the study before breakfast; snatches of leisure from pastoral duties eagerly used, at Bridge of Allan or some quiet spot on the Firth of Clyde; until a complete course of lectures had been fully written. This extra labour extended over four or five years, each year yielding about six hundred pages of closely written manuscript. His pulpit was supplied by Synod during the eight weeks' session of Hall; but otherwise the pastoral charge remained as before, and these two months were more full of work than any others. On five days of the week two hours were spent with the students; and sometimes there were extra meetings on Saturdays.

For the Professor did not limit himself to delivering lectures on Systematic Theology. Besides hearing exercises and conducting examinations, he gave a remarkable course of lectures on Homiletics. He held a very decided opinion to the effect that those only who have themselves had some success in preaching ought to be set to train preachers; and he eagerly gave his students the benefit of his large reading, his shrewd acquaintance with human nature, and his ripe experience. These lectures were specially instructive, rich in wisdom, and leaving on our minds a deep sense of the greatness of the preacher's office. The Professor never appeared to greater advantage than when delivering them colloquially, and enlivening them with many a racy anecdote. All the greater is our regret that, unless some student may have preserved copious notes, they exist now only in the shape of a fleshless skeleton,—neat and orderly jottings, but scarcely intelligible even to one who heard them.

The following letter shews how fresh the impressions left on the mind of a student remain after twenty years :—

"36 Cumberland Street, Glasgow,
30th June 1879.

"My dear Mr. Symington,—My recollections and impressions of your father are of the most agreeable kind. It was more as a professor than as a minister that I came under his influence. We students were all proud of him as a man, a professor, a friend. As a man, his commanding figure, gentlemanly manner, natural enthusiasm and eloquence, inspired us with respect. As a professor, he approached as near as perhaps is possible to a model. Punctual to the hour, reverent in reading the Word of God, devout in prayer, he fanned in our hearts the flame of devotion. Then these Lectures on Systematic Theology, what a treat to our opening minds! so comprehensive, methodical, demonstrative, elevated and elaborated, brimming with information, all poured forth with such glowing energy as at once revealed the sympathy of his own mind with his theme and fixed ours. I would give much to be able to listen to them again. The Homiletic Lectures, which were only occasional, gave outlet to his abounding humour. Many a mirth-provoking story is still remembered illustrative of the foibles of preachers in the selection and division of texts. But these sallies served only to impress on our softened natures an all-important truth. 'Gentlemen,' he would add, 'be powerful preachers. Some are known as funny, fine, flowery, pretty, sweet, and so forth: be you mighty. Aim at being known as men of power.' Such, doubtless, was his own ideal. Having chosen a substantial text, he spared no pains on the matter, style, spirit and delivery to make the truth tell on the hearts and minds of his audience; and he had a corresponding reward.

"As a friend dispensing hospitality in his own house, he could admirably adapt himself to students. Books new and old, articles from and for the press, presents from lands far and near, were made to interest us nearly as much as himself. A finer combination of the gentleman, the preacher, the professor, the friend, it would be hard to find.—I am, my dear Sir, sincerely yours,

JOHN EDGAR."

Some of the rules which he often pressed upon his students remain in our memory. Although no originality can be claimed for them, they are given here to illustrate his character and perpetuate his usefulness.

1. Never use a text in praying or in preaching without having read it in your own Bible. By this means accuracy is secured, much light is often found in the context, and mastery of Scripture is at length acquired.

2. Begin every piece of study and composition with solemn prayer. If interrupted, on resuming the pen lift up your heart afresh.

3. Be superior to moods. Do not wait on an afflatus before beginning to work. Seek strength, and go at your work with courage; the mood will come. (The example and words of Chalmers used to be quoted to enforce this.)

4. Be always *natural* in speaking. Study elocution, of course, but the best thing such study can do for you is to make your utterance perfectly natural. For an example of the natural expression of earnestness, go to the Saltmarket and watch the fish-wives bargaining and scolding.

The work of his large congregation was carried on with unabated vigour during the last years of Dr.

Symington's life. He maintained it in conspicuous prosperity—numerous, united, warmly attached to himself, and with considerable evangelistic fruitfulness—to the very last. An offshoot on the south side of the city, kindly cherished by him in 1853, has for many years been a considerable and fruitful congregation, under the bountiful and genial pastorate of the Rev. John M'Dermid. The mission in Green Street grew apace in the hands of Mr. Edgar (whose admirable letter has just been quoted); and from it, in 1863, a congregation was formed in the extreme east of the city, which is still highly prosperous. A third congregation in the west end, although formally constituted by a disjunction from West Campbell Street, derived a good part of its strength from the old church in the east without diminishing the attendance in its pews or the vigour of its congregational life.

So much toil brought with it occasional illness, a frequent sense of weariness, and the fear that while one part of his work was done well, other parts might be left undone. Not that any part was left undone: he preached as earnestly and visited as assiduously as ever. But, although he maintained his habitual cheerfulness—which was not easily affected, because it had its roots in Christian simplicity of heart and genuine goodwill to men—the double work of minister and professor was carried on at a serious expense of vital energy. This is a thing which congregations and churches, when they see a man going on earnestly with his work, do not, alas! understand. He craved assistance, not that he might do less, but that more might be done; and his congregation at length took steps to procure him a colleague. Their choice fell, in March 1857, on his oldest son, who had for thirteen years been minister at Castle Douglas,—a man of culture and wisdom, with a singular power of winning hearts, well fitted by his gifts as a preacher to sustain the character of the Great Hamilton Street pulpit. But the opposition made by his attached flock, and his own deep conviction, retained to the last, that he was not suited for a charge in a large city, led my brother to decline this call. Our father was sorely disappointed; but he neither murmured nor was disheartened: and on the 3d of March 1859, the call having been renewed, he was granted the desire of his heart in seeing his first-born son inducted as his colleague and successor.

One evening (the date cannot be precisely fixed) our father returned in very good spirits from dining with a Christian merchant, and told us that as soon as his name had been announced, the Rev. Rajah Gopaul had come to him and asked if he were the author of a book on the Atonement, saying that was the first treatise on theology put into his hands after he had begun to study for the ministry in Madras. Later in the evening, Mr. Anderson, the missionary under whom the Brahmin had been brought to Christ, had taken him aside and asked whether he remembered having preached at Springholm, in the open air, from a certain text. He had preached often there, he said, but could not recall the occasion or the text. "But I can," said the missionary, "for I was on the outskirts of the crowd, and my attention was then for the first time seriously fixed on divine truth." It was the only time they met here. Our father told us this with simplicity and gladness, but not without emotion.

When the breath of revival began to move with gracious quickening over all parts of the church, Dr. Symington was among the first to hail it. We find him reading Arthur's "Tongue of Fire;" rejoicing in Spurgeon's Puritan soundness and astonishing energy of faith; circulating a pastoral address on revival which Mr. M'Gill had prepared at the instance of the Synod; and taking part in special meetings for prayer.

It is impossible to convey to those who did not know him a just idea of what our father was in private life and in the family. Great knowledge of human nature was accompanied by an indescribable pleasantness, the product of love and humour. The look of gravity which might be caught when his features were at rest, changed instantly when one spoke to him into the sunniest of smiles. He told a story admirably, and laughed heartily at the wit of others if it was anything genuine. Every inch a Christian gentleman in the best sense of the word, his distinguished courtesy appeared quite as much at home as in general society: it was his nature. One who gave and received the love of a son— the Rev. Dr. Goold—has felicitously described him :—

"The power and value of system was notably exemplified by our departed father. He owed most of his usefulness in life to what we may designate his peculiar love and faculty of order. His very study was the image of his thoughts—a place for everything, and everything in its place. It was the same principle that gave him success in that walk which he chiefly cultivated—systematic theology. He was in his own person a living refutation of the folly of the modern prejudice against it. It was with him no dead herbarium, but a living garden—no fetter cramping the native elasticity of his thoughts, but the wing with which he soared upward, till he could take more accurate survey of the whole domain of divine truth.

"It is but right to add, that he 'adorned' the doctrine of his Saviour, as well as professed and believed it. In private habits he was eminently devout. His delight was communion with God. His closet could testify to his prayerfulness. But yet there was nothing of the morose about him. Genial and buoyant with the glee of childhood, he was the life and spirit of every company in which he mingled; in wit and repartee never rivalled, but never losing in the joyousness of his nature the dignity which became the Christian and the minister; the youngest of his grandchildren hailed him as a companion, while they revered him as a patriarch."

The home at Annfield Place became in these latter years strangely lonely, yet had a pathetic beauty about it. All their six children were, after 1856, settled in families of their own; and our parents were left with only a very faithful servant, Sarah, one of the good old sort that is getting too rare, and without any domestic society except that of one another. None of the family, it is true, was far away, and two sons and a daughter had their homes in Glasgow, so that the old house was frequently enlivened by the presence of children and children's children. But the beautiful thing was, that it was not dull even when none of these were there. The old folks, as they sometimes called themselves, laughingly said they were beginning life again, and renewing the happiness of a youth forty years past. It was quite true: they understood if any ever did the secret of renewing youth by joy in God and glad thankfulness for his abounding mercies.* Our father contrived to spend less time in the study that he might spend more with our mother, and watched over her failing strength with the gallantry of a bridegroom. It may seem a singular expression, but it is the only one that will suit. Both hailed each grandchild as it was born with a warmth of love which could not be exceeded; and after her death the following paper—her only will!—was found in our mother's workbox. The date shows it to have been written at a time when she was called to look death in the face: it is inscribed now on more than twenty little Bibles, and her prayer has been signally answered in the case of some who received them.

"GRANDMAMA SYMINGTON'S DYING GIFT TO HER GRANDCHILD (WILLIAM SYMINGTON).

"*May* 1858.—Should it be the Lord's will to take me away suddenly and soon, I add my wish that every grandchild may

---

* Ps. ciii. 1-5.

get a BIBLE as my *dying gift*, and marked so; and that they may read it daily and make it the rule of their life. And, oh! may their heavenly Father pour out his Spirit upon them, opening their eyes to see clearly his GREAT LOVE, and thus drawing them unto him through Jesus Christ their Lord."

Our mother survived her husband for a few months, and was, she said, as well and happy as a person could be with a broken heart. When the end came she said, "My anchor was cast long ago, and it is holding firm now;" and so composed herself to sleep.

But while the sunset was bright, it was the brightness of grace shining against clouds. At the close of 1861 his first serious illness required his son and colleague to go to Leamington for prolonged rest. The following is the last entry in his private record:—

"*January* 1, 1862.—The year which has just closed, like its predecessors, has been a chequered one. The last month the darkest of all, from illness first of my son and latterly of my wife. The amount of anxiety, distress, and watching compressed into the last four or five weeks has been all but overwhelming. The Lord, however, has upheld me. And now the invalids are both in a state of promising convalescence. The Lord has had mercy on them, and not on *them* only, but on *me* also, lest I should have sorrow upon sorrow. Blessed be his gracious name! May we be prepared for whatever shall fall out during this period on which we have entered! We would rest on the Lord and wait patiently for him. . . .

"A gloom hangs over our country from the death of great public men, the prevalent commercial stagnation, and the possibility of a war with America. May the Governor of the nations dispel the cloud and send prosperity, by giving grace to repent and reform."

The only words omitted from the above extract are those recording work done and books read.

The whole of the very last entry in his diary is this—

"*January* 14.—Still weak as ever."

On the first Sabbath of 1862 Dr. Symington preached two sermons on the words "Occupy till I come." On Friday the 10th he was attacked with influenza; but rose from bed on the 12th and insisted on preaching all day. His text in the forenoon was Matthew vi. 19-21: "Lay not up for yourselves treasures upon earth, where moth and rust doth corrupt, and where thieves break through and steal; but lay up for yourselves treasures in heaven, where neither moth nor rust doth corrupt, and where thieves do not break through nor steal: for where your treasure is, there will your heart be also." The feelings of weakness and depression with which he was bravely struggling, may explain the striking fact that his text in the afternoon, his last text, was the same from which he had preached nearly a quarter of a century before at Stranraer, when permitted to return to his pulpit after long affliction—"It is of the Lord's mercies that we are not consumed, because his compassions fail not" (Lam. iii. 22).* He appeared feeble in the forenoon, but had much of his old fire and unction in the afternoon.

He returned from the pulpit to bed, but rose on Monday and wrote to his youngest son at Dumfries, who was to occupy his pulpit on the 19th, asking him to come prepared to lecture to the Young Men's Society, as he feared his cold would prevent him keeping that engagement. Although he never rose after the 14th,

* See p. lix.

nothing more serious than influenza was suspected for some days; and everything which the highest medical skill could do in the hands of warm Christian friends, Dr. George Wilson and the late Dr. Harry Rainy, was done. His son preached again in his pulpit on the 26th, and by that time hope was quite gone. Extreme and mysterious exhaustion, for which there was no apparent cause, baffled all skill: it was only after death that an aneurism, the result of a strain years before through slipping on ice, was discovered, which had been allowing the life blood to ebb away from a large artery under the skin. The parting from his old Christian friend Dr. Rainy, after the beloved physician could no longer conceal that his hopes were gone, was a scene not to be forgotten: friend could still help friend.

During these two weeks our father frequently asked that certain psalms and chapters should be read to him, with prayer. When his faithful old beadle, Robert Walker (a man of remarkable gifts), called one morning, he said, "Robert, have you ever had any desire to depart from this world? . . . I had sweet meditations last night on departing hence." "Save for the friends you hold so dear," said Robert. "Oh yes," our father answered, "but it is my dear old wife that I am thinking of: the children are all settled in their own families." He then named several of the elders to whom he wished Robert to go and ask their prayers for him, adding, "You and Mrs. Walker should set apart some time and remember your minister at the throne of grace." The good old man, after setting down these things in writing, says: "The meekness and familiarity of his conversation struck me much: his soul seemed to me like a weaned child."

It was truly so. The pen that writes these closing words trembles at the remembrance of a ten days' conflict with the last enemy, in which he saw an unclouded mind winning decisive victory every hour through the simplicity of faith. No description shall be ventured. Let it only be said that there was not a single murmur nor one longing toward earth; that he was surrounded by wife and children, and took a Christian's leave of them; that his constant desire was for the Word of everlasting life. One day in the first week he said to me, "I think if I were taken away in this illness I could exercise a calm trust in the Redeemer." Near the end he repeated old Rowland Hill's lines—

> "And when I'm to die
> 'Receive me,' I'll cry;
> For Jesus hath loved me,
> I cannot tell why:
> But this I can find
> We two are so joined
> He'll not be in glory and leave me behind."

And the very last words were—

"THERE REMAINETH A REST TO THE PEOPLE OF GOD."

The remembrance of such a victory is beyond all price. Still my heart turns rather to two sayings of our father that fell from him in talking with me some years before, when he was in full health.

"OF COURSE NO ONE GETS A PARTICLE OF TRUE PEACE EXCEPT IN LOOKING STRAIGHT OUT TO JESUS."

And on another occasion, when the matter we were

speaking about was the case of one called on to relinquish his own likings for the advancement of the cause of Christ—

"A MAN'S LIFE IS WORTH NOTHING AT ALL UNLESS IT BE FRUITFULLY JOINED TO THE KINGDOM OF CHRIST. NOTHING ELSE IS OF VALUE, BECAUSE NOTHING ELSE WILL LAST."

William Symington's life, from an early period of it, was fruitfully joined to the kingdom of Christ. The lesson and the comfort for us, who so sorely miss that life now, are that its issues remain with the KING whom he served, and serves, and shall serve for ever, " seeing his face and having His name in his forehead."

MESSIAH THE PRINCE.

AUTHOR'S PREFACE.

THE present may be regarded as a sequel to the work on the Atonement and Intercession of Christ, published by the author some few years ago. The subjects, as will be seen from the introductory pages of this volume, have an intimate connexion with each other. The glory of the divine Redeemer is deeply involved in both. The writer is not aware of the existence of any work on the exact plan of that now offered to the public. It has been his object to present a condensed, yet comprehensive, view of the nature, properties, extent, and duration, of the kingdom of the Messiah.

Two departments—the church and the nations—have received a large share of attention. But their paramount importance, apart from other considerations, is sufficient to account for this, and to render any apology unnecessary. In adverting, as was unavoidable in the discussion of these topics, to questions that are keenly agitated at the present time, the author has studied to keep clear of all allusion to matters, purely of a party nature, which have been unhappily mingled up with the discussion of a great and vital principle. Having no party purpose whatever to serve, he hopes he may have been enabled to escape, in some considerable degree at least, that bitterness of feeling, and obliquity of judgment, which the spirit of party naturally engenders. It is one of the painful and unhappy results of controversy, especially when it happens to involve points in which the immediate interests of the respective parties are supposed to be concerned, that it is almost sure so to pervert the mind, and awaken animosities, as to be greatly unfavourable to the detection and establishment of truth.

The author commits his work to the candid judgment of all who love that Redeemer, whose princely glory he has attempted to delineate; and to the promised blessing of the Spirit of Christ, who can give efficacy to the feeblest of human efforts.

W. S.

CHAPTER I.

NECESSITY OF CHRIST'S MEDIATORIAL DOMINION.

The question of Paul, *Is Christ divided?* is one to which professing Christians have not given sufficient heed, and the evil consequences are abundantly apparent.

It was deemed essential to the salvation of men that their Redeemer should possess the powers at once of a prophet, a priest, and a king. These offices, while essentially distinct, are necessarily and inseparably connected with one another. Such a union has been by some utterly denied; and its denial has laid foundation for some capital errors, which have exerted a pernicious influence on the Christian church. By others it has been criminally overlooked; and the neglect with which it has been treated has occasioned vague and conflicting conceptions regarding the great work of man's deliverance from sin and wrath by the mediation of the Son of God.

If, as we presume will be readily admitted, the whole of Christ's offices are necessary to the salvation of fallen man, it follows that they are all essential to the character of the Saviour, and that, of course, we cannot suppose him to have existed for a moment without any one of them, as this would suppose him to have been, for the time at least, no Saviour. This fearful result might itself be deemed sufficient to put Christians on their guard against fancying either that Christ was invested with his different offices at different times, or that he acts at one time according to one and at another time according to another. From the very first he must have possessed the powers of all his offices; and in every part of his work all must have come into operation. For example, when he taught his disciples, he acted not only as a prophet, but also as a priest and a king; inasmuch as the doctrine which he taught brought fully to view his sacerdotal character, and the authority with which his instructions were enforced distinctly recognised his regal power. Again, when as a priest he offered himself a spotless sacrifice to God, he gave to the world as a prophet a new revelation of the character of God, and of the principles of the divine moral government; at the same time that as a king he triumphed gloriously over his enemies. In like manner, his royal achievements not only manifest his majesty and his power, but serve to publish the clemency of his grace, and to recognise the merit of his atoning sacrifice as the ground on which they proceed.

This doctrine of inseparable union does not by any means confound the distinction subsisting between the various offices of our Mediator, any more than the union of persons in the Godhead amounts to a denial of the essential distinction between the Father, Son, and Holy Spirit; or than the union of natures in the person of the Son of God is at variance with the ascription, by the inspired writers, of some things to the one nature, and of other things to the other nature. Without confounding the distinction between them, we may, therefore, safely maintain the inseparable union of Christ's mediatorial offices—a union which obtained in every pain he endured, and in every act he performed or will ever perform in behalf of the elect; and which it becomes the believer joyfully and gratefully to recognise and acknowledge, as the absence of any one of them would disqualify him for performing the work of our redemption.

In proceeding to consider the kingly office of Christ, it is to be borne in mind that it stands in inseparable connexion with his sacerdotal office. He sits *a Priest upon his throne.* Nor will any enlightened subject of Sion's King feel that there is any incongruity, in his case at least, between the mitre and the crown, the altar and the throne, the censer and the sceptre, the smoking incense and the shout of victory. 'We have a great High Priest, that is passed into the heavens. This man, after he had offered one sacrifice for sin, for ever sat down on the right hand of God; from henceforth expecting till his enemies be made his footstool.'[1]

The kingly office of Christ forms an interesting part of the Christian system, and as such both merits and requires extensive illustration. We may judge of its importance from the frequency with which Christ is spoken of in the sacred writings under the character of a King. Is the advent of Messiah announced to the ancient church? It is in these words: 'Rejoice greatly, O daughter of Zion; shout, O daughter of Jerusalem; behold, thy KING cometh unto thee.'[2] Are the members

---

[1] Heb. iv. 14; x. 12, 13.   [2] Zech. ix. 9.

of the church invited to behold his excellences? Such is the character in which he is discovered: 'Go forth, O ye daughters of Zion, and behold King Solomon, with the crown wherewith his mother crowned him in the day of his espousals, and in the day of the gladness of his heart.'[3] Is a gracious discovery of the Saviour promised? It is thus conveyed: 'Thine eyes shall see the King in his beauty.'[4] Are the saints required to exult in the Redeemer? It is in these terms: 'Let the children of Zion be joyful in their King.'[5] Does the believer record the effect produced by some singular manifestation of the divine presence to his soul? This is his language: 'Woe is me! for I am undone; because I am a man of unclean lips, and I dwell in the midst of a people of unclean lips: for mine eyes have seen the King, the Lord of hosts.'[6] Or is the church required to celebrate the ascension of her Lord? In strains borrowed from the triumphant entrance of an earthly monarch into the capital of his kingdom, she exclaims: 'Lift up your heads, O ye gates; and be ye lift up, ye everlasting doors; and the King of glory shall come in.'[7] Such being the frequent allusion made in the Scriptures to this particular feature of the Saviour's character, an examination into the mediatorial government of Christ presents peculiar attractions to every true disciple of Jesus; and as the theme is ample, as well as inviting, it requires the patient, candid, and believing attention of all who would be wise unto salvation.

The sovereign authority of Christ may be viewed

[3] Song iii. 11. [4] Isa. xxxiii. 17. [5] Ps. cxlix. 2.
[6] Isa. vi. 5.   [7] Ps. xxiv. 7.

either as *necessary*, or as *official*. Viewing him as *God*, it is necessary, inherent, and underived: viewing him as *Mediator*, it is official and delegated. It is the latter of these we are now to contemplate. The subject of our present inquiry is, the MEDIATORIAL DOMINION of the Son; not that which essentially belongs to him as God, but that with which, by the authoritative act of the Father, he has been officially invested as the Messiah. It is that government, in short, which was *laid* upon his shoulders—that power which was *given* unto him in heaven and in earth.

In proceeding to the consideration of this interesting and momentous subject, the first thing which claims attention is the NECESSITY of Christ's kingly office. This takes precedence of all other points, inasmuch as its establishment will tend to prepare for the more careful investigation of the other parts of the subject, by impressing the mind with a higher sense of its importance. '*For he* MUST *reign till he hath put all enemies under his feet*' (1 Cor. xv. 25).

1. The kingly office of Christ is necessary to the *fulfilment of God's gracious purposes* respecting the elect. The right of dominion over all things necessarily belongs to him as God. Had his kingdom embraced nothing but the material and the moral worlds, generally considered, there should have been no room, because no need, for the mediatorial rule, all the purposes of his government being perfectly subserved by his essential control as God. But there is something else than the material and moral world, generally considered, under the government of the Almighty. Man, having

broken the original moral constitution under which he was placed, and become liable, in consequence, to judicial displeasure and punishment, and God having determined to rescue a number of the human family from the fearful consequences of such a state, that this might be done honourably and successfully, it became necessary that the government of these, and of others on their account, should be committed to him who was chosen to be their Saviour. God, from the very perfection of his nature, could not, in his absolute character, deal with rebel sinners in any way with a view to their salvation. In this character he must seek their punishment, for he is just: and not only could he not *procure* or offer pardon and deliverance from the curse of the broken covenant, but he could not even *bestow* it, nor could he actually deliver them, or conduct them to any of the blessings of salvation. Hence the necessity of another being appointed, not only to purchase and to offer redemption through his blood, but to apply it, to give it effect, to bestow the benefits of grace on the destined subjects of salvation.

2. Indeed, to *complete the mediatory character itself*, such an office was requisite. Jesus, the chosen of God, is of course a perfect Saviour. But this he could not be without being invested with regal dignity and power. The work given him to do, supposes him to be so invested. It is SALVATION; and what is that? It is not merely, as we are apt to suppose, paying a ransom, by which the claims of the divine moral government shall be satisfied; it is not merely making announcement that such satisfaction has been given and accepted, and

offering redemption to the guilty on this ground. These are certainly important and essential parts of salvation; nor would we be understood as wishing to disparage either the one or the other. No; we can never enough appreciate or extol them. Still they do not, in themselves, constitute salvation; if there were nothing more, not a single sinner could ever be saved. The ransom must be *applied* as well as *paid;* the offer must be not only *made*, but *accepted;* and to secure this the Mediator must be invested with regal power.

Each office of Christ has its own peculiar province, in which it is essential and indispensable. Generally speaking, it may be said that his province as a priest is to purchase; as a prophet, to publish; as a king, to apply. In the first, he procures; in the second, he makes known; in the third, he gives effect. They are all alike essential: not one of them can be dispensed with. The regal office can as easily be supposed to supersede the sacerdotal or the prophetical, as the sacerdotal or the prophetical can be supposed to supersede the regal. It were absurd to talk of applying what had not been procured; but not less so to talk of procuring what could not be applied.

Let us, for the sake of illustrating and confirming the point under consideration, try what consequences would follow from supposing government or dominion to be expunged from the mediatorial functions of Christ. As priest, he makes atonement for the sins of the chosen of God, procures pardon, purchases deliverance from condemnation, pays the ransom due for their sins, and completely removes all legal obstructions to their salvation. As priest, also, he represents their case to the Father, pleads the merits of his sacrifice, and expresses his will that they may be put in possession of the purchased benefits of redemption; and the Father is pleased to hear and sustain the validity of his claims. As prophet, he makes known to men that all this has been done, informs them plainly that the curse of the law has been removed, God reconciled, and heaven opened for their reception. Yet will these avail for their salvation? All this may be conceived to be done, and yet not one sinner rescued from the pit, not one rebel restored to the favour of the Almighty, not one child of Adam exalted to glory. Without something more, the benefit arising from these interpositions is lost; without another office, the functions of these two are neutralised. Without regal authority, the sacrifice, however meritorious, has no power; the intercession, however powerful, has no efficacy; the doctrine, however clear, has no saving influence; and the Son of God must be content to see the whole human race perish for ever in their sins, as if his blood had never been either shed on Calvary, or carried within the veil. Such being the case, we can appreciate the import of the answer returned by the Saviour to the question of Pilate—'Art thou a king then? Thou sayest that I am a king. *To this end was I born, and for this cause came I into the world.*' [8]

This view of the necessity of the kingly office in particular to the perfection of the others, agrees well with the account given in Scripture of the work of the

[8] John xviii. 37.

Messiah. The purchase of redemption having been effected, the ransom for sin paid, the decease at Jerusalem accomplished, what step does he take next? Does he surrender all further concern in the salvation of men? Does he abandon all mediatorial actings, and retire into the bosom of the Father? No. Follow him in his ascension to heaven; see him pressing forward into the presence of God and presenting his petition, 'Father, glorify thy Son, that thy Son also may glorify thee.' Ere it is asked it is granted. This is the address with which the Father salutes him as he enters the heavenly places not made with hands: 'Sit thou at my right hand, until I make thine enemies thy footstool.' As if he had said to him—Thou hast established thy right to that rebel world: I surrender the government of it into thy hands: go through it and find out thy redeemed: gather them from the four winds of heaven: for this purpose institute ordinances, promulgate laws, issue commands, appoint servants, subordinate whatever exists to the gracious and magnificent ends of thine appointment. And what is the result? Why, the mitre becomes a crown; the censer a sceptre; the Mediator passes from the altar to the throne; heaven becomes at once a temple and a palace, while its walls echo with the loud acclaim of welcome bursting spontaneously from the whole celestial host to the newly inaugurated monarch.

3. The kingly dignity of the Mediator is necessary, *as a reward of his obedience unto the death.* Never was service so meritorious, whether we consider the sacrifice made or the end contemplated. In estimating the

sacrifice made in performing this service, we must remember that the Son of God left the bosom of his heavenly Father, the region of uncreated light, and all the attractions of celestial society; that he put the essential splendour of his perfections in eclipse, and assumed the likeness of sinful flesh; that he tabernacled with men on the earth, and there submitted to poverty, reproach, and pain; that he endured the persecution of men and devils, and suffered the most awful and mysterious agony, springing from the hiding of his Father's countenance. Then, the end contemplated was nothing less than this: that men might be saved from everlasting destruction, made fit for heaven, reinstated in the society of angels and of one another, and restored to the favour of God. When or where was there ever service to compare with that of Christ? Who ever delivered from misery so profound? Who ever exalted to bliss so dignified? Who ever made sacrifices so self-denied, in order to accomplish a benevolent undertaking? Here is merit transcendent, overwhelming, which beggars description and sets comparison at defiance.

Should not such service be rewarded? Every principle of moral rectitude says that it should. *'Ought not Christ to have suffered these things, and to enter into his glory?'* (Luke xxiv. 26). This is not more a maxim of inspiration than a dictate of right moral feeling; and with this the stipulations of the eternal covenant, inspired predictions, the testimony of the Mediator himself, and the assertions of his apostles, all cordially harmonise.

But in what shall this merited reward consist? Not merely in the satisfaction of his own bosom, and the approbation of his heavenly Father. These are great, indeed, but they are not enough. They are inward, and, however fit to be appreciated by the Saviour himself, inadequate for giving expression to others of a sense of the value of his work. There must be something substantial, visible, outwardly glorifying, in the mediatorial reward; something to attract the notice, and call forth the applause of men and angels. Regal exaltation, absolute and unlimited, meets exactly the requirements of the case. If men, who have been faithful over a few things, are to be rewarded by being made 'rulers over many things,' surely it is due to him who, 'as a Son, has been faithful, like Moses, over all his house,' that he be made 'ruler over all.' Having, as a part of his humiliation, suffered himself to be made subject to rulers, to be placed at their bar, to be judged by their laws, to be counted worthy of death by their unrighteous decree, it is fitting that, in reward of what he has effected, he should be invested with sovereign rule over the princes of this world, and, in his turn, demand of them obedience to his authority, punish them for their proud and obstinate rebellion, and subordinate all their measures and movements to the gracious purposes of his reign.

4. Nor is this dominion less requisite *to counteract the opposition made to the work of man's salvation by its enemies.* 'For he must reign, till he hath put all enemies under his feet.' That a work of such grace and benevolence as that of man's salvation should provoke

hostility, seems strange; but it is not more strange than true. It has many enemies—enemies to its internal operations in the heart; and enemies to its outward administration in the world. Against those internal operations in the heart which salvation supposes, there rise up a host of adversaries. The law, as a covenant of works, by demanding the punishment of the guilty violator, slays the peace of the soul. Indwelling corruptions wage incessant warfare against the quickening, sanctifying, and comforting work of the Spirit. 'I find then a law that when I would do good, evil is present with me.' Satan and his emissaries, numerous, subtle, and powerful, assail by their temptations, accusations, and persecutions. 'We wrestle not against flesh and blood, but against principalities, against powers, against the rulers of the darkness of this world, against spiritual wickedness in high places.' The world, with its allurements and terrors, its smiles and frowns, tries to undermine the principles of stability. 'Because ye are not of the world, but I have chosen you out of the world, therefore the world hateth you.' Death, by threatening to execute the curse of the broken covenant, awakens slavish fears; deprives of tranquillity; maintains in ignoble and distracting bondage. He must be a king in order to threaten to hold the body in corruption, and then to engulf in final ruin both soul and body for ever: 'to deliver them who, through fear of death, were all their lifetime subject to bondage.'[9] In opposition to the outward administration of the work of Christ in the world, also, a

[9] Rom. vii. 21; Eph. vi. 12; John xv. 19; Heb. ii. 15.

whole host of enemies stand forth. Wilful ignorance, unblushing infidelity, hardened profanity, open idolatry, Mohammedan delusion, Jewish obstinacy, antichristian domination, and civil misrule, form a combined phalanx of portentous breadth and depth; an unholy alliance of discordant materials, yet breathing only one spirit of determined enmity to the reign of Christ in the world, and resolved to prevent the progress, and, if possible, to effect the extermination of his kingdom, by every means in their power.

Are these enemies to meet with no resistance? Is the kingdom of the Messiah to fall a prey to their rapacious hatred, and that of his great arch-enemy to be erected on its ruins? Certainly not. It is the prayer of every saint that they may meet with a signal defeat. The honour of the Saviour himself demands their final overthrow; and the word of God assures us that such shall be the ultimate issue of the contest. By whom is this end to be brought about, but by the Messiah himself? 'My sword,' says he, 'shall be bathed in heaven: behold it shall come down upon Idumea, and upon the people of my curse, to judgment. The sword of the Lord is filled with blood; it is made fat with fatness, and with the blood of lambs and goats, with the fat of the kidneys of rams; for the Lord hath a sacrifice in Bozrah, and a great slaughter in the land of Idumea.' Isa. lxiii. 1-4: 'Who is this that cometh from Edom, with dyed garments from Bozrah? This that is glorious in his apparel, travelling in the greatness of his strength? I that speak in righteousness, mighty to save. Wherefore art thou red in thine apparel, and thy garments like him that treadeth in the wine-fat? I have trodden the wine-press alone; and of the people there was none with me: for I will tread them in mine anger, and trample them in my fury; and their blood shall be sprinkled upon my garments, and I will stain all my raiment. For the day of vengeance is in mine heart, and the year of my redeemed is come.' [10]

To the accomplishment of this work, investment with regal power and authority is indispensable. In this capacity it is that Jesus encounters his enemies. It is not on the *white* horse merely, but on the *red*, the *black*, and the *pale*, that he goes forth conquering and to conquer, and bearing back with him from the field of battle the palm of victory. Nor is there anything in this at variance with his general character as Mediator. The saviour of his people, and the conqueror of their foes, are not incompatible features. The prosperity of the people of God is intimately connected with the destruction of their enemies. These things go necessarily hand in hand. At the deluge, the preservation of the true seed and the destruction of those who had corrupted their ways, were inseparably conjoined. The rescue of the Israelites from Egypt stood connected with the overthrow of the Egyptians; and when the Jews were restored from Babylon their Chaldean oppressors were spoiled.

5. The kingly office is not less necessary *to meet the needy circumstances of Christ's own people.* They are all of them, by nature, rebels, enemies to Christ, both

---

[10] Isa. xxxiv. 5, 6; lxiii. 1–4.

in their minds and by wicked works; their bosoms rankle with every hostile feeling; the carnal mind is enmity against God, and by nature all are carnal, sold under sin. It is not possible, such being the case, that they should embrace of themselves the overtures of reconciliation, accept without hesitation the offers of mercy, and acquiesce with cordiality and esteem in the terms of salvation. No; they treat them with despite, they spurn them from them with scorn. They must *be* reconciled—they must be *made* willing—their imaginations must be *brought* down. And how but by the Saviour's rod of omnipotent strength sent forth out of Zion; by the irresistible sceptre of his grace, swayed with authority for this very end; by the sharp arrows of conviction which penetrate the heart of the King's enemies only when propelled by him whose right hand teaches terrible things, and who, in regal majesty, rides prosperously, because of truth, and meekness, and righteousness! They are all by nature guilty, and stand in need of pardon; but to dispense forgiveness is a royal prerogative, and Christ could never have exercised it had he not been a king. They are naturally unruly, and need to be governed; nor can they frame or execute laws for themselves:—the Lord is their lawgiver; and to promulgate laws, to enact statutes, belongs to one invested with regal dignity. They are, moreover, weak and defenceless; exposed to the combined opposition of the enemies formerly specified, they have, in themselves, no ability to withstand either their artifices or their strength:— that he may not only restrain and conquer all their enemies, but rule and defend themselves, Christ must hold the office of a king.

Such is the varied necessity that exists for the regal office of the Mediator. A review of the several points by which it is established, may serve to strengthen our conviction of the importance attaching to this feature of the character of our Redeemer. Without Christ's kingly work, the gracious purposes of God could not be executed; the mediatorial character itself would not be complete; the work of salvation must continue unrewarded; the enemies of truth and holiness should finally triumph, and the necessities of the children of God remain for ever unsupplied. Such things cannot—shall not be. 'The Lord is our king, and he will save us' (Isa. xxxiii. 22). The exalted Redeemer is at once 'a Prince and a Saviour' (Acts v. 31).

CHAPTER II.

REALITY OF CHRIST'S MEDIATORIAL DOMINION.

That Christ, besides the dominion which belongs to him originally and essentially as God, is invested with a delegated and official dominion as Mediator, is capable of being established by a variety of cogent proof. The necessity of such dominion to the work of salvation, established in the preceding chapter, itself constitutes an argument of some weight on this point. But other evidence is at hand.

1. Long before his advent in the flesh, there were *prefigurations* of this feature of the Saviour's character. Whether *all* the kings of Israel and Judah are to be regarded as express types of Messiah the Prince or not, it cannot be questioned that *some* are to be looked upon in this light. This was certainly the case with *Melchizedek*. That *he* was a type of Christ, is affirmed:—'Thou art a priest for ever after the order of Melchizedek.'[1] The points of accordance are manifold and striking. The very name signifies 'king of righteousness,' and points directly to him who, righteous in himself, wrought out for his people a justifying righteousness, works a sanctifying righteousness within them by his Spirit, and sways them with a sceptre of righteous-

[1] Ps. cx. 4; Heb. v. 10.

ness. His designation 'king of Salem,' that is 'king of peace,' fitly enough points out one who, whether as regards the disposition for which he was distinguished, the blessing he died to procure, or the effects of his administration, is well entitled to be called 'the Prince of peace.' What he did, in bringing forth bread and wine to Abraham and his army returning from the slaughter of the kings, is no unapt emblem of the spiritual nourishment and refreshment which the Messiah affords to his soldiers engaged in warfare with the enemies of their salvation. But the point which, most of all, marks him out as typical of our mediatorial king, is his combining in his own person the regal and sacerdotal offices. Besides being 'king of Salem,' he was 'priest of the Most High God.'[2] He was a royal priest —a sacerdotal king—and thus an eminent type of him who, exerting his power on the footing of his purchase, sits 'a priest upon his throne.' *Moses* resembled Christ, not only in the facts of his personal history and in his official acts as a mediator in general or prophet in particular, but as 'king in Jeshurun.'[3] Jeshurun signifies *upright*, and refers to the people of Israel, who were required, and understood, to possess this character. The Jewish legislator thus typified Him who, being 'king in Sion,' rules among the upright in heart, and governs them with integrity and truth. And as Moses, in the capacity in question, gave his people laws, so Jesus has given *his* laws, not indeed of carnal ordinances, but of steadfast faith and inward spiritual obedience.—*David*, too, to say nothing of the import of his name as the

[2] Heb. vii. 2.   [3] Deut. xxxiii. 5.

beloved, of his personal qualifications, and of his sufferings, cannot fail to strike every one at all acquainted with his history, as a remarkable type of Christ;—in the auspicious commencement of his power by the signal overthrow of the vaunting champion of the Philistines;—in his valour in war, and his wisdom and humanity in peace;—in the principles and character of his administration, in which he led his people according to the integrity of his heart, and guided them by the skilfulness of his hands;—and in the covenant of royalty made with him and his seed for ever. So close is the resemblance, that the Messiah himself is more than once spoken of by the prophets, under the very name of David.[4]—But by none was the mediatorial dominion more strongly prefigured than by *Solomon*. In the wisdom of his administration—in the extent of his territory—in the wealth of his subjects—and in the peacefulness of his reign, he was a remarkable type of the Messiah; so much so, that in that mystic epithalamium in which the Saviour's excellency and love are so fully set forth, this is the very name by which he is designated: 'Go forth, O ye daughters of Zion, and behold King Solomon, with the crown wherewith his mother crowned him in the day of his espousals, and in the day of the gladness of his heart.'[5]

2. *Prophecy*, as well as type, bore testimony to this view of the Saviour's character. The very first prediction is conceived in terms which allude to the ancient way in which victorious kings expressed their conquest,

---

[4] Jer. xxx. 9; Ezek. xxxiv. 23, 24; Hos. iii. 5.
[5] Song iii. 11.

namely, by placing their feet on the necks of their foes.[6] When the dying patriarch foretold that the 'sceptre should not depart from Judah, nor a lawgiver from between his feet, until Shiloh come,'[7] his language clearly enough imports, that on him of whom he spake, should devolve, at his coming, that judicial and legislative authority which had been previously exercised by others. Balaam prophesied: 'There shall come a star out of Jacob, and a SCEPTRE (the emblem of regal power) shall rise out of Israel.'[8] David said: 'Yet have I set my king upon my holy hill of Zion,'—a prediction which is expressly applied in the New Testament to Christ.[9] The forty-fifth Psalm undoubtedly refers to the Messiah. The circumstances which it details were not verified in the history of Solomon's reign, besides being, many of them at least, inconsistent with the tenor of his private life, and at variance with the fortunes of his family. The titles by which the person spoken of is saluted, the multitudinous character of his progeny, and the perpetuity of his kingdom, all show that a greater than Solomon is here. Now, in this Psalm, the regal character is sustained throughout: 'I speak of the things which I have made touching the king. Gird thy sword upon thy thigh, O most Mighty, with thy glory and thy majesty. Thy throne, O God, is for ever and ever; the sceptre of thy kingdom is a right sceptre.'[10] But time would fail to enumerate particularly all the prophecies bearing on this point, and we must content

---

[6] Gen. iii. 15.
[7] Gen. xlix. 10.
[8] Num. xxiv. 17.
[9] Ps. ii. 6; Acts iv. 25, 26.
[10] Ps. xlv. 1, 3, 6.

ourselves with referring to some others in the margin.[11]

3. Many of the *titles* which are applied to Christ in the Scriptures, bear on this subject. He is designated LORD :—' God hath made that same Jesus, whom ye have crucified, both *Lord* and *Christ*.—LEADER and COMMANDER :—' Behold, I have given him for a witness to the people, a *Leader* and *Commander* to the people.' — JUDGE : — 'The Lord is our *Judge.*' — RULER :— ' Thou, Bethlehem Ephratah, out of thee shall he come forth unto me, that is to be *Ruler* in Israel.' [12]

4. The Saviour *laid claim himself* to this character. The passage in which this is related deserves particular attention. ' Then Pilate entered into the judgment-hall again, and called Jesus, and said unto him, Art thou the king of the Jews ? Jesus answered, My kingdom is not of this world. If my kingdom were of this world, then would my servants fight, that I should not be delivered to the Jews ; but now is my kingdom not from hence. Pilate therefore said unto him, Art thou a king then ? Jesus answered, THOU SAYEST THAT I AM A KING. To this end was I born, and for this cause came I into the world, that I should bear witness unto the truth.' [13] It had been generally rumoured that Jesus was king of the Jews. The jealousy of the Roman government was excited. Pilate feels himself bound, from his office, to call him to account on this point. Jesus, while he explains the sense in which his regal character was to

---

[11] Ps. lxxii.; lxxxix. 19-24; cx. 1-3; Isa. ix. 6, 7; xi. 1; Jer. xxiii. 5, 6; Ezek. xxxvii. 24; Zech. ix. 9, &c.

[12] Acts ii. 36; Isa. lv. 4; Isa. xxxiii. 22; Mic. v. 2.

[13] John xviii. 33, 37.

be understood, does not deny the fact. On the contrary, he explicitly avows it. No sinister motive could induce him to decline acknowledging it. Nor does he content himself with a mere simple avowal; but he speaks of it as closely connected with the great purpose of his appearance in our world.

5. We find that *others* recognise the validity of his claim. It is acknowledged by intelligent and moral beings of every class and rank. At the head of these, stands *God* the Father himself:—'Thou settest a crown of pure gold on his head'—'God also hath highly exalted him, and given him a name which is above every name; that at the name of Jesus every knee should bow, of things in heaven, and things in earth, and things under the earth.'[14] Next come *angels*, tuning their harps of gold to the praises of Zion's King:—'And behold thou shalt conceive in thy womb,' said the angel to Mary, 'and bring forth a son, and shall call his name JESUS. He shall be great and shall be called the Son of the Highest: and the Lord God shall give unto him THE THRONE of his father David: and he shall REIGN over the house of Jacob for ever; and of his KINGDOM there shall be no end.' 'And I heard the voice of many angels,' says John, 'round about the throne, saying, Worthy is the Lamb that was slain to receive POWER, and riches, and wisdom, and strength, and honour, and glory, and blessing.'[15] Then follow the *saints*, with notes less high, perhaps, but not less distinct or sincere. 'The star-led wizards' inquire for 'the heaven-born child,' in these words, 'Where is he that is born KING

[14] Ps. xxi. 3; Phil. ii. 9, 10.   [15] Luke i. 31-33; Rev. v. 11, 12.

of the Jews?' while, as an act of lowly homage, they unfold their ordoriferous treasures and lay them at his feet. Nathanael witnessed this good confession:—'Rabbi, thou art the Son of God; thou art the KING of Israel.' And the Apostle of the Gentiles, as he exhibits Jesus Christ 'for a pattern to them who should hereafter believe on him to life everlasting,' exclaims, 'Now unto the KING eternal, immortal, invisible, the only wise God, be honour and glory for ever and ever, amen.'[16] His *enemies* are reluctantly compelled to bring up the rear of witnesses to his royal claims. The Jewish multitude rent the air with their shouts, as he entered into Jerusalem, crying, 'Hosanna, blessed is the KING of Israel that cometh in the name of the Lord.' The Roman soldiers unwittingly bore their part, as they 'bowed the knee before him and mocked him, saying, Hail, KING of the Jews!' And Pontius Pilate must needs cause to be put on his cross, written in Hebrew, and Greek, and Latin, the unalterable title, 'JESUS OF NAZARETH, THE KING OF THE JEWS'—a title which was read, we may conclude, with profit by many of the multitude, and which was, perhaps, the principal means of conveying to the malefactor that knowledge of the Saviour's character which led to his conversion.[17]

6. In harmony with all this evidence, is the circumstance that *royal appendages* are described as belonging to him. We say nothing here of his *kingdom*, as this will fall to be spoken of afterwards. He wears royal *titles*. As expressive of his being the inherent source,

---

[16] Matt. ii. 2; John i. 49; 1 Tim. i. 17.
[17] John xii. 13; Matt. xxvii. 29; John xix. 19.

the meritorious author, and liberal bestower and supporter of spiritual and eternal being, he is called the 'PRINCE OF LIFE':—to denote his dominion and authority, he is spoken of as 'KING OF SAINTS':—and, as indicative of his absolute and universal supremacy, he is represented as having on his vesture and on his thigh the splendid inscription, 'KING OF KINGS, AND LORD OF LORDS.'[18] He occupies a *throne*,—the seat of royalty, from which the king dispenses his laws, and on which he receives the homage of his subjects:—'Thy THRONE, O God, is for ever and ever. To him that overcometh, will I grant to sit with me on my THRONE.'[19] His head is adorned with a *crown* of purest radiance, surpassing in worth and beauty the most costly diadem ever worn by earthly monarch, composed of the richest material, and studded with the brightest gems—*its* substance being true honour, and *its* jewels immortal souls. 'Thou settest a CROWN of purest gold on his head. Thou hast CROWNED him with glory and honour. Upon himself shall his CROWN flourish. They shall be mine in that day when I make up my JEWELS.'[20] He wields a *sceptre*, the rod of office, the symbol of regal authority, and the instrument by which the monarch at once gathers and governs his people, and smites and subdues his enemies. 'The SCEPTRE of thy kingdom is a right SCEPTRE. The Lord shall send the ROD of thy strength out of Zion. Thou shalt break them with a ROD of iron; thou shalt dash them in pieces like a potter's vessel.'[21] *Laws* are essential to dominion; it cannot exist long without

---

[18] Acts iii. 15; Rev. xv. 3; xvii. 14; xix. 16. [19] Ps. xlv. 56; Rev. iii. 1, 2.
[20] Ps. xxi. 3; viii. 5; cxxxii. 18; Mal. iii. 16. [21] Ps. xlv. 6; cx. 2; ii. 9.

them; and there can be no administration where they are entirely wanting. The Messiah is not without these; the Scriptures are the law of the Lord—a code at once righteous, suitable, extensive, and efficacious:—'The law is holy, and the commandment holy, just, and good' —'being not without law to God, but under law to Christ.'[22] Numerous and glorious are his *attendants*. At the giving of the law they are thus described: 'The Lord came from Sinai, and rose up from Seir unto them: he shined forth from Mount Paran, and he came with TEN THOUSANDS OF SAINTS.' At his advent: 'Suddenly there was with the angels a multitude of the heavenly host, praising God and saying, Glory to God in the highest, and on earth peace, good will toward men.' During his life: 'ANGELS came and ministered unto him.' At his ascension: 'The chariots of God are twenty thousand, even THOUSANDS OF ANGELS: the Lord is among them as in Sinai, in the holy place. Thou hast ascended on high, thou hast led captivity captive.' And, at his second coming, when the judgment shall be set and the books opened: 'THOUSANDS, THOUSANDS shall minister unto him, and TEN THOUSAND TIMES TEN THOUSAND stand before him. Behold the Lord cometh with TEN THOUSAND OF HIS SAINTS.'[23]—Then, he has his *servants* and *ambassadors*. Of the elements, it is said: 'He maketh his MINISTERS a flaming fire.' Of the angelic tribes: 'Are they not all MINISTERING SPIRITS sent forth to minister for them who shall be heirs

---

[22] Rom. vii. 12; 1 Cor. ix. 21.
[23] Deut. xxxiii. 2; Luke ii. 13, 14; Matt. iv. 11; Ps. lxviii. 17, 18; Dan. vii. 10; Jude 14.

of salvation?' Of the ministers of religion: 'Now, then, we are AMBASSADORS for Christ, as though God did beseech you by us: we pray you in Christ's stead, be ye reconciled unto God. Let a man so account of us as of the MINISTERS OF CHRIST.'[24]—How shall we describe his *revenues*—the honour, and glory, and worship, and respect, and esteem, and constant obedience, which he exacts as tribute from all the subjects of his dominion? 'He is thy Lord, and worship thou him. Give unto the Lord the glory due unto his name: bring an offering, and come into his courts. Oh worship the Lord in the beauty of holiness: fear before him all the earth.'[25]—And all the royal prerogatives of apprehending and liberating, of condemning and acquitting, of life and death, of pardon and execution, belong to him without reserve: 'I kill and I make alive; I wound and I heal: neither is there any that can deliver out of my hand.'[26]—Such, if we may so speak, are the *ensignia* of the Mediator, ensignia of transcendent value and matchless splendour. No titles like his titles;—no throne of such peerless majesty;—no crown of such overpowering radiance;—no sceptre of such resistless might;—no laws so equitable or beneficent;—no retinue so large or so illustrious;—no ministers so dignified;—no revenues so rich;—no prerogatives so absolute, as his! 'Who in the heaven can be compared to the Lord? who among the sons of the mighty can be likened unto him?'

Of the reality of Christ's mediatorial dominion there

---

[24] Ps. civ. 4; Heb. i. 14; 2 Cor. v. 20; 1 Cor. iv. 1.
[25] Ps. xlv. 11; xcvi. 8, 9.   [26] Deut. xxxii. 39.

can thus be no doubt. Great must be the guilt of those who deny it. To do so is to nullify types; to contradict prophecy; to blot out the Saviour's titles; to give the faithful and true Witness himself the lie; to convert his regalia into empty baubles; and to reduce his prerogatives to mere mockery and show. While we profess to recognise and acknowledge the Prince of life, let us not, by reducing our acknowledgment to an empty form, be guilty of re-acting the impious mockery of those who, in derision of his claims, placed on his head a crown of thorns, put on him a purple robe; and as they shouted, 'Hail, King!' smote him with their hands. Rather let us place on his head the crown of our salvation, submit cheerfully to be governed by his laws, and look forward to being honoured to sit with him on his throne of glory in the heavens.

CHAPTER III.

CHRIST'S QUALIFICATIONS FOR THE KINGLY OFFICE.

1. *Personal dignity* forms a primary and conspicuous feature in the regal qualifications of the Messiah. This, if not always deemed essential in a king, is generally regarded as fit and proper. This general sense of its propriety may be inferred from the ease with which men in every age have gone into the principle of hereditary government. A degree of personal dignity or natural majesty, either real or adventitious, seems essential to qualify for rule. That the reins of government should be placed in the hands of one entirely destitute of everything of this nature, is repugnant to all our feelings of propriety. On this principle proceeded the answer to the question put by Gideon to Zebah and Zalmunna :—' What manner of men were they whom ye slew at Tabor? As thou art, so were they; each one resembled the children of a king.'[1] To the same purpose is the reflection of the wise man :— ' Woe to thee, O land, when thy king is a child, and thy princes eat in the morning. Blessed art thou, O land, when thy king is the son of nobles!'[2] Now, great is the personal dignity of our mediatorial King. He is the SON OF GOD—a title by which he is designated

[1] Judg. viii. 18.   [2] Eccl. x. 16, 17.

times without number in the Scriptures. Into the question, whether his sonship be personal or official, we cannot be expected fully to enter here. The remark we have made, however, proceeds on the supposition that it is *personal;* for, if he were the Son of God only in an official or figurative sense, sonship could never be adduced as qualifying for the very office from which it derived its own existence. Sonship cannot both be derived from, and qualify for, office at the same time. But that the title in question may safely be viewed as denoting personal dignity, as involving something supernatural or divine, as implying a constructive assumption of such dignity as belongs only to God, is borne out by the circumstance, that his assuming this title was considered, by the highest legal and ecclesiastical authorities of the Jews, as sufficient to expose him to the charge of blasphemy, because by doing so he thus made himself equal with God;—an inference which he never once attempted to deny, while he vindicated himself from the imputation which it was falsely understood to involve. 'Therefore the Jews sought the more to kill him, because he not only had broken the Sabbath, but said also that God was his Father, making himself equal with God.'[3] The sonship and office of Christ are, also, frequently spoken of as different; they are often set in opposition to one another, and even introduced as distinct parts of the same simple propositions; as, for example, when it is said, 'He preached Christ in the synagogues, that he is the Son of God'—'I believe that Jesus Christ is the

[3] John v. 18.

Son of God.'[4] Besides, official sonship is a common thing, but that of Christ is spoken of as peculiar and exclusive; whence he is called God's 'own Son,' and his 'only begotten Son'[5]—language expressive of a relation supreme in dignity, unique in nature, without a parallel, absolutely his own. That he is qualified for mediatorial dominion by his personal dignity as the Son of God is very impressively set before us in the words of the angel to Mary:—'He shall be great, and shall be called the Son of the Highest: and the Lord God shall give unto him the throne of his father David.'[6] If the land may be pronounced blessed whose king is 'the son of nobles,' how greatly blessed must that kingdom be whose ruler is 'the Son God!'

2. The personal dignity, however, is not, in this case, such as to prevent a *near relationship* to the subjects of his spiritual kingdom. 'Thou shalt in any wise set him king over thee, whom the Lord thy God shall choose: one from *among thy brethren* shalt thou set king over thee: thou mayest not set a stranger over thee, who is not thy brother.'[7] Such was the law respecting the appointment of the supreme ruler among the Jews. It was founded in reason and in accurate views of human nature, as only one who is related by natural ties can enter fully into the feelings of the people, participate in all their troubles, and sympathise with them in all their joys and sorrows. Reason revolts at the idea of a man ruling over angels, or of an angel ruling over men; and it is the same

[4] Acts ix. 20; viii. 37.
[5] Rom. viii. 32; John i. 14.
[6] Luke i. 32.
[7] Deut. xvii. 15.

general principle which dictates the impolicy and impropriety of appointing a foreigner to the supreme government of a nation.

To qualify him for ruling over man, it would thus appear to be necessary that Christ should possess human nature. The height of his personal dignity as the Son of God, seems to preclude the possibility of natural relationship to his subjects. By the mystery of the incarnation, however, this difficulty is overcome. A human nature, miraculously provided by the power of the Holy Ghost, was, by a voluntary act of assumption on the part of the Son of God, taken into close and indissoluble union with his person: the Son of God became also the Son of man. The Word was made flesh. He who, as God, was removed far above everything human, as man became qualified for exercising all the sympathies of humanity; and, touched with the feeling of our infirmities, was thus fitted for ruling in the hearts of his people with all the sensibilities of a brother. When his incarnation was announced by the angel, he was spoken of in his regal character. 'Thou shalt bring forth a son, and he shall reign over the house of Jacob for ever.'[8] His personal dignity is not in this way lessened; the lustre of his divine majesty is not diminished: but there is something superadded which gives us greater boldness in approaching him. When we come to our King with perfect freedom, pressing our suit with eagerness and expressing our confidence that the petition we present shall be granted, were we questioned as to what

[8] Luke i. 31.

it is that gives us all this case, we might reply in the words of the men of Judah to the men of Israel of old—*Because the king is near of kin to us.*[9]

3. Jesus is farther qualified for mediatorial dominion, by his *knowledge* and *wisdom*. These are indispensable regal qualifications. That authority of any kind, particularly supreme authority, should be held by one who is ignorant or foolish, shocks all our sentiments of propriety. 'Be *wise*, O ye kings' (Ps. ii. 10). The kings of Israel were required to read in the book of the law; and Solomon, the most distinguished king of antiquity, and one of the most remarkable types of Christ in his regal office, was wiser than all the men of his day. We speak now, not so much of knowledge in general, as of that which qualifies for rule;—knowledge of the principles of government; of the laws of the kingdom; of the character, state, and necessities of the subjects; and of the nature and bearing of foreign relations. Such knowledge is essential to the useful exercise of power. The knowledge of Christ, in all these respects, is extensive and perfect. He knows well the principles of the government which he is delegated to administer; for they are founded on the nature of God and man, and on the relation subsisting between them; and with these, being Immanuel, God with us, he cannot but be most thoroughly acquainted. He knows well the laws of his kingdom, being himself the lawgiver by whom they were all framed and promulgated, and having himself yielded perfect obedience to them all. He knows all his subjects, in the minute variety of their

[9] 2 Sam. xix. 42.

circumstances, characters, necessities, and desires; 'he needs not that any should testify of man, for he knows what is in man, and he searcheth the reins and hearts.'[10] He is thoroughly acquainted with the rival kingdom of this world, from which he has to reclaim his subjects, and against whose assaults he must defend them; with the kingdom of darkness, from which he has to save them; and with the kingdom of light, with which he has to induce them to form, not a partial or temporary confederacy merely, but a final and permanent alliance.

Nor is wisdom less important than knowledge. Wisdom to foresee, judgment to contrive, prudence to execute, are essential to a ruler. Jesus, 'the king eternal,' is at the same time 'the only *wise* God' (1 Tim. i. 17). His understanding is infinite. He can lay down the best plans and devise the best measures for promoting at once the enlargement, the usefulness, and the happiness of his kingdom.

In short, nothing can fail either from ignorance or from indiscretion. There is no lack of information or of prudence. No event can occur unforeseen by him. He is prepared for every occurrence. Nay, such is his wisdom, that what his enemies design for injury, he, by skilful management, can cause to operate powerfully for good.

4. But all these qualities will be of no avail without *power*. Dignity to adorn, relationship to sympathise, and wisdom to project, can be of no use, unless there be also energy to execute. Force of mind, energy of character, and powerful resources are requisite in a king.

[10] John xxi. 17; ii. 25; Rev. ii. 23.

Besides skill to plan for the good of his subjects, he must have ministers, finances, armies, to enable him to realise his schemes. Uncontrollable power is one of the regal qualifications of Christ. 'Wisdom and *might* are his' (Dan. ii. 20). He possesses all the resources of omnipotence. He is 'the Mighty God,' 'the Lord which is, and which was, and which is to come—the Almighty.' Creation, providence, regeneration, and resurrection, proclaim the extent of physical and moral energy that he has at his command, in order to conduct the administration of his mediatorial kingdom. His ministers are qualified, by their numbers and endowments, to execute his sovereign pleasure. He can call to his aid all the perfections of Godhead, and all the fulness of the new covenant. The elements of heaven, apostate spirits, and angels of light, are under his control, advancing his cause and opposing his enemies. At his command, the stars in their courses fought against Sisera; a messenger of Satan was sent to buffet an apostle, in fulfilment of his gracious designs; and it was no empty boast, that he could have commanded more than twelve legions of angels. With such vast might, with such immense resources, no purpose can fail from inability to carry it into execution. His people shall be willing in the day of his power. He is mighty to save. Where the word of this King is, there is power.

5. High *moral excellence* is another indispensable qualification. Without this, dignity serves only as a passport to iniquity; relationship and knowledge confer only greater capacity of mischief; wisdom degenerates

into low cunning; and power becomes mere physical force, more to be dreaded than the hurricane or the lightning. Rectitude of intention, justice of administration, and exemplary conduct, are the constituents of that moral excellence which Scripture, reason, and common sense concur in demanding as necessary to qualify for conducting a proper and effective government. These elements of moral worth meet, in the highest degree and in perfect combination, in the character of Prince Messiah. 'The sceptre of thy kingdom is a right sceptre' (Ps. xlv. 6); 'Just and true are thy ways, thou King of saints' (Rev. xv. 3). Rectitude of intention characterises all his plans. Everything is designed for the good of his people and the glory of the Godhead. Other kings may have sinister ends to serve: even when doing what is right in itself, they may have an ultimate respect to their own personal aggrandisement, or to the advancement of some favourite courtier; or, supposing them moved solely by a regard to the good of their subjects, they may be seeking this at the expense of some neighbouring state. No defect of this nature can ever attach to him of whom we are speaking. He can have no intentions but what are benevolent and righteous; nor can he, even for the fulfilment of these, ever overlook what is due to the honour and glory of God. His administration, too, is perfectly equitable. When the intentions of men are the best that can be supposed, the administration is not always such; while, in other cases, both the intention and the administration are the reverse of just. The rights, and liberties, and property of the subjects, are too often sacrificed, by unprincipled rulers, to schemes of lawless ambition or iniquitous favouritism. The administration of Christ, on the contrary, is impartial, righteous, infallible; no one is wronged that another may be benefited; and every act is such as entitles it to meet with ready and implicit submission.

Exemplary behaviour is necessary to give due moral effect to official administration. Laws however wise, acts however equitable, intentions however pure, cannot have the same influence on others when they proceed from persons who are themselves destitute of moral character. No government, however good in itself, can be expected to be successful, which is administered by a known profligate. It is wisely required that he that ruleth over men must be 'just, ruling in the fear of the Lord.' It were unreasonable to expect principles to be acted upon, and laws to be obeyed, which are inculcated by persons who are themselves violating them every day. He is likely to be most useful who can appeal, as Samuel did of old, to his people: 'I have walked before you from my childhood unto this day. Behold here I am; witness against me before the Lord and before his anointed, whose ox have I taken? or whose ass have I taken? or whom have I defrauded? whom have I oppressed? or of whose hand have I received any bribe to blind mine eyes herewith?'[11] Jesus set his subjects an example of perfect holiness. His conduct was unimpeachable; his behaviour was unaffected with the slightest moral obliquity. All the laws of his kingdom, whether personal, relative, or religious, were recom-

[11] 1 Sam. xii. 2, 3.

mended by his example, as well as enforced by his sovereign authority. Perfect moral excellence adorns his character. He is not only the righteous Lord who *loveth* righteousness, but he *practised* it so fully and so constantly, as to entitle him, in presence of his most inveterate enemies, to put forth the challenge: 'Which of you convinceth me of sin?'

6. Nor is Jesus deficient in the more gentle qualities of *meek compassion, tender mercy, and munificent bounty*. Great wisdom and stern integrity may be combined with a harsh, repulsive, and unfeeling disposition, but such a combination can be regarded only in the light of a defect. '*Mercy* and truth preserve the king, and his throne is upholden by *mercy*.'[12] In the qualifications of Sion's King, the combination in question is complete. In him, justice and compassion honourably harmonise. 'Mercy and truth are met together, righteousness and peace have kissed each other' (Ps. lxxxv. 10). While 'he loves righteousness and hates wickedness,' all 'his garments smell of myrrh, and aloes, and cassia' (Ps. xlv. 7, 8). To the daughter of Sion, her King is announced at once as '*just* and having salvation, *lowly* and riding upon an ass, upon a colt the foal of an ass' (Zech. ix. 9). He can have compassion upon the ignorant and them that are out of the way. Although having all the resources of destruction at his command, he bears patiently with the disobedience and rebellious insults of his subjects. He waits to be gracious. To the most worthless criminal he extends the golden sceptre of his love. His munificence is

[12] Prov. xx. 28.

exhaustless; his bestowments most bountiful and liberal. Plenty, liberty, honour, are dispensed with open hand. What shall be done to the man whom this King delights to honour, cannot be told or conceived. 'He shall judge the poor of the people, he shall save the children of the needy, and shall break in pieces the oppressor. He shall come down like rain upon the mown grass; as showers that water the earth. In his days shall the righteous flourish; and abundance of peace so long as the moon endureth. He shall deliver the needy when he crieth; the poor also and him that hath no helper. He shall spare the poor and needy, and shall save the soul of the needy.'[13]

7. *Authority* is necessary to the valid exercise of power. Other qualifications cannot confer this; nor can the abundance in which they may be enjoyed make up for the want of it. There are two ways in which legitimate authority may be conveyed—divine appointment and popular choice. The latter, however just and proper among men, cannot obtain here; as it is one of the peculiarities of the case before us, that the king chooses the people, and not the people the king. 'Ye have not chosen me, but I have chosen you.' Divine appointment, therefore, is here the only proper source of authority. Not that his right to rule is not confirmed by purchase and by conquest; but these are not in themselves sufficient; in their very nature they presuppose an authority founded on the appointment of God. This, then, is the origin of that authority by which the Messiah is qualified for the exercise of media-

[13] Ps. lxxi. 4, 6, 7, 12, 13.

torial dominion. It is a matter of such importance, and admits of such amplitude of proof and illustration, that we shall devote a section to it by itself. 'The Father loveth the Son, and hath given all things into his hand' (John iii. 35).

Such is the beauty of Christ's regal qualifications. Here, dignity and condescension, grace and majesty, are admirably blended. There is nothing redundant, nothing defective. There is nothing present that can be wanted, nothing wanting that is required, and every part is in due proportion and delightful harmony.

CHAPTER IV.

APPOINTMENT OF CHRIST TO MEDIATORIAL DOMINION.

This is a topic of great importance, and deserving of being fully investigated and distinctly understood.

1. Christ was *formally* appointed to the kingly office *by his Father from all eternity in the covenant of grace.* 'Yet have I SET my king upon my holy hill of Zion.—I appoint unto you a kingdom, as MY FATHER HATH APPOINTED UNTO ME.—As the Father hath life in himself, so hath HE GIVEN to the Son to have life in himself; and hath GIVEN HIM AUTHORITY to execute judgment also because he is the Son of man.'[1] It belonged to the Father to do this formally, as the representative of Deity in the economy of redemption. Absolutely speaking, Christ's appointment proceeded from the sovereign act of the divine will essentially considered. The designation of all the divine persons to their respective economical characters and offices, can only be referred to such an act. To conceive it as proceeding from the Father necessarily or originally, is at variance with the perfect *equality* subsisting among the divine persons themselves. It must, therefore, be viewed as flowing *absolutely from God essentially considered* in the first instance; and, then, that of the Son and the Holy

[1] Ps. ii. 6; Luke xxii. 29; John v. 26, 27.

Spirit as proceeding *formally from the Father*, in whom all power and authority have been economically vested for this end. To him, therefore, the formal appointment of the Mediator to government or rule must be ascribed. This formal appointment took place in the covenant of grace. 'I have made a COVENANT with my chosen, I have sworn unto David my servant, thy seed will I establish for ever, and build up thy THRONE to all generations.'[2] It took place from eternity—in anticipation of the fall and consequent helplessness and danger of man. Hence, after the announcement 'Yet have I set my king upon my holy hill of Zion,' it is added, 'I will declare the DECREE: the Lord hath said unto me, Thou art my Son; this day have I begotten thee.'[3] To the same purpose is the declaration—'I was set up FROM EVERLASTING, from the beginning, or ever the earth was:'[4] while he who was to be 'Ruler in Israel' was spoken of by Micah as having his 'goings forth from of old, from everlasting.'[5] How solemn and indubitable this act of formal appointment!

2. Christ's appointment from eternity to the kingly office, was *significantly intimated, in the fulness of time, by the unction of his human nature*. In order to our feeling an interest in, and becoming acquainted with, what took place in the everlasting covenant, it required to be made known. This was effected by his being solemnly anointed. To anoint, was the ancient way of denoting regal designation. 'The trees went forth on a time *to anoint* a king over them.—The bramble

[2] Ps. lxxxix. 3, 4.
[3] Ps. ii. 6, 7.
[4] Prov. viii. 23.
[5] Mic. v. 2.

said unto the trees, If in truth you *anoint* me king over you.—Samuel also said unto Saul, The Lord sent me *to anoint* thee to be king over his people, over Israel. —Thou shalt *anoint* unto me him whom I name unto thee.—The house of Judah have *anointed* me king over them. *Anoint* Hazael to be king over Syria.'[6] Similar language is used respecting Christ: 'Yet have I set (Heb. *anointed*) my king upon my holy hill of Zion. God, thy God, hath *anointed* thee with the oil of gladness above thy fellows. I have found David my servant; with my holy oil have I *anointed* him. I have ordained a lamp for mine *anointed*. Of a truth against thy holy child Jesus, whom thou hast *anointed*, both Herod and Pontius Pilate, with the Gentiles, and the people of Israel, were gathered together. How God *anointed* Jesus of Nazareth with the Holy Ghost, and with power.'[7] What idea was intended to be conveyed by this phraseology, the passages formerly quoted enable us to determine. There cannot be a doubt, that regal appointment is designed by the unction which Jesus is said to have received; an unction which consisted not, as in the case of kings among men, of literal oil and aromatic perfumes applied to the body by the hand of a prophet, but of the Spirit of grace poured out upon him in rich abundance by the Father. This was the 'holy oil, the oil of gladness,' with which he was anointed 'above his fellows.' These expressions may refer, in part, to his blessed qualifications; but they must be viewed principally as denoting his authoritative ap-

---

[6] Judg. ix. 8, 15; 1 Sam. xv. 1; xvi. 3; 2 Sam. ii. 7; 1 Kings xix. 15.
[7] Ps. ii. 6; xlv. 7; lxxxix. 20; cxxxii. 17; Acts iv. 27; x. 38.

pointment, in respect of which, all his garments may be said to 'smell of myrrh, and aloes, and cassia, out of the ivory palaces.'

3. Christ's appointment was still farther intimated by his *actual investiture with regal power at and after his resurrection.* This might be called the inauguration solemnity of the mediatorial King. What took place in the counsels of eternity was made known in the fulness of time; but it was still more largely and clearly exhibited when the Son of God rose from the dead. The kingly office of Christ being essential to the mediatorial character, must of course have existed from eternity, and must also have been exercised from the beginning of time; yet the Scriptures speak of it as conferred in reward of his obedience unto death. 'Being found in fashion as a man, he humbled himself, and became obedient unto death, even the death of the cross. Wherefore God also hath highly exalted him, and given him a name which is above every name, that at the name of Jesus every knee should bow, of things in heaven, and things in earth, and things under the earth.'[8] Its having been conferred at his resurrection may seem inconsistent with having existed from the beginning. They are, however, both true. The Holy Spirit always existed in the church, and yet was not given until Christ was glorified. After Christ was glorified there was a more copious manifestation, a more full dispensation of the Spirit. In like manner, at his resurrection, there was a more ample display, a more extensive exercise of Christ's regal power. His power

[8] Phil. ii. 8–10.

was, from the first, exercised on the footing of his meritorious death. But when the death had really occurred, it was fitting that there should be a display of the power which resulted from it, and which had all along a regard to it. In short, the exercise of the kingly office *before* and *after* Christ's resurrection, bear much the same relation to one another, as the exercise of the same office before and after the coronation of an earthly king. The ceremony of coronation makes a public, solemn, august display of the sovereign's investiture with regal power; but the power itself existed before;—in an hereditary government, from the moment of the demise of his predecessor; in an elective government, from the time of his being chosen by the people. After the resurrection of our Redeemer from the grave, there was a more full, explicit, and expressive recognition than before of his appointment to mediatorial rule. Then did it appear that all power was given unto him in heaven and in earth. 'His being by the right hand of God exalted,' was the means of 'letting all the house of Israel know assuredly that God had made that same Jesus whom men had crucified both Lord and Christ' (Acts ii. 33, 36). 'When he raised him from the dead, he set him at his own right hand in the heavenly places, far above all principality, and power, and might, and dominion, and every name that is named, not only in this world, but in that which is to come' (Eph. i. 21, 22). 'When he had by himself purged our sins, he sat down on the right hand of the Majesty on high' (Heb. i. 3). He was King from eternity; from the entrance of sin into our world he exercised the regal functions; in the lowest depths of his humiliation, occasional signs of dignity and power appeared. But not until his resurrection from the dead and ascension to the throne of the Father, was his investiture with this power publicly and formally recognised. Then, however, did his regal splendour come out from the cloud of obscurity in which it had been formerly wrapped; his diadem shone forth with transcendent lustre; his sceptre, the weight of which had before been comparatively unfelt, began now to be wielded with new power; angels sang his coronation anthem:—

> 'Ye gates, lift up your heads on high;
> Ye doors that last for aye,
> Be lifted up that so the king
> Of glory enter may;'

And, amid the loud acclaim of these celestial attendants, he ascended his throne, and entered on the formal administration of his kingdom.

4. This appointment is *attested by many distinct and indubitable witnesses.* The Father gives formal proof of the fact, when he says, 'Yet have I set my King upon my holy hill of Zion' (Ps. ii. 6). The Saviour himself bears this testimony, 'All power is given unto me in heaven and in earth' (Matt. xxviii. 18). The spirit of Old Testament prophecy declared, 'I beheld in the night visions, and behold, one like the Son of Man came with the clouds of heaven, and came to the Ancient of days, and they brought him near before him, and there was given him dominion, and glory, and a kingdom, that all people, nations, and languages should serve him: his dominion is an everlasting dominion,

which shall not pass away, and his kingdom that which shall not be destroyed' (Dan. vii. 13, 14). Apostles, under the New Testament, concur in the evidence they furnish: 'God hath highly exalted him, and given him a name which is above every name' (Phil. ii. 9). And every creature in heaven, and on the earth, and under the earth, and such as are in the sea, and all that are in them, are heard saying, 'Blessing, and honour, and glory, and power, be unto him that sitteth upon the throne, and to the Lamb, for ever and ever' (Rev. v. 13). Such united, harmonious, unequivocal testimonies, leave us no room to doubt the interesting fact, and render inexcusable every feeling of scepticism on the subject.

Yet, this matter is not without its difficulties.

The appointment of Christ to the kingly office has been represented as inconsistent with his divinity. It is supposed to imply inferiority. But the economical character of the Son removes the difficulty at once. It is not as God absolutely considered, that it takes place; but as Mediator. In this capacity it is easy to suppose him invested with authority; and, considering the deep humiliation to which he voluntarily submitted in this character, there can be no difficulty whatever in understanding either the fact or the nature of his exaltation.

Nor did he, in assuming the mediatorial kingdom, divest himself of anything belonging to him as God. This it were impiety to suppose. Deity is unchangeable. His being, perfections, character, and government, as God, remained the same as they ever were.

They might be obscured in appearance, but they were the same in reality. His moral authority over all creatures could never be laid aside. It is essential to his very being and character. The mode of its exercise only was changed: it was now administered in an economical instead of an absolute character, for the good and salvation of his church.

Neither does the appointment of Christ to the regal office suppose that God is deprived of that necessary and essential dominion which belongs to him. If it does not take from Christ his own essential power as God, it cannot be understood as taking it from God absolutely considered. That springs naturally from the inseparable relation subsisting between God and his creatures. The delegation of power does not suppose the surrender of it, on the part of him from whom the delegation proceeds. When a king appoints a plenipotentiary to act for him, he does not divest himself of the inherent right to reign. And if this is the case where the person appointing and the persons appointed are essentially different, why should we find any difficulty in a case where they are 'the same in substance, and equal in power and glory?' Nay, so far from God's essential dominion being subverted by the mediatorial appointment, it might easily be shown to be confirmed and established by it in a variety of particulars.

If the view given, in this chapter, of the appointment of Christ to mediatorial power be correct, there can be no difficulty in understanding how his regal acts were possessed of validity in the earliest ages of the church. This appointment had, as we have seen, a special respect to his death; it was conferred as the reward of his sufferings; and, hence, he was not fully inaugurated till after his resurrection. Still, the administration of mediatorial rule existed from the time of the entrance of sin into our world. The Son of God then entered on the administration of all his mediatorial functions; on this, as well as others. The voice of the Lord God, walking in the garden in the cool of the day, announced him as a *prophet:* the institution of sacrifices, which there is reason to think was coeval with the fall of man, exhibited him as a *priest:* and the warfare betwixt the seed of the woman and the seed of the serpent, which then commenced, unfolded his *regal* character. In this latter capacity, he never ceased afterwards to act. The formation of the church in Eden; the translation of Abel's righteous soul to glory; the re-organisation of the church with Noah; the covenant made with Abraham, and renewed with Isaac and Jacob; the establishment of the Jewish economy under Moses; the many interpositions made on behalf of the armies of Israel, by which they were rendered victorious over their enemies; the appointment of judges; and the raising up of kings in the line of David, to dispense the benefits of civil government to God's ancient people—are all so many regal acts of Prince Messiah. Accordingly, when he came in the flesh, he was recognised, not as entering upon, but as in the full possession of, royal prerogatives: 'Where is he that IS BORN KING of the Jews?'[9] And, even during the period of his humiliation, as has been before remarked, he claimed and received royal honours, as well as per-

[9] Matt. ii. 2.

formed regal acts. Now, what we have said regarding his appointment, shows the validity of all these acts from the beginning. His appointment took place in the eternal counsels. It was, therefore, not only what he did after his resurrection, but all the acts which preceded it, that were possessed of valid authority. His sovereignty must never be doubted. Whether he erects or destroys, plants or plucks up, kills or makes alive, implicit submission is due to his righteous sceptre; we must acknowledge his title to do according to his will in the army of heaven and among the inhabitants of the earth; and, instead of seeking to impede the regular flow of his administration, it becomes us to shout from the heart, 'O King, live for ever.'

Christ's appointment gives him a rightful claim to the implicit and conscientious obedience of every moral creature. 'Hereby we do know that we know him, if we keep his commandments. He that saith, I know him, and keepeth not his commandments, is a liar, and the truth is not in him. But whoso keepeth his word, in him verily is the truth of God perfected.'[10] It is as mediatorial King that all his commands are given, and in this capacity is it that he is to be obeyed. Let men be convinced of this. He is no usurper. Great must be the guilt of refusing him submission; it is to resist lawful authority, to reject the appointment of God.

This appointment affords ample security for the overthrow of all Christ's enemies, and the ultimate establishment of his kingdom in the world. Has God appointed

[10] John ii. 3-5.

him to rule, and shall any one be able to hinder his success? No; we have, in this, sufficient security that no opposition shall ever be able to prevent the progress of his reign. The counsel of the Lord, it shall stand. The heathen may rage, and the people imagine a vain thing; the kings of the earth may set themselves, and the rulers take counsel together, against the Lord and against his Anointed, saying, Let us break their bands asunder and cast their cords from us. But, having respect to the decree by which he has been set King on the holy hill of Zion, He that sitteth in the heavens shall laugh; the Lord shall have them in derision; he shall break them with a rod of iron, he shall dash them in pieces like a potter's vessel; and the heathen shall be given to him for his inheritance, and the uttermost parts of the earth for his possession. Much reason, then, have the people of God to rejoice in the appointment of Christ to mediatorial dominion. Let them make themselves intelligently acquainted with the evidence by which it is supported, and exult in the stability of the foundation on which it rests—a foundation which no force of earth or hell can ever overthrow. 'The Lord said unto my Lord, Rule thou in the midst of thine enemies; thy people shall be willing in the day of thy power.'

CHAPTER V.

THE SPIRITUALITY OF CHRIST'S MEDIATORIAL DOMINION.

The subjects which have hitherto engaged our attention may be viewed as preliminary. The necessity, reality, qualifications, and appointment of Christ's kingly office, prepare the way for an inquiry into the *nature* of the mediatorial dominion itself. This we are now to consider. Nor can it be more clearly expressed than by saying, in one word, that the government of the Son of God, as Mediator, is strictly and properly *spiritual*. His kingdom is not an earthly or temporal kingdom, like the kingdoms of this world. It has a higher origin; it interferes, in no respect, with the exercise of lawful civil authority; and the means by which its advancement is effected are different from those which the rulers of this world employ.

1. The *origin* of the mediatorial dominion illustrates its distinction, in respect of spirituality, from the kingdoms of this world. These all originate in what is natural. Lawful civil authority in general, is, doubtless, an ordinance of God; but, as respects the immediate origin of each individual kingdom, it is an ordinance of man. Whether taking rise from the elective power of the people, from hereditary succession, from conquest, or from usurpation, dominion

among men is natural in its origin. To some the crown descends by lineal succession from ancestors from whose heads it has just been displaced by the hand of death. Others have the sceptre bestowed on them by the unconstrained suffrage and cheerful acclamation of a free and happy people. Others, again, establishing right by might, assert their claims by the power of the sword, wade to sovereignty through seas of blood, and mount to the throne on the slaughtered bodies of the men whom they seek to govern. It is otherwise far with the dominion of which we are now treating. The crown of our Mediatorial King was worn by no other; he is its original and exclusive possessor. He enjoys, it is true, the welcome of his spiritual subjects, but this is the result of his administration, and not the source of his authority; and, although blood be connected with the establishment of his reign, it is not the blood of his subjects or enemies, but his own blood, the very shedding of which presupposes an existing right to rule and act as a king. His dominion originates solely in immediate divine appointment, in the spiritual grant of his Father from all everlasting in the covenant of grace. *My Father hath appointed unto me a kingdom.* To such an origin, no kingdom of this world can lay claim; to such a grant, no monarch among men can pretend. These are of the 'earth, earthy;' this is 'from above.' *The Father loveth the Son, and hath given all things into his hand.*

2. The *ends* contemplated by this dominion are spiritual. The immediate ends for which kingdoms

are set up among men, are of course worldly ends. The administration of public justice, the preservation of peace, the advancement of morals, and the establishment of social order, are immediately contemplated by civil authority. These, right and proper in themselves, are different from, and inferior to, the ends of Christ's mediatorial dominion. Those bear a closer relation to the value of the soul, the greatness of the human mind, the vastness of human desires, the immortal destiny of man. To give light to them that are in spiritual darkness, to rescue from the tyranny of sinful passions, to purge the conscience from dead works, to renovate the heart, to sanctify the life, to swallow up death in victory, and to shut the mouth of the infernal abyss,—in one word to save the soul, is the grand end of the mediatorial dominion. A worldly kingdom has to do with the lives and property of men, that of Christ with their hearts and consciences. The one has a respect to their interests in the world that now is, the other to those in the world that is to come. The one aims at making men good subjects, the other at making them true saints. The ends contemplated by the kingdoms of this world terminate in time, but those contemplated by the dominion of the Mediator point forward to, and can be consummated only in, an eternal state of being. Not but that earthly dominion may be so conducted as to subserve the interests of the soul and of eternity, just as the dominion of the Mediator cannot but produce the temporal interests and social advantages of mankind; but we speak now, not of the collateral or indirect tendencies of each, but of their direct and immediate ends,—which are in the one case worldly, and in the other spiritual. 'For the kingdom of God is not meat and drink, but righteousness, and peace, and joy, in the Holy Ghost.'

3. The *administration* of Christ's kingdom is spiritual. It is administered, as are the kingdoms of this world, by office-bearers, government, and laws; but these are of a character different from those which obtain in other cases. Here, the officers are not persons invested with magisterial authority, and armed with civil weapons; but pastors and teachers, elders and deacons, endowed with ministerial authority, whose weapons are not carnal but spiritual. The government and discipline they administer address themselves to the understandings, and hearts, and consciences of men; they aim at something more than laying restraints, as civil government does, on the persons and overt acts of men; their object is to influence the motives of action and to restrain the inward passions of the soul. The ministers, to whom the management of this government is committed, are made overseers by the Holy Ghost. They assume no right, like civil rulers, to enact, command, or enjoin in their own name; they are 'not lords over God's heritage.' When they issue their counsels, it is in the name of the Lord, being prefaced with 'Thus saith the Lord' or 'It seemed good to the Holy Ghost and to us to lay upon you those necessary things.' They claim not to have dominion over their people's faith, but to be helpers of their joy. Instead of the stern voice of authority, which, at the peril of property, liberty, or life, must be obeyed, they appeal to the law and to the

testimony, and invite a strict scrutiny of whatever they utter. *We speak as unto wise men, judge ye what we say.* They claim no power over the persons or purses of men. The penalties they denounce are not fines, imprisonment, and death. They bear not the *sword;* but, entrusted with the *keys* of the kingdom of heaven, view it as their prerogative to 'open or shut' the doors of ecclesiastical privilege, according to character. Instruction and advice, censure and remonstrance, are the only weapons they feel themselves at liberty to employ. They reprove, rebuke, exhort with all authority. When repeated admonition has failed to produce the desired effect, they reject; when milder measures have proved insufficient, they proceed in the name of the Lord Jesus to deliver over the offender to Satan for the destruction of the flesh: but physical violence they may never use, to produce a constrained submission. The conscience, with which alone they have to do, cannot be influenced by fire or steel. Standing armies, well-stored magazines, swords, and muskets, form no part of their equipments. No. 'If my kingdom,' says Christ, 'were of this world, then would my servants fight: but now is my kingdom not from hence.' The instruments, the use of which He recognises as legitimate, are:—the *Bible;* the word of God which is quick and powerful, sharper than any two-edged sword, the sword of the spirit, the sharp two-edged sword which goeth out of the mouth of him who is Alpha and Omega:—the *Cross;* the preaching of which is the most effectual means of turning men from darkness to light, of thinning the ranks of Satan, and increasing the number of true adherents to the

Captain of Salvation:—the *example* of Him who is the great pattern of perfection, whose contempt of the world appeared in that he 'had not where to lay his head;' his meekness, in 'bearing the contradiction of sinners;' his patience, in that 'when he was reviled he reviled not again;' and his active benevolence, in continually 'going about doing good.' These, under the hallowed influence of the Holy Spirit of all grace, are the means of enlightening, renewing, sanctifying, and consoling men, and of thus bringing them to be, and qualifying them to act as, subjects of Christ's spiritual kingdom. 2 Cor. x. 4: 'For the weapons of our warfare are not carnal, but mighty through God to the pulling down of strong-holds.' Zech. iv. 6: 'Not by might, nor by power, but by my Spirit, saith the Lord.'

4. The *principles* of Christ's kingdom are spiritual principles. It disclaims all sympathy with the maxims on which the governments of this world are too often administered, maxims which are, not seldom, infidel, fallacious, and ungrateful. Instead of the common and pernicious sentiment, that personal virtues are not necessary in public men, it is an established maxim here that 'he that ruleth over men must be just,' and that trust is to be committed only to 'faithful men.' Instead of supposing that, if the laws of the nation are only understood and acted upon by men in power, it matters not how much the law of God is overlooked and contemned, it is provided that rulers shall have a copy of the law, and shall read in it continually. Instead of regarding it as a matter of inferior moment how much private wickedness may abound in a land, provided only

that public tranquillity and obedience to the laws can be preserved, it is a first principle that 'righteousness exalteth a nation, and that sin is a disgrace to any people.' In the kingdoms of the world it is a principle too much acted upon, that a state of warfare warrants us to treat an enemy without pity, sincerity, or even humanity; but, in the kingdom of Christ, it is an immutable law that 'all things whatsoever we would that men should do to us, we should do even so to them.' But there is no end to the contrast; the longer it is pursued it becomes not more evident that 'the kingdom of Christ is not of this world,' than that 'the kingdoms of this world' are *not yet* 'the kingdoms of our Lord and of his Christ.'

5. In short, almost *every thing* connected with this kingdom is spiritual. The King himself is no worldly prince, but the Lord from heaven, who is a quickening spirit. The subjects are a spiritual community, consisting of persons who have been regenerated by the Holy Spirit as an essential and indispensable qualification to their admission; for 'except a man be born again, he cannot enter into the kingdom of God.' The laws by which they are governed are spiritual laws, which take cognisance of the heart. The homage paid to the sovereign Lord, instead of vain and empty ceremonies, consists in the sincere and pious devotion of the soul. His throne is such as no king of this earth ever occupied, an eternal heavenly throne; 'thy throne, O God, is for ever and ever.' His sceptre is a righteous sceptre, even the rod of strength sent out of Zion, by which he rules in the midst of his enemies. His courtiers

are not those who, by intriguing complacence and mean arts of adulation, contrive to bask in the sunshine of royal favour, but 'whosoever shall do the will of his Father, who is in heaven.' His attendant retinue is composed, not of fawning sycophants and feigned friends, but of the immortal sons of light, angels and archangels ten thousand strong.

Thus, in whatever light we contemplate it, the spirituality of Christ's kingdom stands forth as a prominent and well-established feature. Nor is it possible not to be impressed with the affecting confirmation this view of the matter received from his appearance on earth. He steadfastly resisted every attempt to invest him with the attributes of an earthly sovereign. 'When Jesus perceived that they would come and take him by force to make him a king, he departed into a mountain himself alone.' With temporal aggrandisement and the showy trappings of royalty, he would have nothing to do. The only occasion on which he enjoyed anything approaching to a triumphal procession, was when he entered into Jerusalem, and then he rode upon an ass. The only robe of office, in which he was ever arrayed, was a cast-off military cloak, thrown around him by his enemies in derision of his regal claims. The only sceptre he ever handled was a reed. The only diadem, he ever wore, was a crown of thorns. For a throne he had assigned him a cross. And the homage offered him by the men of the world, consisted only in pointing at him with the finger of scorn, spitting on him, and striking him with the palms of their hands. Well mightest thou say, O Jesus! 'My kingdom is not of this world.'

But when we speak of the dominion of the Mediator as spiritual, it is necessary to guard against supposing that it can have no sort of connexion with the world, or with things that are secular. Such an idea it is not at all our intention to convey. From not sufficiently attending to certain distinctions proper to be observed on this subject, mistaken and pernicious conclusions have been drawn. Because the dominion of Christ is spiritual in its nature, to conclude that everything connected with his kingdom must be spiritual also, and that nothing earthly or secular can have any relation to it, is an inference alike illogical in reasoning, and unsupported by fact. The subjects of this spiritual kingdom, after being separated by grace from the world lying in wickedness, continue for a length of time in this lower region of human existence, before they are prepared for being transferred to that brighter, and higher, and more spiritual sphere in which they are to exist for ever. Although not *of* this world as to their character, they are *in* this world as respects their place of abode. While, as *saints*, they number among the ranks of Christ's spiritual subjects, as *men* and as *citizens* they occupy their places and act their parts in the offices and institutions of civil society. While here, they have bodies which require to be fed, and clothed, and protected; and, even when their souls at death are taken to heaven, their material frames, redeemed by Christ and destined to undergo a remarkable change at the last day, sleep till then in the lower parts of the earth, where they are ever contemplated with interest, watched over with ceaseless care, and faithfully preserved by that Saviour-king, who claims dominion over their persons in both their constituent parts, material and immaterial. So long as the saints have bodies, this kingdom can never be so strictly spiritual as to exclude all sort of connexion with matter.

Besides, the kingdom of Christ has a visible as well as an invisible form. This distinction is founded in fact, and is, we believe, universally admitted. Now, a visible church must have visible laws, visible ordinances, visible subjects, and visible office-bearers. And what but this world is the sphere where these laws are promulged, these ordinances observed, these subjects located, and these office-bearers find room for their labours? While God has a visible church in the world, there will be required outward erections for the ordinances of worship, and temporal emoluments for the support of its ministers and institutions.

Nay, more; we may venture to affirm, that, connected with the spiritual kingdom of the Mediator, there are some things which are in themselves strictly and literally worldly or secular. The dominion of Christ, as we shall have occasion afterwards more fully to explain, is universal. It includes ALL creatures without exception; not merely the church, visible and invisible, but all things, animate and inanimate, rational and irrational, moral and immoral, individual and social, ecclesiastical and political. It may suffice, at present, to remind the reader of one or two Scripture passages by which the assertion is fully borne out. 'All power is given unto me in heaven and in earth—He hath put all things under his feet—And hath put all things under his feet, and gave him to be the head over all things to the church, which is his body, the fulness of him that filleth all in all.'[1] If, according to these expressions, the mediatorial rule extends over all things, many things strictly secular and worldly must be somehow or other connected with Christ's kingdom ; and such a view of its spirituality as is incompatible with any sort of connexion with the things of this world, is thus shown to be manifestly erroneous and untenable.

The kingdom of Christ is truly spiritual ; yet, connected with this kingdom, it seems there may be many things which are properly secular. The kingdom of Christ is not of this world ; yet many worldly things are connected with Christ's kingdom. These statements are not inconsistent. We may find it difficult to reconcile them ; we may feel ourselves at a loss to find out a harmonising principle ; but we must neither, on the one hand, deny the fact, nor, on the other, impute contradiction to the words of Christ or the language of Scripture. We must not think ourselves warranted, to avoid the difficulty in question, in substituting a quibble for a sober interpretation, or in proceeding to restrict the mediatorial rule agreeably to our own partial and limited views, by cutting off from his economical prerogative whatever is not strictly of a spiritual character. Such would be to use an unwarrantable liberty with the word of God, to interpret the Bible as no other composition will admit of being interpreted, and to take an ungenerous advantage of the mere sound of words. The

---

[1] Matt. xxviii. 18; 1 Cor. xv. 27 ; Eph. i. 22.

two ideas are capable of being perfectly reconciled. All that is required for this purpose, is, that whatever is connected with Christ's kingdom be understood to be somehow or other *subservient* to spiritual objects,— objects not terminating with, but superior to, and outliving in duration, the present world. Although every thing connected with it may not be in itself spiritual, every thing connected with it may be subservient to what is spiritual. The grand aim and purpose of the whole may be of this description, while many things of a different nature may be subordinate to this end. The dominion of the Messiah may extend over many things besides the church, and may comprehend many creatures besides the saints, and yet embrace nothing but what is somehow or another fitted to be of service to these. The Father has given him to be head over *all* things; but the reason of this does not terminate in these things themselves; it points to a higher and more spiritual object; He has given him to be head over all things TO THE CHURCH which is his body. Whatever power the Mediator possesses is for the good of the church; is given and exercised for this purpose. But what, we ask, is there that is not for the good of the church? But for the church would the sun continue to shine, the rain to fall, the earth to vegetate? Would the wheels of providence continue to revolve, or the pillars of the universe to be upheld? No. The church is the great conservative element of the world and all that is in it; nor is there any thing which is not capable of being rendered, by infinite wisdom and power, subservient to the interests of God's covenant society. Here, then, we are furnished with a solution of the difficulty. Every system derives its character and designation from that which constitutes its ultimate end or aim, and not from any inferior or subordinate appendage. We call that an enlightened and virtuous kingdom, whose constitution and administration have for their direct object the promotion of knowledge and morality, notwithstanding that some of the subjects may be wicked, ignorant, or even insane. We call that person spiritual, who gives evidence, from the obvious tendency of his general demeanour, that he is born from above and destined for glory, although many of his thoughts and pursuits may have a relation to this world, and even some of his actions be sinful. Thus it is with the kingdom of Christ. We call it a spiritual kingdom, inasmuch as the great design of its existence is spiritual, notwithstanding that, among the things connected with it, there may be many that are material, and perhaps even worldly.

Christ said of the church, 'My kingdom is not of this world.' But, if this means that his kingdom is so absolutely spiritual as to have no connexion whatever with what is secular or earthly, then when he said of his disciples 'ye are not of the world,' he meant that Christians could lawfully hold no worldly property, engage in no worldly enterprise, nor enter into any political connexion whatever. The phrases are in both cases precisely similar; and as, in the latter instance, it would be absurd, and contradictory both to Scripture and common sense, to contend for the exclusive interpretation in question, so must it be in the former.

Thus much to prevent misconception, and to obviate

a common mistake. It will now be understood that when we speak of the dominion of the Mediator as spiritual, we mean that its nature and design are wholly celestial, that it is of a character different from the kingdoms of this world, and destined to higher and more glorious purposes.

The view now given of the kingly office of Christ is one of great importance. The tendency to take a carnal view of his kingdom is deeply seated in the human heart, and has appeared in various forms.

It was the radical error of the unbelieving Jews. The prophecies respecting the glory of the Messiah they interpreted literally. They expected him to appear as a temporal prince, to put himself at the head of his countrymen, to rescue them from the yoke of Romish subjection, and to restore the kingdom to its original and rightful possessors. Because Jesus of Nazareth did not fulfil these expectations, they could not look upon him as the true Messiah. To them he appeared as a root out of a dry ground, having no form nor comeliness; they saw no beauty in him for which they should desire him. Blinded by their carnal prejudices, they could not bring themselves to believe, that the prediction that the Messiah should wield a sceptre was fulfilled in one who held only a reed—that the prophecy that the Messiah should wear a diadem, was fulfilled in one who was crowned only with thorns—or that the statement that the Messiah should occupy a throne, was fulfilled in one who occupied only a cross. The event, instead of correcting their error and suggesting to them the true interpretation, instead of leading them to spiritual ideas of his character and reign, only drove them to the mad extreme of contemptuous rejection. Their descendants to the present day adhere to their opinion and follow their example, solely from the influence of the same carnal views. It becomes those to whom God has given more scriptural and spiritual ideas, to pity their mistake; to pray for their illumination; and to do everything in their power to reclaim them from so fatal an error. Ye sons of Abraham! ye wandering tribes of Israel!—still beloved for the fathers' sakes—be entreated to abandon the prejudices by which you are held in mental bondage; burst your ignoble thraldom; and, giving a spiritual interpretation to the glowing imagery of your prophets, behold the fulfilment of their predictions in the despised Nazarene!

The error of those who look for a *literal advent* of Christ, and a literal reign upon earth during the millenium, must be traced to the same source, namely, to their overlooking the spirituality of the mediatorial dominion. They expect a visible descent of the Redeemer in his glorified human nature, to erect a local court, to sit upon a literal throne, and to conduct a temporal reign for at least a thousand years. If we have been at all successful in proving that the kingdom of Christ is a spiritual kingdom, this system must fall to the ground, for its whole tendency is to represent his kingdom as a temporal one, to revive the exploded rites and opinions of carnal Judaism, and to bring back upon the church the yoke of beggarly elements from which Christ has made us free. Let those who are in danger of being seduced by the doctrine in question, ponder well the evidence furnished in support of the spirituality of the kingdom of Christ. Let them be jealous of the tendency there is, in the human heart, to be carried away with what strikes the senses in preference to that which appeals to faith. Let them profit by the case of the unhappy Jews, who, by yielding to this natural tendency, have been plunged into the gulf of unbelief, and are still suffering the just award of their iniquity. 'The letter killeth; the spirit giveth life.'

It is impossible here to overlook the means with which we are thus furnished, of forming a right estimate of the church of Rome, and of determining the question whether that church be Christian or anti-Christian. It pretends to be Christ's kingdom upon earth, and to be the only church which can lay claim to this distinction. Well, Christ's kingdom is not of this world—it is a spiritual kingdom;—a kingdom of truth, and righteousness, and love, and peace; a kingdom whose office-bearers, ends, administration, and appendages, are all of a spiritual character. How does the state of things in the Romish church accord with this view? Look at the Roman pontiff,—the assumed representative on earth of Him who strenuously refused to be made a king by men, who studiously avoided all interference with the civil authorities, who wore a crown of thorns, and expired on a cross. You see on his head a triple crown, glittering with gold and sparkling with diamonds; his vestments are of the most costly and gorgeous materials; at his side hang golden keys; grasping the sword of temporal power, he lays claim to a universal, civil, as well as ecclesiastical, authority; and adding the imperial diadem to the sacerdotal mitre, he prostrates even monarchs at his feet. Enter the Vatican,—the habitation of the pretended successor of Him whose kingdom is not of this world, and who had not where to lay his head,—and what do you behold but the unequivocal insignia of temporal power, the gaudy paraphernalia of earthly pomp and grandeur? Visit a cathedral,—where the highest acts of devotion are professedly engaged in to Him who is a Spirit, and who requires such as worship him to worship him in spirit and in truth. There you have lofty domes, massive pillars, pictorial decorations on which the most accomplished artists have expended their skill, splendid vestments, voluptuous music, smoking incense, sparkling lights;—everything, in short, to strike the senses rather than to affect the heart, to glitter in the eye rather than to impress the conscience. These are scandalous departures from the character of that kingdom which is not of this world; they are standing proofs that the church of Rome has no title to be regarded as a church of Christ at all, much less as *the* Church of Christ: they are the unequivocal, ineffaceable marks of anti-Christianism.

May not this subject be of use, farther, in enabling us to test the character and claims of even Protestant systems of religion? The diversity of sentiment existing among Protestant churches, is painful and bewildering; and it is desirable to be furnished with some principles by which we may estimate their respective conflicting claims. Here is one—the degree of spirituality they possess. The system which has the least of worldly pomp, which least depends on the smiles of the world, which has fewest attractions for the carnal heart; the system which, at the same time, pays most respect to the spiritual principles, and best subserves the spiritual ends, of Christ's kingdom, is surely that which has the strongest claims on our regard. This is a test that few churches can well stand.—The episcopal church of England, weighed in this balance, will be found wanting. In her present half-reformed state, she retains many of those worldly appendages and outward ceremonies by which the church of Rome is characterised; and a thorough purgation of these, together with a more spiritual system of preaching and administering the sacraments, and a revival of discipline, are required to bring her into even a decent show of conformity to the kingdom which is not of this world.—The Scottish establishment also, though far from being in the same situation with that in England, would do well to subject itself to a searching application of the criterion of which we are now speaking. Although unexceptionable in her doctrinal standards and forms of worship, it may be worthy of being considered, whether there be not things, both in the tone of preaching which extensively prevails, and in the appendages of some of her courts, which will not bear the rigid application of a strictly spiritual test. —Nor let communities which exist in a state of separation from the national church, think that *they* have no need to try themselves in this way. In all of them, even the purest, will be found, we fear, a measure of the spirit of the world, and departure from the simplicity and spirituality of the primitive model, sufficient to warrant humiliation and call for amendment. In choosing an ecclesiastical profession, perhaps no principle of guidance can be more safe than the degree of spirituality of which a church may be possessed. We cannot be too much on our guard against being deceived by worldly glare, or by the worldly advantages which connexion with a particular community may offer. Are there not many who deceive themselves in this respect;—many who, in joining a church, are influenced in their choice, by the worldly respectability it possesses, or by the ease with which, in its communion, they can indulge the love and pursuit of the world; while the reasons by which they are determined against other churches, are their poverty, their simplicity, their strictness, or their spirituality?

To persons as well as churches, the principle in question furnishes a means of trial. It is well fitted to aid in examining into our own personal character. Who are the subjects of Christ's kingdom? Such only as are spiritual. Not the vain, the sensual, the passionate, the worldly; but the humble, the meek, the mortified, the self-denied. Such as adopt, not the maxims of the world, but the principles of the gospel. Not such as permit their hearts to be engrossed with the things of earth, and lavish their attentions on its possessions, its grandeur, pomp, and parade; but such as, looking on the world and all things that are in it as transitory, content themselves with little, and cherish a heavenly spirit. Not such, in fine, as restrict their views to time; but such as, while they live, look steadfastly forward to an eternal state of being, and expect, when they die, that an entrance shall be ministered to them abundantly into the everlasting kingdom of the Lord and Saviour Jesus Christ. Soon shall this world and all that belongs to it be at an end; and it concerns those who have no hope beyond the present, to consider what they shall do when old age arrives, or when death knocks at the door of their chamber, and summons them away. Then, true wisdom will be found with those who have obeyed the command of the Saviour: 'Seek ye first the kingdom of God, and his righteousness, and all these things shall be added unto you.'

CHAPTER VI.

THE UNIVERSALITY OF CHRIST'S MEDIATORIAL RULE.

The topic on which we are now to descant is of great importance, yet it is one on which much misconception exists. There are some who deny the fact altogether; and there are others, who, though compelled to admit the fact, have most inadequate ideas of the place which it is entitled to hold in estimating the offices of the Mediator. There is one short clause, in the writings of the Apostle Paul, which both these classes would do well to consider. It is that in which, speaking of Christ's exaltation by the Father, he uses the expression, 'AND GAVE HIM TO BE HEAD OVER ALL THINGS TO THE CHURCH' (Eph. i. 22)—language which asserts at once the unlimited extent of the mediatorial power, and the high and glorious end for which such power has been conferred.

1. The connexion of Christ's universal power with the honour awarded him by the Father for the work of man's redemption, is sufficient to attest its IMPORTANCE. That which entered into the stipulations of the eternal covenant, and which occupied the mind of the Saviour throughout the whole period of his sufferings, his last mysterious agony not even excepted, cannot be deemed a matter of inferior moment. Now, we are assured, that 'for the joy set before him he endured the cross' (Heb.

xii. 2); and that this joy included that of which we are speaking, the language of the same inspired writer clearly imports, 'He humbled himself and became obedient unto death, even the death of the cross, wherefore God also hath highly exalted him, and given him a name *above every name*, that at the name of Jesus *every knee should bow, of things in heaven, and things in earth, and things under the earth*' (Phil. ii. 8, 10).—Besides, the doctrine of his universal supremacy was one of the last things which Christ taught his disciples. Just before his ascension, in the concluding interview he held with his apostles on earth, in which surely nothing but what is of the highest importance could find a place, he said, 'ALL power is given unto me in heaven and on earth' (Matt. xxviii. 18).—Moreover, the possession of universal power must, on a moment's reflection, appear to be intimately connected with the interests of the church. Power beyond the church, is essential to the existence, increase, and welfare of the church itself. That the members of his mystical body may be complete in him, he must have dominion over all principalities and powers. The overthrow of the church's foes, the fulfilment of the church's prospects, and the final victory of every member over death and the grave, suppose him to rule with uncontrollable sway in the midst of his enemies. 'For he must reign till all enemies be put under his feet' (1 Cor. xv. 25).—These things may be sufficient to convince the unprejudiced mind, of the vast importance of the feature of the Mediator's kingly office of which we are now to treat. But, should there still remain a single sceptical doubt on the reader's mind, it cannot fail to be removed when he is reminded that the fact of Christ's universal reign enters into the praises of heaven, and is echoed from the arches of the celestial temple. 'And I heard,' says John, 'the voice of many angels round about the throne, and the living creatures, and the elders, saying with a loud voice, Worthy is the Lamb that was slain to receive power, and riches, and wisdom, and strength, and honour, and glory, and blessing. Blessing, and honour, and glory, and power, be unto the Lamb for ever and ever. Alleluia, for the Lord God omnipotent reigneth' (Rev. v. 15; xix. 6).

2. No doctrine in Scripture is supported by clearer or more abundant EVIDENCE than the universality of Christ's mediatorial supremacy. Before exhibiting the passages in which it is expressly affirmed, it may be proper to state, that what determines that the passages in question refer to the mediatorial, and not to the essential, kingdom of the Son of God, is the circumstance that the power spoken of in these passages is said to be *given* him. His essential authority can in no sense be said to be *given*. That which is delegated, conferred by gift, bestowed by another, can belong to him only as Mediator. Nor is it necessary that the territory over which the sovereignty is exercised by inherent right, and that over which it is exercised by delegated authority, should be actually different in matter or extent. They may in reality be the same in substance, and of course equal in extent; the difference consisting in this, that the kingdom over which he, as the Son of God, rules by inherent and original right, he,

as Mediator, is authorised to manage and direct for a new end, namely, the salvation of men, and the best interests of the church. His investiture with mediatorial authority, thus means his having had conferred on him a right to employ the power, which he always possessed as God, for the specific objects of his mediatorial work. The essential and the mediatorial kingdoms of Christ may, therefore, be co-extensive; and we need not wonder to find the inspired writers ascribing the gift of universal power to Him whose essential dominion is absolute and unlimited. These things premised, we are prepared to look at the Scripture proof for the universality of the mediatorial dominion.

'All things are delivered unto me of my Father.'[1] These are the words of Christ to his disciples. The connexion shews that it is of his mediatorial power he is speaking, as it is in this character that he is said to know and to be known by the Father, and to reveal the Father to others. The very word 'delivered' carries in it the same idea, as his power as God is not delivered to him, but essentially and intrinsically possessed. Now, the affirmation respects universal power—'all things,' παντα — no exception being so much as hinted at.

'And Jesus came and spake unto them, saying, All power is given unto me in heaven and in earth.'[2] This is, if possible, still more decided. Here, as in the former instance, both the context, which relates to the apostolical commission, and the language itself, 'given,' shew that the mediatorial character is meant. And, as

[1] Matt. xi. 27.   [2] Matt. xxviii. 18.

to the extent of what he attributes to himself in this character, the words are, 'All power in heaven and in earth'—πασα εξουσια εν ουρανω και επι γης—expressive of universality in the largest sense.

To the same purpose are the words of Peter in his discourse at Cesarea. Speaking of Jesus Christ in connexion with the peace which is preached through him, and of course as Mediator, he says, in an emphatic parenthesis—'He is Lord of all,' παντων Κυριος.[3] The term 'Lord' denotes authoritative power, and the 'all' may be either persons, or things, or both.

'And hath put ALL things (παντα) under his feet, and gave him to be head over ALL things (παντα) to the church.'[4] The terms 'put' and 'gave' mark, with sufficient precision, the character in which Christ is here spoken of by the apostle, while the extent of grant is abundantly explicit.

Not less decisive is the language of the same inspired writer in another epistle :—'And ye are complete in him which is the head of ALL principality and power,' η κεφαλη πασης αρχης και εξουσιας.[5]

'For he hath *put* ALL things under his feet. But when he saith all things are put under him; it is manifest that he is excepted which did put all things under him.'[6] This is the only instance in which an exception is stated to the universality of the mediatorial dominion; and the exception strengthens greatly our position. The only exception stated is the Father, who confers on him the mediatorial dominion; and the specifying of this shews that there is not another, proves

[3] Acts x. 36. [4] Eph. i. 22. [5] Col. ii. 10. [6] 1 Cor. xv. 27.

that the mediatorial dominion embraces everything in the universe but God.

One more direct Scripture proof may suffice. And it is of such a character, that, had there not been another in the Bible, it were itself sufficient. Its phraseology seems purposely framed, to place it beyond the power of any one to find a plausible pretext for setting the slightest limit to the official dominion of the Son of God. 'But one, in a certain place, testified saying, What is man that thou art mindful of him? or the Son of man, that thou visitest him? Thou madest him a little lower than the angels; thou crownedst him with glory and honour, and didst set him over the works of thy hands: thou hast put ALL things in subjection under his feet. For in that he put all in subjection under him, HE LEFT NOTHING THAT IS NOT PUT UNDER HIM.'[7] The reference is to the eighth Psalm. The purpose for which the words of the Psalm are quoted by the apostle, shews that it is the Messiah who is spoken of. The universality of dominion ascribed, cannot be affirmed of man in the ordinary sense of the term; other worlds and angels not being made subject to *him*. Besides, a part of the Psalm is applied elsewhere to the Redeemer.[8]

Here, then, we have ample proof in support of our position, to which every believer in the Scriptures must pay respect. We can conceive of nothing more decisive or complete. Nothing but the blinding influence of prejudice, interest, or error, can account for such plain testimony being resisted. Whatever some may find it

[7] Heb. ii. 6-8. [8] Matt. xxi. 15, 16.

convenient to maintain, it is clear that neither Christ nor his apostles entertained the most distant thought of the mediatorial power being limited, but that they rejoiced in the truth that ' his kingdom ruleth over all.'

3. It might be added, that every thing which renders the mediatorial dominion necessary to all, requires it to be of universal extent. It could easily be shewn that, to the fulfilment of the purposes of the divine will respecting the elect—to the completion of Christ's character as a Saviour — to his being fitly rewarded for his obedience unto the death—as well to his successful overthrow of his enemies, nothing less than universal power could suffice. But these things are so palpable, that to dwell upon them at length would be only to weaken their force. It will serve a better purpose to CLASSIFY and particularise some of the 'all things' that are put under Christ's feet.

Inanimate and *irrational* creation is placed under the Mediator. 'Thou madest him to have dominion over the works of thy hands: thou hast put all things under his feet; all sheep and oxen, yea, and the beasts of the field, the fowl of the air, and the fish of the sea, and whatsoever passeth through the paths of the sea.'[9] This passage is, as we have seen, quoted in the epistle to the Hebrews, with express application to Jesus Christ.[10] The objects specified are the inferior parts of creation, but of these there is no exception. The language comprehends matter in every form, organised and unorganised: the planetary bodies in

[9] Ps. viii. 6–8. [10] Heb. ii. 6–9.

general, the earth with its water and dry land in particular, the mineral kingdom, and the vegetable world, are all included in 'the works of God's hands:' while inferior animals of every tribe are expressly enumerated,—' the beasts of the field, the fowl of the air, and the fish of the sea.' Nor was it unnecessary that the mediatorial grant should embrace such particulars as these. Far from it. The material world owes its preservation to this circumstance. It is the Mediator who 'upholds all things by the word of his power.' But for the dispensation of divine mercy of which this earth is the theatre, we have no reason to believe that it would have survived the fall. This is the grand conservative element by which it is enabled to withstand the destructive tendency of the dreadful penalty denounced on man's disobedience. When the guilty pair put forth their hands, plucked the forbidden fruit, and ate,—

> 'Earth felt the wound ; and Nature from her seat,
> Sighing through all her works, gave signs of woe
> That all was lost.
> Earth trembled from her entrails, as again
> In pangs ; and Nature gave a second groan ;
> Sky lowered, and muttering thunder, some sad drops
> Wept at completing of the mortal sin
> Original.'[11]

But, while clouds obscure the horizon, and thunders roll in tremendous peals alongst the sky, while the earth quakes to its very centre, and everything portends immediate and inevitable destruction; when the earth, and the inhabitants thereof, are about to be dissolved, the divine Mediator steps forth, grasps

[11] Paradise Lost, book ix.

it with his almighty hand, and 'bears up the pillars of it.'[12] Without this interposition, the interests of the church at large could not have been subserved, either in the way of protection or of propagation; nor could her members individually have been fed, clothed, and preserved, or their bodies have been raised up at the last day.

With regard to the *inferior animals*, the right of dominion over them, given to man at his creation, was forfeited by sin. They are no longer his willing subjects; the service he receives from them he has to extort by constraint. They flock not now around him, as in innocence, but flee from his presence. They dread him as their enemy, instead of loving and revering him as their lord. Many of them, assuming superiority in their turn, cast upon him a glance of hostile defiance, and compel him to betake to flight, that he may escape falling a victim to their merciless ferocity. And to what but to the mediatorial interposition is it owing, that man retains any control over the lower animals, and that the members of the church have secured to them, among other privileges, 'a covenant with the beasts of the field, and with the fowls of heaven, and with the creeping things of the ground?'[13] No other satisfactory account can be given of this, than that which is supplied by the fact of God's having put under the feet of his Son 'all sheep and oxen, yea, and the beasts of the field, and the fowls of the air, and the fish of the sea.'

Scripture history amply and beautifully illustrates

[12] Ps. lxxv. 3.   [13] Hos. ii. 18.

this department of mediatorial rule. It is no dream that the sun, moon, and stars, do obeisance to our New Testament Joseph. At what but his command was it, that the sun stood still for a time on the dial of Ahaz? To what but to his power can it be ascribed that the strange order was exactly obeyed—Sun, stand thou still upon Gideon, and thou moon, in the valley of Ajalon?' Or to what but to this was it due that 'the stars in their courses fought against Sisera?' The winds and the waves, too, acknowledge his power. He it was who made the waters of the Red Sea to stand up on a heap till his people passed through, and then to collapse for the destruction of their enemies. At his command it was, that Jordan was dried up, to make a way for the ransomed of the Lord to enter into their promised inheritance. His power over the element of fire, appears in his preserving unhurt the three children whom the incensed monarch of Babylon caused to be thrown into the burning fiery furnace, heated seven times more than it was wont to be heated. And his power over the opposite element, appears in his casting down upon the Canaanitish kings, at Beth-horon, great stones from heaven, so that there were more who died with hailstones than they whom the children of Israel slew with the sword. The *beasts of the field*, whether domestic or untamed, obeyed his command. When he wanted a colt, on which, in fulfilment of prophecy, to ride into Jerusalem, he had only to send his disciples to a particular spot, where they found one standing ready for his use, which they appropriated unchallenged, because 'the Lord had need of him.' When his servant

Daniel was thrown into the den of lions, he sent his angel to shut their mouths, and when he was taken up out of the den, no manner of hurt was found upon him. The *fowls* of the air are no less subject to his control. When the inhabitants of the ark were becoming anxious for the abating of the waters, he it was who commissioned the dove with an olive leaf in its mouth to intimate that they had begun to be assuaged. When the prophet by the brook Cherith was hungry, and had no means of obtaining food, ravens, under the same infallible and resistless guidance, brought him bread and flesh in the morning, and bread and flesh in the evening; their own natural appetites being restrained to prevent their consuming these supplies themselves. Nor are we without examples of his power over the *fish* of the sea. He ordered his disciples to let down the net on the right side of the ship, and immediately there was inclosed a great draught of fishes. When he was in want of money to meet the demand of temple tribute, he instructed one of his attendants to go to the sea and cast a hook, and the fish which first came up had in its mouth the coin required. That even reptiles and insects felt his authority, appears from some of the plagues sent on the Egyptians, from the fiery serpents by which the rebellious Israelites were so severely chastised, and from the viper fixing on the hand of an apostle without doing him harm. How true is it that the mediatorial dominion extends over the inanimate and irrational parts of creation; and how fully do the facts of the church's history illustrate this extent of power!

2. If from the lower parts of creation we ascend to

the highest, we shall still find traces of the mediatorial dominion. Christ exercises rule over *angels*. These constitute the highest order of intelligent and moral creatures with which we are acquainted. Of their character, rank, attributes, and employments, we know but little. But this we know that, in all their orders and degrees, they are without exception put in subjection to the Messiah. It is only necessary here to view them in their two grand divisions, of good and bad, or fallen and unfallen.

(1.) Christ's mediatorial dominion extends to holy angels—those who, when their fellow-spirits rebelled, kept their first estate. Paul, in writing to the Ephesians, represents him as seated ' far above all principality, and power, and might, and dominion,' [14] terms which are understood to denote the different orders of angelic creatures. Peter also speaks of him as He ' who is gone into heaven, and is on the right hand of God; ANGELS, and authorities, and powers, being made subject unto him.' [15] As God he has an undoubted essential right of dominion over such: but that something different from this is meant in these passages is plain from the context, and also from the phraseology employed, especially in the latter case. Angels could be *made subject* to Christ, only in his mediatorial capacity. The account given in Scripture of the services of these bright and happy beings, both to the Head of the church, and to the members of his mystical body, throws the clearest light on the general statements to which we have just referred. Holy angels surround the throne of the

---

[14] Eph. i. 21. [15] 1 Pet. iii. 22.

mediatorial King :—'In the year that king Uzziah died,' sings the son of Amos, 'I saw the Lord sitting upon a throne, high and lifted up, and his train filled the temple. Above it stood the seraphims.'[16] They offer him the tribute of their lofty adoration at the command, 'Let all the angels of God worship him,' for they cry with a loud voice, 'Worthy is the Lamb that was slain to receive power, and riches, and wisdom, and strength, and honour, and glory, and blessing.'[17] They attended him at Sinai, when the law was 'ordained by *angels* in the hand of a Mediator.'[18] When, in the fulness of time, he

> 'Forsook the courts of everlasting day,
> And chose with us a darksome house of mortal clay,'

an 'angel choir' descended on the plains of Bethlehem, and sung the hymn of his nativity :—'And suddenly a multitude of the heavenly host, praising God and saying, Glory to God in the highest, and on earth peace, goodwill toward men.'[19] Angels ministered to him in his state of humiliation: when the devil left him in the wilderness, 'Behold angels came and ministered unto him' (Matt. iv. 11). And, during his mysterious agony in the garden, 'there appeared an angel unto him from heaven, strengthening him' (Luke xxii. 43). On the first day of the week when he rose from the dead, 'Behold, there was a great earthquake, for the angel of the Lord descended from heaven, and came and rolled back the stone from the door of the sepulchre' (Matt. xxviii. 2) ; and, taking his station there, was the first

[16] Isa. vi. 1, 2.
[17] Heb. i. 6 ; Rev. v. 1, 12.
[18] Gal. iii. 19.
[19] Luke ii. 13, 14.

to announce the tidings of his resurrection to the disciples who visited his tomb. Angels accompanied him at his ascension to the Father's right hand:—'The chariots of God are twenty thousand, even thousands of angels' (Ps. lxviii. 17). And when, at the last day, he shall come again to judgment, 'The Lord Jesus shall be revealed from heaven with his mighty angels, in flaming fire, taking vengeance on them that know not God, and that obey not the gospel of our Lord Jesus Christ' (2 Thess. i. 7, 8).

Holy angels are commissioned by the Mediator to perform a variety of important services to the members of the church. 'Are they not all ministering spirits sent forth to minister for them who shall be heirs of salvation?'[20] The 'heirs of salvation' are, of course, those on whom God has chosen to bestow deliverance from all evil, and the possession of all good, as a rich, manifold, extensive, and imperishable inheritance, freely bequeathed to them as children. To such the holy angels minister in holy things, in a variety of ways. Setting aside the learned fancies of certain ancient philosophers, regarding the peculiar occupations of these celestial beings; discarding, as without foundation in the word of God, the Socratic notion of one guardian spirit being assigned to each saint; the following ideas respecting the ministry of angels, may be gathered from the Scriptures of truth.

Holy angels, under the Mediator, exercise a certain inspection over the people of God. 'Suffer not,' says Solomon, 'thy mouth to cause thy flesh to sin; neither

[20] Heb. i. 14.

say thou *before the angel,* that it was an error: wherefore should God be angry at thy voice, and destroy the work of thy hands?'[21] If the angel in this passage means, as is supposed by some, one of the celestial hierarchy, such are plainly to be considered as taking cognizance of the sayings and doings of men. The most plausible interpretation of an obscure passage in the writings of Paul, proceeds on the same supposition:—'For this cause ought the woman to have power on her head because of the angels,'[22]—angelic inspection being here urged as an inducement to female decorum in the matter of dress, especially in the public congregation. The same consideration gives point and emphasis to a clause in Paul's solemn appeal to Timothy: —'I charge thee, before God and the Lord Jesus Christ, and *the elect angels,* that thou observe these things without preferring one before another, doing nothing by partiality.'[23] It would thus seem to be one of the functions of angelic ministry, to exercise an inspection over the worship, and sufferings, and obedience of the saints, that they may be ready to yield them assistance when required, be prepared to carry tidings respecting them to the company of interested fellow-spirits on high, and be qualified to bear witness in their behalf at the last day.

Holy angels, under the Mediator, are employed in making suggestions to the people of God. The following passage may perhaps warrant the idea that they performed an important part in communicating to the sacred writers the matter of the Scriptures:—'The

[21] Eccl. v. 6.   [22] 1 Cor. xi. 10.   [23] 1 Tim. v. 21.

revelation of Jesus Christ, which God gave unto him, to shew unto his servants things which must shortly come to pass, and he sent and signified it by his angel to his servant John.'[24] But, however this may be, now that suggestion of this extraordinary kind is at an end, it is interesting to think that they may still be employed in directing the mind to duty and to comfort, and in calling up thoughts of a spiritual and improving character. The thing is at least possible. It is rendered even probable, by what we know of the power of bad spirits, in suggesting evil thoughts, imaginations, and desires. But the experiences of the people of God, respecting the sudden occurrence of ideas and states of feeling, whose origin cannot possibly be referred to the mind itself on any known laws of mental operation, would seem to give it a character of certainty. This cannot be understood as interfering with the work of the Divine Spirit, whose prerogative it is to guide into all truth; it only supposes him to work by means, the means in such case being created spirits, while the sole efficient agency is reserved exclusively to himself. It may be difficult, or impossible, to discriminate between the suggestions of the mind itself and those of angelic ministers; but the difficulty is not greater, here, than in the case of the workings of evil spirits; and, in neither case, does the difficulty in question militate in the least against the fact.

Protection is afforded to the saints by holy angels. 'There shall no evil befall thee, neither shall any

[24] Rev. i. 1.

plague come nigh thy dwelling. For he shall give his angels charge over thee, to keep thee in all thy ways. They shall bear thee up in their hands, lest thou dash thy foot against a stone.'[25] Agreeably to this general statement, we find them employed in delivering Lot and his family from the destruction of Sodom:—'And when the morning arose, then the angels hastened Lot, saying, Arise, take thy wife and thy two daughters which are here, lest thou be consumed in the iniquity of the city.'[26] Daniel's safety from the lions is another instance:—'My God,' says the prophet, 'hath *sent his angel*, and hath shut the lions' mouths that they have not hurt me.'[27] If we may judge from what occurred in the case of the Saviour himself, at the time of his being tempted by Satan, when angels came and ministered unto him, we may conclude that the protection they afford extends to spiritual as well as outward dangers. Nor is it irrelevant, here, to observe the services they discharge, in the way of counteracting the plots of the church's enemies, and inflicting upon them the judgments of the Lord, inasmuch as these are connected with the safety of his people. Thus, with respect to Sennacherib's army, it is said:—'And it came to pass that night, that the angel of the Lord went out, and smote in the camp of the Assyrians an hundred fourscore and five thousand: and when they arose early in the morning they were all dead corpses.'[28]

Holy angels, under the Messiah, exercise a salutary

---

[25] Ps. xci. 10-12.   [26] Gen. xix. 15.   [27] Dan. vi. 22.
[28] 2 Kings xix. 35. See also Zech. i. 8-11; Dan. x. 13; xi. 1.

vigilance over the people of God. They are employed in frequent embassies of mercy to them while they live. When they die, they carry their disembodied spirits to the regions of bliss :—' The beggar died, and was carried by angels to Abraham's bosom.' And have we not reason to think that even their bodies will be taken in charge by the same powerful servants at the period of the resurrection? ' He shall send his angels with a great sound of a trumpet; and they shall gather together his elect from the four winds, from one end of heaven to the other.'[29]

Such are some of the services performed by the angelic tribes to the members of the church of Christ. The wide space betwixt heaven and earth is not, as we are apt to imagine, an unoccupied void, but crowded with a busy throng of active beings employed in ministering to them who are to be heirs of salvation. And who is the master of these servants? By whom are they 'sent forth'? From whom do they derive their commission? From Him whose mediatorial kingdom ruleth over all; who has removed the moral barrier which sin interposed to obstruct the intercourse of men and angels; who hath 'gathered together in one all things, both which are in heaven and which are in earth,' and thus opened the way for our being introduced to 'an innumerable company of angels.' Had he not assumed the character and discharged the functions of Mediator, none of the benefits conveyed through the medium of angels, could ever have been enjoyed by the people of God; nor could men ever have undergone that trans-

[29] Luke xvi. 22; Matt. xxiv. 31.

formation and elevation of moral character which are necessary to fit them for intercourse with such pure and dignified creatures.

Important purposes are served by the subjection of angels to the Messiah. Foundation is thus laid for the restoration of a useful, happy, honourable, and lasting friendship betwixt men and these celestial spirits. The whole honour and glory of man's salvation are thus secured to Christ, no service being performed to the saints, or benefit received by them, but emanates, be the instruments who they may, from the sacred fountain of his authority and love. Had the angels not been put under his feet, the services they perform, supposing them to have taken place, must have been independent of him, and consequently believers should have had a class of precious benefits for which they were under no obligation to Christ, and the glory of which they could never have ascribed to him. In this way, also, provision is made for a high example of obedient subjection to Messiah being set before saints; as well as for the overthrow of evil spirits by beings of their own order, which cannot fail to contribute to the completeness of their defeat by increasing their torment and mortification.

(2.) And this leads us to remark, that fallen angels, as well as those who kept their first estate, are placed under the Messiah. He possesses power over infernal spirits, not only as God, but as Mediator. The very object of his mediatorial character requires this; for, as the elect of God are, by nature, exposed to the assaults of Satan and of his emissaries, it is important that He, who is to act as their Saviour, should be invested with power to rescue them from their spiritual adversaries. That he may bind the 'strong man,' and spoil him of his goods, by delivering those whom he has led captive at his will, he must have a right to enter his house and place him in fetters. The god of this world, the prince of the power of the air, worketh in the children of disobedience; and He who is to restore them to the love and practice of holiness, must have power to cast out the prince of this world. Even after the children of God are rescued from the yoke of Satan's dominion, they are still liable to be assailed and subjected to partial and temporary bondage. Either on the one hand to protect his people from such assaults, or on the other to render them subservient to good, it is necessary that the devil and his angels be placed under the control of the Mediator. It is here not a little interesting to observe, that the very first announcement given of the Saviour exhibits him as the conqueror of the prince of the bottomless pit —*the seed of the woman bruising the* SERPENT's *head.* Such was the object contemplated in his advent. 'For this purpose the Son of God was manifested, that he might destroy the works of the devil.'[30] When the saints are exhorted to 'be sober, be vigilant, because their adversary the devil, as a roaring lion, walketh about, seeking whom he may devour,'[31] to whom but to their divine Mediator can they look for wisdom and strength, to resist his attacks and continue steadfast in the faith? When the devil is permitted to cast them into prison that they may be tried, He only can enable

[30] 1 John iii. 8. [31] 1 Pet. v. 8.

them to 'be faithful unto death, that they may receive a crown of life.'[32]

Nor is it for the individual members of his mystical body alone, that this extent of mediatorial power is necessary, but also for his church in her collective character. As for those systems of iniquity, religious and civil, with which she has to contend, we are assured that 'the dragon gave them their power and their authority;' and, of course, without some such control as we are supposing, things could never be so ordered as to bring about the issue which is predicted. 'And the great dragon was cast out, that old serpent, called the Devil, and Satan, which deceiveth the whole world: he was cast out into the earth, and his angels were cast out with him. And I heard a loud voice saying in heaven, Now is come salvation, and strength, and the kingdom of our God, and the power of his Christ: for the accuser of our brethren is cast down, which accused them before God day and night.'[33] Nay, these infernal agents, it would seem, are employed by the Mediator as instruments of inflicting merited punishment on the enemies of the church; but this they could not be, unless under his dominion. 'Woe to the inhabitants of the earth and of the sea! for the devil is come down unto you, having great wrath, because he knoweth that he hath but a short time. And I saw three unclean spirits like frogs come out of the mouth of the dragon, and out of the mouth of the beast, and out of the mouth of the false prophet: for they are the spirits of devils, working miracles, which go forth unto the kings of the

[32] Rev. ii. 10.   [33] Rev. xii. 9, 10.

earth and of the whole world, to gather them to the battle of that great day of God Almighty.'[34] Thus the church's salvation, safety, peace, and prosperity, require that her Head be possessed of a rightful dominion over fallen spirits of every order.

This branch of his official rule is not less fully illustrated in the history of the Redeemer's life, and death, and mediatorial government, than is his dominion over holy angels. His miracles filled the infernal spirits with dread, and extorted from them a deprecation of the exercise of his power: 'Art thou come to torment us before the time?'[35] By his personal conflict with Satan in the wilderness, the arch-fiend of hell was subjected to the mortification of a threefold defeat. Such was the influence exerted by his ministers, that 'even the devils were subject to them through his name;' and, as they proceeded in their work of mercy and benevolence, 'Satan was beheld falling as lightning from heaven.'[36] But his death, his vicarious and meritorious death, was what shook the foundations of Satan's kingdom, and gave the fatal blow to the reign of the God of this world: 'Having spoiled principalities and powers, he made a show of them openly, triumphing over them in his cross.'[37] Let me illustrate this a little, as it involves a point of some nicety which is not always well understood.

The power possessed by the devil and his angels over the human race, may be regarded in two lights—either as an unrighteous usurpation, or as a judicial calamity.

---

[34] Rev. xii. 12; xvi. 13, 14.
[35] Matt. viii. 28.
[36] Luke x. 17, 18.
[37] Col. ii. 15.

As regards Satan himself, the former is the view we are to take of it: as regards the overruling providence of God, the latter is the light in which it is to be contemplated. Satan is a usurper; he possesses no lawful authority; as far as he himself is concerned, he can point to no authority from God for the exercise of his wicked and malicious control over man. Yet, notwithstanding this, it is obvious that, without the permission of God, he could have no such control, for a single moment, as that which he actually exercises. He could have no power unless, in this sense, it were given him from above.[38] Nor can we suppose, that a righteous God would even permit him to have such power, unless for the punishment of those who have violated his law, and exposed themselves to his judicial displeasure. Satan, in himself, has, indeed, no regal right to inflict torment on men; he has no direct moral authority from the Supreme Governor, to execute the threatening of his holy law against transgressors; he holds no such place as even that of *authorised executioner* of the divine vengeance: yet his wrath and malice are, as in the case of wicked men, made to praise God, by being overruled for the punishment of the guilty violators of his law. In this view it is the guilt of men which gives Satan power. His dominion, usurped though it be on his part, springs from human transgression. But for this, the righteous Lord who doeth righteousness, would never have tolerated, for an instant, the unrighteous usurpation of the prince of this world. This being understood, it must be obvious that the overthrow of Satan's power,

[38] John xix. 11.

required, first of all, that legal satisfaction should be given to the claims of the divine law for the sins of men. When this is done, his throne is undermined—his sceptre broken—his arm of might paralysed; and any efforts he can ever afterwards make, are but the feeble attempts of a vanquished foe to recover his lost influence, or the spiteful manifestations of unsubdued but impotent malice. Now this is just what was effected by the death of Christ; and we have here an illustrious display of the inseparable connexion subsisting betwixt his regal and sacerdotal offices. It was on his *cross* that he triumphed over the principalities and powers of darkness. It was on his Cross that he bruised the serpent's head. All legal ground for permitting Satan to continue to exercise his lawless usurpation being at an end, the triumphant Saviour could forthwith exert his power in destroying his influence over the chosen of God. From this point, then, does the victorious Mediator go forth, on his glorious undertaking of destroying the works of the devil. The death of the Cross effected, he is prepared to enter the territories of the prince of darkness; to overthrow his dominion in the hearts of men, and in the institutions of society; to rescue his own children from the fangs of the destroyer; to bind and loose Satan at his pleasure; and to order everything so as best to bring about the period, when 'the devil shall be cast into the lake of fire and brimstone,'[39] and when 'he who has the keys of hell and of death, who openeth and no man shutteth, and shutteth and no man openeth,' shall so hold him in eternal

---

[39] Rev. xx. 10.

durance, that he shall not torment his people any more.

3. A middle place, betwixt inanimate creation and angelic intelligences, is occupied by *men*; and they also are under the government of the mediatorial King. 'The Father has given him power over ALL FLESH'[40] —a phrase which in this, as in other parts of Scripture,[41] signifies the whole of mankind, the human race at large. That he possesses authority over the righteous, the elect, those whom the Father has given to him, cannot be doubted. But that his power, as Mediator, should extend to the non-elect, the ungodly, the world lying in wickedness, may not seem so obvious. A little reflection, however, is all that is required to produce conviction on this point also. Those who are given to him, are mingled up for a time with the rest of the human family; they are themselves, at first, ungodly and unrighteous; and, that they may be changed, as well as gathered out from a sinful and apostate race, he, whose work it is to accomplish these objects, must have power over the wicked as such. Nay, the ungodly may often be rendered instrumental in contributing to the interests of the church and people of God. The earth helps the woman, as Egypt supplied the children of Israel with support during the years of famine, and as Cyrus assisted the Jews in their return to their own land and the rebuilding of their temple. The very enmity of the wicked may be overruled for the good of the righteous. Now, it is Christ who, in virtue of his mediatorial power, thus establishes the

[40] John xvii. 2.   [41] Luke iii. 6, &c.

wicked for correction, and makes the wrath of men to praise him. Even to restrain and keep back what would not be for the good of his chosen, the Redeemer must be possessed of such power. And, in addition to these, his power must be thus extensive, for the purpose of inflicting on the ungodly the punishment due to their sins. As the Father hath committed all judgment to the Son, it is his to 'make his enemies his footstool,' and to put into the hand of them that afflict his people 'the cup of trembling, even the dregs of the cup of his fury.' [42] On all these accounts, there can be no greater mistake than to limit the Mediator's power to the members of the church, or to exclude any class of men whatever from his authority.

Enemies as well as friends are put under his feet :— 'Rule thou in the midst of thine enemies' [43] Heathens as well as Christians are subject to his authority :—'The heathen are given to him for his inheritance;' 'He is head of the heathen.' [44] Persons, in their civil not less than in their ecclesiastical capacity, are required to acknowledge his power :—'Be wise, O ye kings; be instructed, ye judges of the earth. Serve the Lord with fear, and rejoice with trembling. Kiss the Son lest he be angry, and ye perish from the way.' [45] The dead, not less than the living, are under his control :—'For to this end Christ both died, and rose, and revived, that he might be Lord both of the dead and living.' [46] The wretched inhabitants of the pit, as much as those who are in heaven, feel his sway :—'He has the keys of hell and of death;

---

[42] Isa. li. 22, 23. [43] Ps. cx. 2. [44] Ps. ii. 8; xviii. 43.
[45] Ps. ii. 10–12. [46] Rom. xiv. 9.

he openeth and no man shutteth, and shutteth and no man openeth.'[47] Among the human family, not one is exempted from the government of Messiah; none so high as to be beyond his reach, none so low as to be beneath his notice. He has power over all flesh.

4. Nor is it over men as individuals merely that Christ possesses power. His authority extends to *associations* of every description, domestic, civil, and ecclesiastical. The social principle is deeply lodged in the constitution of man, and makes its appearance in a thousand varied forms. Individuals, by forming themselves into societies, may make themselves powerful for good or evil, for purposes of aggression or defence. Societies, like persons, are under the government of God, and subject to the divine law. Bodies-politic or corporations are to be regarded as large moral subjects. To suppose that men, as individuals, are under the moral government of the Almighty, and bound to regulate their conduct by his law, but that, as societies, they are exempted from all such control, is to maintain what involves the most absurd and pernicious consequences. According to this, those who wish to free themselves from the restraints of moral obligation, have only to enter into alliance with one another,—they have only to band themselves together, to have their proud wish of independence fully gratified. This conclusion is too glaringly impious, not to shock every reflective mind. But if associations are under the moral government of God, and God has committed all government to the Son, it follows that associations are as much under the mediatorial sovereignty as

[47] Rev. i. 18; iii. 7.

individuals. Indeed it would not be difficult to shew, that no species of society can exist whose proceedings do not bear more or less directly on the interests of the Redeemer, so that, without having such under his control, he could not fully accomplish the ends for which he is invested with the mediatorial character. While this is true of all associations, there are two, the church and the state, over which the mediatorial authority in a very particular manner extends. These are so important, both in themselves and in their relation to the subject now under discussion, that we must give to each a separate consideration afterwards.

5. But before leaving the present department, it is proper to remark that all the *dispensations of providence,* as well as the various departments of creation, are under the dominion of the Mediator. This is proved, not only by the universal language employed by the inspired writers when speaking of Christ's rule in general, but by the express terms of Scripture with reference to this particular subject, and also by the necessity of the thing itself. The vision of the wheels, in the first chapter of Ezekiel's prophecy, is generally understood to refer to the dispensations of divine providence in their nature, aspects, intricacy, and perfect consistency and wisdom. These dispensations were represented to the prophet as under the direction of one who sat upon a throne, and whose likeness was as 'the appearance of A MAN above upon it.'[48] We are not left to doubt that 'the man Christ Jesus' is here meant, for it is afterwards said, 'This was the appearance of the likeness of the glory of THE LORD.'

[48] Ezek. i. 26.

We have here, then, an explicit proof from Scripture that the affairs of providence are managed by the Mediator: managed, too, with perfect wisdom, as indicated by the rings of the wheels being 'full of eyes round about;' and with special reference to the covenant of grace, as indicated by the appearance of the brightness being 'as the day of rain.' Indeed, the necessity of the thing requires that the Mediator's power be of such extent as to embrace all the affairs of providence. How, else, could he remove those obstacles which prevent the success of his gospel, and make way for the advancement of his spiritual kingdom? How, but for this, in a world in which 'there are many adversaries,' could 'a great door and effectual be opened up' to his servants in furthering his cause? How, without this, would it be possible to render the train of events in operation at any time, subservient to the interests of the church? How could things merely secular, such as learning, and wealth, and the common relations of life, be ever ultimately Christianised, and have inscribed on them the motto *Holiness to the Lord?* Or how could the whole scheme of providential concerns be brought to that glorious consummation at the final judgment, to which it is his prerogative to bring it, seeing 'the Father judgeth no man, but hath committed all judgment to the Son'? It is *his*, in short, to open the seven-sealed book—to blow the seven trumpets—and to pour out the seven vials, in which all the events of divine providence toward the church and her enemies are comprehended. The measures of providence are best studied in the light of Calvary; and there is no surer key to the interpretation of the apocalyptic symbols than the Cross.

Such is the varied proof, to which we invite attention, on the subject of the universal extent of the mediatorial rule. It embraces every thing animate and inanimate, rational and irrational, moral and immoral, individual and social;—every thing, in short, in heaven, on earth, and under the earth. All things are put under his feet. He only is excepted who did put all things under him. To such an extent of mediatorial power, however, several OBJECTIONS have been started.

1. One of these objections, founded on the spirituality of Christ's kingdom, has already been obviated. But, it may be said that such an extent of dominion as we have supposed to belong to the Son as Mediator, tends to *exclude the Father and the Holy Spirit from the government of all things.* By no means. However mysterious in itself and difficult to be explained, the fact is not to be denied that the work of one person of the Godhead, in any department of operation, does not preclude that of the others; creation, providence, and grace being alike ascribed in Scripture to each. The inspired writers represent the Father and the Son, accordingly, as occupying the same throne:—'Even as I am set down with my Father in his throne,'—'the throne of God and of the Lamb shall be in it.'[49] Nor can it fail to strike an intelligent person that the very same mode of reasoning might be directed against the Saviour's dominion over the church. If the circumstance

[49] Rev. iii. 21; xxii. 3.

of the government of *the world* at large being vested in the Son goes to exclude the Father and the Spirit from the dominion of all things, it will follow that the circumstance of the dominion of the *church* being vested in the Son, must, on the same principle, go to exclude the Father and the Spirit from all control over the church. And, if the management of the church may be delegated to the Son without interfering with the essential right of dominion belonging to the other persons of the Trinity, why not also the management of all things besides? If a part may be delegated without annulling the right of the other persons to dominion over that part, why may not the whole, without annulling their right of dominion over the whole?

2. It has also been supposed to *confound the essential and the mediatorial rule of Christ.* In confirmation of, and in addition to, what was formerly observed on this point, it may here be remarked that there may be a formal distinction where there is a material identity. The same thing may be viewed in different aspects. Things, the same in themselves, may be viewed as under the dominion of Christ both essentially as God and officially as Mediator. In the latter case, they are invested with a new power, and directed to a new end. He is not only 'head over all things,' but 'head over all things *to the church* which is his body.' In the order of God's creatures, the lower are subordinate to the higher, and the highest include all that are under them. Things natural are subordinate to things moral, and things moral to things gracious; but the interests of those things which are gracious necessarily suppose the

subordination both of those that are natural and of those that are moral. Thus the two latter classes, which are under the Son essentially considered, must, for the sake of the former class, which is under him officially, be placed under him officially too. The result of the whole, then, is that the essential and the mediatorial dominions of Christ, so far from being subversive the one of the other, are absolutely commensurate and perfectly harmonious; yet not so blended as to destroy the distinctive character of either.

3. It has been thought an objection to our doctrine that, if Christ be possessed of such an extent of official power, it must *lay foundation for the ascription of divine honours to him as Mediator.* He who rules over all is certainly entitled to the homage of all. But, so far from believing that divine honours should not be paid to Christ as Mediator, we are at a loss to see to what evil it can possibly give rise, or how, indeed, it can be avoided. His divine and his mediatorial characters are, it is true, distinct. That is to say, we can suppose the former without the latter. But it is carefully to be observed that we cannot suppose the latter without the former. His divinity is essential to his mediatorship. He could not have been Mediator unless he had been God. He is a Divine Mediator. Apart from his divinity, his mediatorial character is not only without validity, but without being,—a mere figment of imagination. Where, then, lies the danger of ascribing divine honours to the Mediator? Was it not as Mediator that the disciples, in the days of his flesh, fell down and worshipped him? Is it

not as the Lamb slain, that every creature in heaven is represented as ascribing to him blessing, and honour, and glory, and power? And might not the payment of divine honours to the Father, viewed as *Creator* or *Preserver*, be as reasonably objected to, as the ascription of divine glory to the Son as *Mediator?* The former characters are not more essential to the being of God than the latter; or rather they are all alike non-essential. God might have existed without assuming the character of Creator or Preserver, as well as the Son without taking to himself that of Mediator. This last is not more the result of an act of divine will than the others; and if these, as is admitted, do not preclude but call for divine homage, why should not this?

4. It is equally inconclusive to maintain, that such an extent of mediatorial dominion must suppose *the wicked to be somehow interested in the work of Christ, and partakers of the benefits of his death.* We appeal, in reply, to what is matter of fact; we have already shown, that there are many things under the power of Christ besides those which are the immediate objects of his purchase. Angels, devils, reprobate men, and things irrational and inanimate, are all put under the feet of the Mediator: yet not one of these can be said to have been redeemed by his blood. There are some benefits enjoyed by the wicked of the world, which, as they result from the mediatorial economy, may be said to be, indirectly at least, the fruits of Christ's death. Such is the case with the divine forbearance, with temporal favours,

and with the outward dispensation of gospel ordinances, of which the wicked partake, but which, but for the scheme of salvation, they could never have enjoyed. It is, however, not more difficult to account for such things, than to understand how a general reprieve, and temporary support, may be conferred by an earthly prince on a whole body of traitors, for the sake of some whom it is his design to rescue from the danger that impends them all. 'And the Lord said, If I find in Sodom fifty righteous within the city, then I will spare all the place for their sakes.' 'Thus saith the Lord, As the new wine is found in the cluster, and one saith, Destroy it not, for a blessing is in it: so will I do for my servants' sakes, that I may not destroy them all.' [50] Nor is it irrelevant, here, to advert to the distinction betwixt things viewed simply in themselves, and viewed as blessed by God. The things themselves may be enjoyed when the blessing of heaven is withheld. In the case of temporal benefits, it is, properly speaking, the blessing that springs directly from the mediation of Christ; the things themselves spring from it only indirectly. Things which flow from the natural goodness of God, it will be allowed, were forfeited by sin; and, if so, they can be restored only through the Mediator. It is commanded, 'Take no thought for your life, what ye shall eat, or what ye shall drink; nor yet for your body what ye shall put on. Is not the life more than meat, and the body than raiment? But seek ye first the kingdom of God and his righteousness,

[50] Gen. xviii. 23; Isa. lxv. 8.

and all these things shall be added unto you.' We are instructed to pray, 'Give us this day our daily bread.' It is said of the believer, 'Bread shall be given him, his water shall be sure.' We are also assured that 'Godliness is profitable unto all things, having promise of the life that now is and of that which is to come.'[51] Now, it may be asked, to which covenant, the covenant of works or that of grace, do these promises and assurances respecting temporal mercies belong? Not surely to the covenant of works, for, through this medium, no good can come to fallen man; the curse is all that he can receive from this source. But if they belong to the covenant of grace, they must have some connexion with the death of Christ, by which this covenant is ratified. The things, viewed in themselves, flow, we admit, from the natural goodness of God, and so may be participated in by more than the saints; yet, viewed as blessed by God, that is, as real blessings, they are to be regarded as flowing from the blood of Christ, by which they are secured, redeemed, and sanctified, for the use of his own people. Nor can it be any more a valid objection to Christ's headship over all things, that the wicked are thus supposed to enjoy temporal benefits, than it is to his headship over the church, that the wicked as well as others enjoy access to the ordinances of the gospel and the means of grace.

5. After all, it may be thought that the doctrine of Christ's universal mediatorial supremacy is at variance with fact. 'We see not yet all things put under him.'

[51] Matt. vi. 25, 33; vi. 11; Isa. xxxiii. 16; 1 Tim. iv. 8.

Devils and wicked men do not acknowledge his authority, or respond to his claims. But his *right* and *title* are unaffected by this circumstance. In the kingdom of a rightful sovereign, there may be rebels. If this objection were of weight against Christ's dominion over all things, it would bear with equal force against his power over the church, inasmuch as, unquestionably, many of those who are included in this department, are yet unsubdued and in arms against his authority. Nay, it would go to exclude the Almighty himself from the rule of the universe; for many there are who refuse to acknowledge or respect his moral government. The reign of the Mediator, however, is not yet ended; in the exercise of the undoubted right he possesses, he is carrying forward the purposes for which it has been conferred. We have only to wait with patience, till he has put down all rule, and all authority and power, and then shall it appear that the Father hath put all things in subjection under his feet, having left nothing which is not put under him.

How delightful the principle thus established and vindicated! It reflects the glory of Christ, on whose head are many crowns. He appears, wearing, not only the crown of dominion over the church, but that of dominion over the kingdoms of nature, providence, and grace—over things physical and moral, rational and irrational, animate and inanimate. Things in heaven, in earth, and under the earth, are thus seen to be put under his feet. His kingdom ruleth over all. Ye saints of the Most High! ascribe to him the glory that is due.

Be not afraid or ashamed to affirm his universal sovereignty. Who would wish to rob him of any one of his crowns, or to see him excluded from any part of his dominions? If some have seemed to do so theoretically, let us hope that it has arisen more from mistaken conception or party prejudice than from real opposition to his honour. This is not a mere speculative matter; it affects the perfection of the Redeemer's character. So much so, that, without such extent of power as is supposed, he could not be our Redeemer at all. To the salvation of men, he must be invested with power, not only over such as *are* saved, but over such as are *to be* saved; he must possess a right to bring them under the influence of means, as well as to render the means efficacious;—a right to subordinate every thing in nature and providence to the accomplishment of this high and glorious undertaking. To limit or restrict the mediatorial rule is thus clearly subversive of the Saviour's glory.

This view of things is fraught with comfort to saints. To such it cannot but afford strong consolation, to know that their Mediator has power over angels, and can employ these celestial beings in watching over them, communicating to them ideas, affording them protection, and transporting them, when they die, to the land of bliss. When assailed by satanic temptations, it must be matter of joyful reflection to the people of God, to know that Christ has dominion over infernal spirits, and can limit and restrain, and overrule for good, all their operations; that they can have no power over these except as it is given them by him; that the power they possess is entirely under his control; and that he possesses the right and the ability, as he stands pledged, to destroy in the end all the works of the devil. As the disciple of Christ looks abroad upon the field of nature, how pleasing the reflection, that it is his Saviour who upholds all things by the word of his power, causing the sun to shine, the stars to twinkle, the rain to fall, the earth to vegetate, and food to spring from it for man and beast! Every thing in nature is thus invested with a new beauty, and reflects a brighter splendour to the eye of the Christian, from being placed under the management of his Lord and Saviour. As the wheels of providence revolve, however high their bearing and intricate their movements, he can behold them with perfect calmness and security, knowing, as he does, that they are all under the infallible guidance of the God-man Mediator, who occupies the throne which is above the firmament. In short, in whatever situation he may be placed, or whatever view of things he may be led to take, nothing can afford to the believer greater consolation and joy, than the reflection that all are under the power of him who is the Saviour of his soul.

Not less calculated is the subject we are considering, to appal the hearts of the enemies of Christ. In virtue of his universal dominion, he can break them with a rod of iron, and dash them in pieces like a potter's vessel. His Father has said to him, 'Rule thou in the midst of thine enemies.' To such as are in a state of rebellion against him, it may well be said, 'Kiss the Son lest he be angry, and ye perish from the way, when his wrath is kindled but a little.' He has at his command infinite resources of torture, dismay, and ruin. You who are his enemies! think how he can send out your fellow-rebels against you; can scourge you with providential calamities; or let loose legions of infernal spirits to torment and devour you. Think how he swept away the Antediluvians with the flood; how he drowned the Egyptians in the waters of the Red Sea; how he overthrew in succession the heathen monarchies; and how he poured destruction on the guilty inhabitants of Judea. As Lord of all, he can make all things the instruments of his vengeance. He must reign till all his enemies be made his footstool. How much better, by timely submission, to be elevated to his throne, than, by obstinate hostility, to be trodden for ever under his feet! You have before you the alternative. Choose ye that which is good. He extends to sinners the golden sceptre of his grace. Let them tremble at the thought of being exposed eternally to 'the wrath of the Lamb' for refusing to touch it.

CHAPTER VII.

THE KINGLY OFFICE OF CHRIST IN RELATION TO THE CHURCH.

We have seen that the mediatorial rule is strictly universal. It comprehends under it all things, without exception. We remarked * that among the 'all things' are included associations of every kind, civil and ecclesiastical. It was also observed, that there are two associations, which, both from their importance in themselves, and their particular relation to the subject in hand, deserve a separate and more full consideration. The first of these is THE CHURCH, without doubt the most important society in existence, and that in subserviency to whose interests it is that the Mediator has been invested with power over every other thing. He is head over *all things to the church* which is his body.

The fact of Christ's mediatorial rule over the church is plainly testified in the Scriptures. He is 'king upon the holy hill of Sion,—king of Sion—he reigns over the house of Jacob for ever—the husband is the head of the wife, even as Christ is the head of the church—he is the head of the body the church—Moses was faithful in all his house as a servant, but Christ as a son over his own house, whose house are we, if we hold fast the confidence

* See page 97.

and the rejoicing of the hope firm unto the end.' They 'who sing the song of Moses the servant of God, and the song of the Lamb,' address him, besides other titles, by that of 'King of Saints.'[1]

The term *church* is a familiar one. It is in the mouths of all. It is of importance that we attach to it some definite idea. The Hebrew word קָהָל, and the Greek word εκκλησια, which are used by the inspired writers to denote the church, signify an assembly convened by invitation or appointment, being derived from verbs the generic idea of which is *to call*. The nature of the assembly, whether civil or religious, must be determined by the context. In the New Testament the word translated church, when used in a religious sense, is applied:—to the whole body of the elect, as when Christ is said to 'love the church;'—to a small association of private Christians, as when we read of the church in the houses of certain individuals;—to a regularly organised congregation, as when 'the church of Ephesus,' 'the church of Smyrna,' or such like is spoken of;—and to the whole visible catholic society, consisting of all, who, in every age and in every place, make a credible profession of true religion, together with their children, as when 'the church in the wilderness' is spoken of, or when the Lord is said to 'add daily to the church such as shall be saved.' The first and the last of these views are of most importance. In allusion to these it is that the church is commonly spoken of as visible and invisible—the latter epithet

---

[1] Ps. ii. 6; Zech. ix. 9; Luke i. 33; Eph. v. 23; Col. i. 18; Heb. iii. 6; Rev. xv. 3.

referring to the first of the senses above enumerated, the former to the last. 'The catholic or universal church, which is invisible, consists of the whole number of the elect, that have been, are, or shall be, gathered into one, under Christ the Head thereof; and is the spouse, the body, the fulness of Him that filleth all in all.—The visible church, which is also catholic or universal under the gospel (not confined to one nation as before under the law), consists of all those throughout the world that profess the true religion, together with their children; and is the kingdom of the Lord Jesus Christ, the house and family of God, out of which there is no ordinary possibility of salvation.'[2] Both of these views are comprehended, of course, in the one church of which Christ is the Head, and over which he exercises mediatorial rule. But it is the visible church with which we are at present chiefly concerned, and of which we are to be understood as principally speaking in the sequel. This comprehends many, we might almost say all, of the real saints of God who are upon earth, inasmuch as true grace in the heart prompts men to make an open profession of the name of Christ before the world. It does not, of course, include all the saints who are in existence, as many of these are in glory, of the mediatorial rule over whom we shall have occasion afterwards to speak; and it may also include some who are not true members of Christ's mystical body. It is, nevertheless, a most interesting view of the church of Christ, the existence, and structure, and privileges of which are necessarily and most intimately connected

[2] Westminster Confession, chap. xxv. sect. 1 and 2.

with the best interests of the strictly spiritual kingdom of the Messiah. In what follows in this chapter, therefore, we would be understood as having a principal regard to *the visible church catholic, consisting of all, who, in every age and in every place, make a credible profession of true religion, together with their children;* while we would not be understood as overlooking that invisible church, for the promotion of whose interests alone it is that this was ever brought into being or organized.

That the term *church* occurs in this sense in Scripture has been denied by some, whose peculiar views of ecclesiastical government require them to understand it, either in the sense of the whole chosen of God, or in that of a particular congregation assembling for worship in one place. But the word occurs in passages in which it can be understood in neither of these senses. Speaking of Moses, Stephen says in his address:—'This is he that was with the church in the wilderness.'[3] The church here means the Jewish church. It cannot be supposed that all who were comprehended in that church were elect persons, much less that it comprehended all the elect. Nor did the members of that church meet all in one congregation; there were many congregations of Israelites scattered throughout the land of Judea. Again, Peter says:—'The Lord added to the church daily such as should be saved.'[4] The church here cannot mean the whole body of the elect, for to such there is no addition, it is complete from eternity: neither can it mean a single congregation, as the increase of the church was not confined to one town or district. When it is

[3] Acts vii. 38. [4] Acts ii. 47.

said, 'Saul made havoc of the church, entering into every house,'[5] the elect cannot possibly be meant, as the most lynx-eyed persecutor cannot distinguish such from hypocrites; and it is surely not reasonable to suppose that the zeal of such an enemy as Saul of Tarsus would be confined to one congregation. Paul says:—'Gaius mine host, and of the whole church.'[6] Gaius' hospitality could not be exercised only to the elect, as he did not know who were such; nor is it at all probable that a person of such distinguished liberality would confine his attentions to a single congregation. Besides, it is written:—'God hath set some in the church; first, apostles; secondarily, prophets, &c.'[7] It is not over the church of the elect, but over the visible church, that God has appointed visible office-bearers: nor are these functionaries restricted to one congregation. These are a few of the passages in which the term 'church' cannot be understood in either of the senses supposed, and in which it is not easy to see what other sense can be attached to it than that of which we are speaking, namely, the visible church catholic. This, indeed, is the meaning it bears in the common language of Christians. When they speak, for example, of 'the church,'—of the faith of the church, the worship of the church, the sufferings of the church, the progress of the church, or the triumphs of the church,—such is the import of the term.

I. Now, this church, the visible church catholic, owes its existence to Christ's mediatorial authority.

[5] Acts viii. 3. [6] Rom. xvi. 23. [7] 1 Cor. xii. 28.

Without the work of Christ, agreed upon in the eternal counsels, the church could never have had a being. Its entire structure, privileges, and ends, rest on what he did. But for his engagement from eternity, it is impossible to see how such a society as the church of God could ever have existed. Nor is this all. The church owes its existence to the creative authority of the Redeemer. It is not a self-existent, self-constituted association merely, formed by voluntary agreement or mutual compact among its members, with reference even to the work of the Son of God. It is expressly founded by the voluntary and authoritative appointment of the Redeemer himself.

The existence of the visible church may be traced as far back as to Eden, when the primitive ordinances of social worship were instituted, and the blessings of grace began, through them, to be dispensed to our fallen progenitors.

It is true, there are several distinct periods of the church's existence, which have been marked by something peculiar to themselves. In a popular, but improper sense, we speak of the Patriarchal, the Levitical, and the Christian churches. These, however, correctly speaking, are but different states of the same church. The church, the spouse of Christ, is one and the same in every age. God has had but one church in the world, and that church has existed since the revelation of the Seed of the woman at the fall of man. There have been, as above hinted, different periods, when, after suffering declension, it has undergone, so to speak, a sort of re-organization : and, on these occasions, as well as at its formation in the beginning, we find the interposition of the Mediator. When, at first, Adam and Eve united in the act of offering sacrifice, connected with prayer and praise, the visible church catholic was formed, and we cannot doubt that it owed its being to 'the voice of the Lord God,' who was heard in the garden at the cool of the day, calling the attention of the guilty pair to their destitute and sinful state, and to the way by which fallen men were to be rescued from the curse and condemnation of a broken law. The covenant made with Abraham, long afterwards, marks another interesting period. It was without doubt an ecclesiastical covenant, in which the visible church in general was interested. This appears from the fact, that, while some of the patriarch's natural posterity were shut out from its blessings, express provision was made for the admission of others who were not his seed; and from the promise of his being made 'the father of many nations,' which could not have been fulfilled if the covenant had had respect only to the one nation of the Jews. It is not unreasonable, therefore, to suppose that he who proclaimed this covenant to the patriarch, was no other than the Angel of Jehovah, the uncreated Messenger of the covenant; for that covenant, we know, 'was confirmed of God in Christ.'[8] With regard to the solemn and awful transactions at Sinai, when the whole Levitical economy was fixed and arranged, we are assured that the law was 'ordained by angels in the hands of a Mediator.'[9] At the introduction of the New Testament dispensation—that dispensation which is to continue to

---

[8] Gal. iii. 17, εἰς Χριστον, in respect of Christ.   [9] Gal. iii. 19.

the end of time—we are assured that the Lord Jesus Christ himself administered ordinances, authorized and sent forth ministers, countenanced with his presence the social meetings of the church, and, on the day of Pentecost, shed abundantly on his assembled disciples the influences of his Spirit. Whatever, then, may be the period at which the origin of the church is fixed, it will be found that it owed its existence to Christ.

What, it may here be inquired, are the marks by which the visible church catholic, of which we are speaking, may be known? Not every one who makes a profession can claim to belong to this church. What then are the characteristics of the true church—the *notæ veræ ecclesiæ*? They are not those to which the Romish church pretends,—antiquity, universality, continued succession, the power of working miracles, and the like. It would be easy to shew that all these are false, even as respects that very community, and that they are altogether spurious and unfounded as respects any denomination whatever. Antiquity, universality, &c., may be properties of the true church, but they are not *exclusive* properties. The characteristics of the visible church catholic are what belong to it, and to it *alone*. These are—soundness of doctrinal sentiment, a lawful and regular ministry, and the due administration of gospel ordinances. Whatever ecclesiastical society can lay claim to these, has a right to be regarded as a section of the visible church catholic; whatever cannot, has no right to be so regarded.

The church is the pillar and ground of the truth. The exhibition and maintenance of divine truth being one end of its existence, the adoption of gross error, whether with regard to the character of God, the person and offices of the Redeemer, the nature of Messiah's kingdom, the method of salvation, the character of Christian duty, or the doctrine of a future state, must prove fatal to the ecclesiastical standing of any professing body. Gross heretics, of any description, have no right to be regarded as members of the visible church. 'Continuing steadfastly in the apostles' doctrine,' is indispensable to such relationship. Whoever aspires to this honour, must 'have been taught as the truth is in Jesus;' nor must they make any such pretension 'who walk not uprightly according to the truth of the gospel.'

A small association of private Christians may be called, in some sense, a church; but to constitute the visible church, the existence of office-bearers would seem to be requisite. A legitimate ministry, therefore, is another mark of the true church. In order to this, the persons bearing office must be properly qualified, regularly called, and duly initiated. If, in any ordinary case, the individuals who officiate are such as have assumed the office of themselves, or have received only a call from the people without scriptural ordination, or are grossly deficient in ministerial qualifications, this circumstance would seem sufficient to impair the right to being regarded as a part of the visible church. The apostles 'ordained them elders in every church.' And if 'Christ glorified not himself to be made an high priest, but he that said unto him, Thou art my Son, to-day have I begotten thee,' no man surely ought to 'take this honour unto himself, but he that is called of God, as was Aaron.'

'How shall they preach except they be sent?' 'I sent them not, nor commanded them, therefore they shall not profit this people at all, saith the Lord.'[10] If the supply of ecclesiastical offices were left to spontaneous assumption, it must be obvious to every one that they would soon either die away altogether from apathy, or become so debased, by the corruption and inability of those who held them, as to be no longer capable of serving the end of their institution.

To the existence of the visible church there must be, farther, the due administration of gospel ordinances. Preaching, prayer, praise; baptism and the Lord's supper; discipline and government, must be regularly dispensed, that is, must be dispensed by persons properly authorized, and with a view to the purposes for which they were appointed. When the ordinances are either altogether wanting, as is the case in regard to some of them in certain professing bodies—or greatly corrupted, as is the case in others—or prostituted to other than their legitimate ends, as has been done by using them to qualify for civil offices, rather than to promote the salvation of the soul; the evidence that such as do so belong to the visible church catholic, is thus far impaired, if not altogether subverted.

II. Christ's mediatorial rule over the church appears from his organizing it, incorporating it by covenant, and purchasing it with his blood.

[10] Acts xiv. 23; Heb. v. 4, 5; Rom. x. 15; Jer. xxiii. 32.

The church possesses a character of visible organization. It is spoken of in Scripture as 'a body,' the members of which exhibit admirable symmetry, nice adaptation, and wise subserviency one to another;— as a 'house,' all the parts of which are 'fitly framed together;'— as a 'city,' whose streets are distributed with regularity, and whose municipal regulations are calculated to secure the peace and order of the inhabitants;— as a 'kingdom,' and as a 'nation,' figures which suggest ideas of good government, orderly management, and proper subordination. Indeed, the nature of things and the necessity of the case require that the church be considered as a thoroughly organized society. Every society supposes, in its very structure, some kind of organization; and it is anything but honourable to the Head of the church, to suppose that he has left its members to exist as a confused mass of detached individuals, living separately, without any bond of connexion or plan of co-operation. Very different, indeed, is the fact, as the character of the Mediator should have led us to infer, even had we not been told, as we are, that 'from him the whole body fitly joined together, and compacted by that which every joint supplieth, according to the effectual working in the measure of every part, maketh increase of the body, unto the edifying of itself in love.'[11]

The church, thus organized, is incorporated by covenant. It is a covenant-society. Christ has made with his church an everlasting covenant. It is not merely

[11] Eph. iv. 16.

founded on the covenant of grace, but he has made with it an express ecclesiastical covenant. This federal deed was renewed, if not originally made, with the church, in the person of Abraham, the father of the faithful. The transaction is recorded (Gen. xvii. 1-14). This was neither a personal nor a domestic covenant. It had, properly speaking, in view, neither the personal salvation nor the domestic prosperity of the patriarch. The promise, 'I will be a God unto thee and to thy seed after thee,' had respect to an ecclesiastical relation. Nor were they his lineal descendants that were meant by his 'seed;' for, on the one hand, there were several branches of his natural posterity who had neither part nor lot in the covenant, while, on the other hand, there was provision made for admission to its privileges on the part of strangers 'who were not of his seed' (ver. 12). Indeed, the circumstance that it constituted Abraham 'the father of *many* nations,' is decisive on this point, as his natural posterity formed only *one* nation, namely, the nation of the Jews. The same thing furnishes indubitable evidence, that the covenant in question had a respect to the visible church catholic in every age of its existence. Had not the church, whose interests are secured by this covenant, been something else than what is called the Jewish church, the part of the promise of which we are now speaking could never have been fulfilled; because, not till after the introduction of the New Testament dispensation, and the extension of gospel privileges to Gentile nations, could Abraham have become the father of more than the nation of the Jews. Besides, the Scriptures furnish us with sufficient evidence to prove that the Abrahamic covenant was never abrogated, and consequently that it was made with that church which is to continue to the end of time. It was not annulled at the introduction of the Levitical dispensation, as the apostle strongly affirms, when arguing for the continuance of its promises: 'And this I say, that the covenant that was confirmed before of God in Christ, *the law*, which was four hundred and thirty years after, *cannot disannul*, that it should make the promise of none effect.'[12] For the same reason, it could not be annulled at the introduction of the Christian economy, when the ceremonial ritual was abrogated. The apostle expressly argues the calling of the Gentiles, after this period, from the existence and terms of the covenant with Abraham. 'That the blessing of Abraham might come on the Gentiles through Jesus Christ,' he maintains, that 'to Abraham and his seed were the promises made: not to seeds, as of many, but as of one (and to thy seed) which is Christ;' whence he draws the legitimate and consoling inference, 'Ye are all one in Christ Jesus, and if ye be Christ's, then are ye Abraham's seed, and heirs according to the promise.'[13] Indeed, to maintain, either that the Abrahamic covenant was not an ecclesiastical one, or that it was ever annulled, were tantamount to asserting that the church is now an uncovenanted society, in opposition to what both the character of its Founder and the tenor of prophecy regarding it would lead us to expect, and is an idea too gloomy ever to be entertained by any true lover of Zion.

[12] Gal. iii. 17.   [13] Gal. iii. 14, 16, 28, 29.

Christ, as Mediator, secured his right of dominion over the church, by purchasing her with his blood. 'Feed,' said Paul to the Ephesian presbyters, 'feed the church of God which he hath purchased with his own blood.' The elect, the members of the invisible church, are all, we know, redeemed from sin and misery by the precious blood of Christ: but can the same be said of the visible catholic church, of which we are now speaking? With proper explanation, we think it may. We are aware that the saying of the apostle above cited, is commonly understood of the church of the elect—the invisible church. We are, however, inclined to take a different view. The church of God, of which Paul speaks, is that over which visible office-bearers are placed, and the members of which are the proper objects of those external functions which it pertains to such office-bearers to discharge. If it were the elect only whom ecclesiastical overseers were enjoined to feed, a knowledge of who are elect and who not, would require to be imparted to the ministers of religion; nay, persons of the most profligate character would thus have a claim to the highest privileges of the church, as it cannot be denied that many such are included among those who are chosen of God to eternal life. It is only a visible church that can be the object of visible institutions. The duties required of the Ephesian elders were visible duties: the church, therefore, which is the object of them, must be a visible church. But, whether the church of God which Paul speaks of as purchased with his blood, be the visible church or not, we say that the same affirmation may be made with regard to this church. The Mediator purchased the visible church catholic with his blood.

This he may be said to have done, inasmuch as the elect of God, who are in the visible church, were actually redeemed from sin by the blood of Christ. The visible church comprehends within its pale many of God's chosen ones; innumerable real saints belong to the covenant society on earth. Now, all such have redemption through the blood of Christ, and the forgiveness of sins according to the riches of his grace. He has obtained eternal redemption for them. They are redeemed with the precious blood of Christ, as of a lamb without blemish and without spot. As embracing so many who are thus redeemed, may not the visible church be said to be purchased with Christ's blood?

Besides, all who are members of the visible church profess to be real saints, and ought to be such. None else have a strict and proper right to the privileges of Christ's house. Others, it is true, find admission to the visible covenant society. But, in imposing upon the office-bearers by a false and hypocritical profession, they are in no slight degree culpable, while, in making use of sacred things to which they have no right, they bring on themselves the additional guilt of sacrilege. Still, that all the members of the church ought to be true saints, is a position that will not be disputed. Now, it is not uncommon to affirm of individuals and societies, that they are what they ought to be, and what they profess to be. On this principle the members of the primitive churches are addressed, in the inscriptions of the apostolical epistles, as *saints, called, elect, chosen of God*, &c.; when it cannot but be supposed that in many, if not all of these churches, there were some who were only nominal Christians. The apostles knew, however, that real saints they ought all to have been, and they all professed to be; and, so long as there was nothing visible in their conduct to prove the contrary, they felt called upon to speak of them as really such. On the same principle, may not the visible church, though comprehending in it some who are not actually redeemed from guilt and corruption, be said to be purchased with Christ's blood? May we not be warranted in speaking of it as being what, at all events, it ought to be, and what, but for the hypocrisy which the rulers of the church have not the power of detecting, it actually would be.

But, farther, the privileges of the visible church catholic are purchased and secured to its members by the blood of Christ. The church has many privileges peculiar to herself as a covenant society; such as the word and sacraments, fellowship, discipline, and government. They are all appointed, in infinite wisdom, for the gathering in and perfecting of God's chosen ones. They are dispensed on the footing of the covenant of grace, and could only be procured by the blood of Emmanuel. They come not to her by the law of nature; for, even supposing that the members of the church are under that law, these gospel privileges have no sort of connexion with it. They come not by the covenant of works; for men are incapable of meriting any thing by that covenant, and, supposing they were, nothing is now dispensed on this footing but the righteous judgments of the Almighty. The inference is thus plain and irresistible, that the privileges of the church come to its members on the footing of the covenant of grace, which is ratified and sealed by the blood of Christ. On this account may the visible church itself be said to be purchased with the Redeemer's blood.

III. On the church, thus redeemed with his own blood, the divine Mediator has conferred a variety of most interesting and distinguishing properties.

It is a *spiritual* society; consisting of persons professedly separated from the world lying in wickedness, and called to the fellowship of God's own Son. Its head is spiritual: its ordinances and institutions bear a spiritual character: and the purposes for which it exists are altogether of this nature. It may be supposed that spirituality is a property, not so much of the visible as of the invisible church. This, however, is quite a mistake. Not that every one belonging to it possesses an essentially spiritual character; far from it: but every member professes that such is his character; and the character of any society, as distinguished from others, must be taken from its object and bearing, and from what those who compose it profess themselves to be. As distinguished, then, from *civil* society, the visible church is spiritual, men having no claim on the enjoyment of its privileges in virtue of their rights and relations as members of the civil community. The power possessed by its office-bearers is exclusively spiritual power; the object of their jurisdiction is the consciences of men, and not their persons or their property, which belong to the jurisdiction of the magistrate. It is, in this respect, a kingdom which is not of this world.

The church of Christ is strictly *independent*; meaning by this term to designate a feature of its character, and not the form of its government. It is independent alike of human wisdom, human power, and human control. The Lord Jesus Christ alone is its judge, lawgiver, and king. 'One is your master, even Christ; and all ye are brethren. Call no man your father upon the earth; for one is your Father, which is in heaven.'[14] No earthly power—be it king, pope, or prelate—has a right to domineer over the church. It is composed of Christ's freemen, and is itself free from all outward control. The state may extend to it protection, and countenance, and pecuniary support, and friendly co-operation; but has no right to dictate its creed, to institute its laws, to appoint its ministers, or to interfere in any one way with either its constitution or its administration. Whether the civil power may and ought to form a friendly alliance with the church, is one thing; whether such an alliance is necessary to the church's existence, is altogether another thing. The former does not, by any means, imply the latter. It may be the duty of the state to give the church all the advantages of a civil establishment, without such an establishment being essential to the church's existence.

[14] Matt. xxiii. 8, 9.

The church *has* existed without the countenance and support of the civil power. These are by no means necessary to its being. To maintain that they are, is pure and undisguised Erastianism;—a principle degrading to the honour of the church, and subversive of the very ends of its existence. Whatever may be said as to the duty of civil rulers, care must be taken to preserve sacred and untouched the blood-bought freedom and independence of Christ's covenant society. The highest and warmest patronage of the state is procured at too dear a price, if, in order to secure it, the church has to barter away the least portion of her liberties. Every attempt, then, to interfere with its independence, on the part of the civil power, must be regarded as an unhallowed invasion of the rights of the people, and a monstrous usurpation of the inalienable rights and prerogatives of the church's glorious Head. From such interferences have sprung some of the grossest corruptions and severest sufferings of the church; and they cannot be too jealously watched against, or too indignantly repelled.

Though independent of man, the church is *under subjection to Christ*. He is the Head of the body, the church. The doctrines which it is the duty of the church to believe and profess, are such as *he* taught. The ordinances to be observed are *his* institutions. The laws to be obeyed are *his* laws. The matter of faith; the form of worship; the line of conduct, are alike sanctioned by his authority. The ministers of religion, neither individually nor collectively, possess any legislative power. Their authority is wholly ministerial, and is subordinate to that of Christ. They are at best but servants, and whatever they do they are required to do in the name of their divine Lord and Master. Do they preach? Like Paul at Damascus, they must 'preach boldly in the name of Jesus.' Do they pray? They must do so, 'calling upon the name of Jesus Christ our Lord.' Do they baptize? Care must be taken that those to whom they administer the ordinance, like the Ephesians of old, be 'baptized in the name of the Lord Jesus.' Do they inculcate duty? They must teach men to 'observe all things whatsoever Christ has commanded.' Do they exercise discipline? They must proceed on the principle laid down by the apostle,—'In the name of our Lord Jesus Christ, when ye are gathered together, and my Spirit, with the power of our Lord Jesus Christ, to deliver such an one to Satan, for the destruction of the flesh, that the spirit may be saved in the day of the Lord Jesus Christ.'[15] To Christ, and to Christ alone, then, is the church in a state of subjection; and for the church to acknowledge any other authority were to act unfaithfully toward her Lord, as for any other to claim authority over her were daringly to invade the prerogatives of Jesus.

The church has received from the Mediator a character of visible *unity*. The spouse, the undefiled of Christ, is but one. The names by which it is designated carry in them the idea of unity. It is called a 'body;' a 'house,' or 'household;' a 'kingdom.' There may be many members in the body, but the body itself is one; there may be different individuals in the household, but

[15] Acts ix. 27; 1 Cor. i. 2; Acts xix. 5; Matt. xxviii. 20; 1 Cor. v. 4.

the household itself is one; there may be many provinces and subjects in the kingdom, but the kingdom itself is one. Hence, says the apostle, 'There is one body and one spirit, even as ye are called in one hope of your calling. One Lord, one faith, one baptism. We, being many, are one bread and one body.'[16]

The religion which is intrusted to the church being designed for mankind at large, in proportion as this religion is diffused there arises a necessity that those who embrace it should meet in separate congregations, and form particular associations. While they were so few that they could conveniently meet in one place, they did so. But this was not long; and the individual congregations or separate meetings which sprung out of the necessity of the case, were no violation of the church's unity. It is important that all those individual churches which possess the marks formerly enumerated —doctrinal orthodoxy, a regular ministry, and the due administration of the ordinances of God's worship—be regarded as so many integral parts of a great whole; as so many members of one body; as so many individuals constituting one grand society; and, so far as they have opportunities of meeting together, holding free and delightful fellowship with one another. Instead of indulging towards each other the jealousies of rivals, and each claiming for itself the exclusive name and privileges of *the church*, it becomes them to keep the unity of the Spirit in the bond of peace. Nor is it to be deemed enough, to effect this purpose, that there be a unity of interest in Christ the Head; and of love, and sympathy,

[16] Eph. iv. 4, 5; 1 Cor. x. 17.

and duty, among the members. The unity which depends on such grounds as these is invisible. The visible church must have a visible unity. This visible unity springs from its having one Head; from its making profession of a common faith; from its participating in the same ordinances of ecclesiastical fellowship; from its having one mode of conveying authority to its office-bearers; and from the nature of the government instituted for the preservation of its purity and peace. Let us illustrate these points a little.

The church must be one, as it has but one Head. 'Christ is *the head of the church*.' 'He is *the head of the body*, the church.' 'There is *one Lord*.' We nowhere read of *the heads of the churches*. It follows, either that each individual church has no head, or that the churches possess a character of visible unity under one common Head.

There is, besides, a common faith, by the profession of which the unity of the visible church is exhibited and preserved. There is 'one faith.' A profession of faith being a visible thing, is thus fitted to form a bond of visible unity. The doctrinal creed of all who belong to the visible church is substantially the same. A public acknowledgment of belief in the truths which compose the Christian system, not only constitutes the individual by whom it is made a member of the particular congregation with which he connects himself, but unites him with all throughout the world who hold the same sentiments. If he has been before a Pagan, or a Mahometan, or a Jew, the avowal in question, while it severs him distinctly from the community to which he formerly belonged, as surely connects him with that great community which is distinguished by the name of Christian.

The different societies of Christians are united in the participation of the same ordinances of ecclesiastical fellowship. There is 'one baptism' and 'one bread.' By being baptized with water in the name of Christ, a person is not merely admitted into the particular church from which he receives the ordinance, but is proclaimed a member of that great society consisting of all who have had the same common badge of initiation put upon them. And, by joining in the Lord's supper in a particular church, the communicant holds fellowship with all who, in every place, by eating of the same bread and drinking of the same cup, unite in showing forth the Lord's death until he come. 'The cup of blessing which we bless, is it not the communion of the blood of Christ? The bread which we break, is it not the communion of the body of Christ? For we, being many, are one bread and one body; for we are all partakers of that one bread.'[17]

The mode in which office-power in the church is conveyed, namely, by ordination, proceeds on the principle that the church is one. The call to exercise official authority proceeds from the people, but the *power* is uniformly represented in Scripture as proceeding from those by whom that power was formerly possessed. Election and ordination are not to be confounded with one another. Whatever may be the theoretical sentiments of some, all the leading denominations of professing

[17] 1 Cor. x. 16, 17.

Christians recognise this distinction, in practice at least. Without sympathizing at all with such as rigidly stickle for the necessity of apostolical succession to the validity of office in the church, it must be admitted that, in all ordinary cases, the right of ordination lies with those who have been previously ordained. This is the general rule, from which, however, there may be exceptions. If ordination expresses the conveying of official power and authority, it must proceed from office-bearers and not from the people, as the people cannot convey what they do not possess. In this way the *oneness* of the church, in all places and in all ages, is marked and kept up. The particular society over whom the person is ordained, thus declares itself one with those societies over whom the persons ordaining preside, and the act of ordination is regarded as so constituting, on the part of the person ordained, a relation to the whole visible church, as to give validity to his official ministrations in any part of the world. 'In the same manner,' says Principal Hill, 'as every one who is baptized, becomes a member of the catholic church, so every one who is ordained by the laying on of the hands of the office-bearers of the church, becomes a minister of the church universal. He is invested with that character in a manner the most agreeable to the example and the directions contained in the New Testament; and by this investiture he receives authority to perform all the acts belonging to the character. He cannot perform these acts to the church universal, because it is nowhere assembled; and the separation of the church universal renders it expedient, that the place in which he is to perform them shall be marked out to him. But this designation of place is merely a matter of order, which is not essential to his character, which does not detract from the powers implied in his character, and which serves no other purpose than to specify the bounds in which the church universal, by the hands of whose ministers he received the power, requires that the power shall be exercised.' 'By ordination,' says the same learned and perspicuous writer, 'they become ministers of the church universal; for having been tried by a particular branch of the church, acting in the name of Jesus, and in virtue of the trust derived from him, they receive authority and a commission to perform all the acts, which belong to those who are called in Scripture ambassadors, stewards, rulers, and overseers. . . . Whenever ordination is considered as the act of Jesus Christ, by his office-bearers constituting a minister of the church universal, the idea of one great society is preserved. The whole may be diversified in outward circumstances, but it does not cease to be a whole; for, from this principle there result subordination to superiors, which is essential to church government, and a bond of union amongst those who are so far removed in place as not to be amenable to the same earthly superior.'[18]

To these considerations, add the argument for its unity arising from the government of the church. If there were no bond of connexion among the individual congregations that exist, the government of each would of necessity be comprised within itself. In cases of controversy, there could be no constitutional means of

[18] Hill's Lectures, iii. 414-416.

settlement; and, in cases of injury or wrong, no legal mode of obtaining redress. To allay contention and restore peace it would often be necessary to resort to division. But the right of appeal, which at present we take for granted to be sanctioned by Scripture, obviates this difficulty and furnishes an evidence of visible unity. The party making the appeal, and the party to whom the appeal is made, mutually recognise each other as members of one body, in whose wisdom they can confide, and to whose decision they are willing to bow.*

* A note on the margin of the author's copy directs attention to the following passages, as shewing that the unity of the church is not violated even by separate organization :—

"As the Spirit wherever he dwells manifests himself as the Spirit of truth, of love, and of holiness, it follows that those in whom he dwells must be one in faith, in love, and holy obedience. Those whom he guides, he guides into the knowledge of the truth, and as he cannot contradict himself, those under his guidance must, in all essential matters, believe the same truths. And as the Spirit of love, he leads all under his influence to love the same objects, the same God and Father of all, the same Lord Jesus Christ; and to love each other as brethren. This inward, spiritual union must express itself outwardly, in the profession of the same faith, in the cheerful recognition of all Christians as Christians ; that is, in the communion of saints, and in mutual subjection. Every individual Christian recognises the right of his fellow-Christians to exercise over him a watch and care, and feels his obligation to submit to them in the Lord."

"It is on all hands conceded, that there may be difference of opinion, within certain limits, without violating unity of faith; and it is also admitted that there may be independent organization, for considerations of convenience, without violating the unity of communion. It therefore follows, that where such diversity of opinion exists, as to render such separate organization convenient, the unity of the church is not violated by such separation. Diversity of opinion is, indeed, an evidence of imperfection, and, therefore, such separations are evil, so far as they are evidence of want of perfect union in faith. But they are a less evil than either hypocrisy or contention; and, therefore, the diversity of sects, which exist in the Christian world, is to be regarded as incident to imperfect knowledge and imperfect sanctification."

The author's reference is to the "British and Foreign Evangelical Review," Vol. I., in which Dr. Hodge's essay appeared. It will now be found in "The Church and its Polity," recently published (Nelson & Sons). The sentences quoted are taken from pp. 42-44 of that volume.

Nearly allied to unity, and necessarily resulting from it, is another property of the church, namely, its *universality* or catholicity. By this we mean something different from what the church of Rome understands by the same term, when it puts forth the presumptuous and uncharitable claim to be regarded as the only visible church upon earth, into which all its inhabitants are bound to seek admission, and without the pale of which there is no salvation. We set up no claim of this kind in behalf of any one body of professing Christians, even the most pure. By the visible church being universal, we mean that it is not confined to any country, but, in the language of the Westminster divines, 'consists of all those *throughout the world* that profess the true religion.' It is not the church of England, nor the church of Scotland, nor the United Secession church,* nor the Reformed Presbyterian church, any more than the church of Rome, which is entitled to lay claim to universality; but that great community, composed of all those who make a credible profession of true religion together with their children, which we have before described as constituting the visible church. Nor is this church called universal with reference to its actual diffusion, for it embraces but a small portion, comparatively, of the population of the globe, and there are even some regions where it is altogether unknown. But it is adapted to universal diffusion: its ministers are authorized, and even required to make known its

---

* The name then borne by what is now the United Presbyterian Church. The Free Church was a name unknown until four years after the publication of this work.

doctrines and offer its privileges to men of every nation, kindred, and tongue: while the predictions of holy writ, and the grant made to Christ of the heathen for his inheritance and the uttermost parts of the earth for his possession, hold out to us, not merely the encouraging hope, but the confident assurance, that his church shall yet exhibit a character of actual universality;—that its light shall yet beam over all lands, and that all that dwell on the face of the wide earth shall unite in the belief of the same truth, the worship of the same God, the enjoyment of the same salvation, and the practice of the same holy obedience.

.The visible church catholic possesses a duration commensurate with time. It is a *perpetual* society. It has existed, without intermission, from the period of its formation to the present hour, and shall continue to exist, without interruption, to the end of time. Different dispensations, indeed, there have been, but, under them all, the same church; nor was there ever an instant when its being was suspended. It existed from Adam to Moses, during the Patriarchal economy; and from Moses to Christ, during the Levitical economy; as from Christ to the end of the world it shall continue, during what is called the Christian economy. Nothing shall ever be able to effect a suspension, much less an annihilation of its existence. Christ has said, referring to himself, 'Upon this rock will I build my church, and the gates of hell shall not prevail against it.' Not that the church may not degenerate. Both the purity of its doctrine, and the spirituality of its worship, may be greatly corrupted, and the number of its faithful adherents may be few. But it shall never become extinct. The Redeemer shall ever have a seed to serve him. 'The purest churches under heaven are subject both to mixture and error; and some have so degenerated as to become no churches of Christ, but synagogues of Satan. Nevertheless there shall be always a church on earth to worship God according to his will.'[19] In the days of Elijah, when he thought himself alone, the Lord had reserved to himself seven thousand who had not bowed the knee to Baal. During the middle ages, when the horrid corruptions of Popery seemed to have obliterated every vestige of true religion, there were found among the valleys of Piedmont, in Bohemia, Switzerland, and even Britain, some who professed the pure gospel of the Son of God, and practised the simple rites of spiritual worship,—a few names who had not defiled themselves with the abominations of the mother of harlots. The existence of a visible church, since the era of the Reformation, cannot be called in question. Christ's covenant society may yet have to encounter evil days; infidelity and heresy may yet attain an alarming degree of strength and prevalence; the witnesses for truth may yet be slain and lie for a while trampled upon in the streets: but the Lord shall never leave himself without a church; the Head shall never be without a body; and the slain witnesses shall be raised again to carry forward, with fresh vigour, the gracious designs of the Redeemer. The highest point to which the impetuous and over-

---

[19] Westminster Confession, chap. xxv. § 5.

flowing current of opposition can possibly rise, is to 'reach even unto the neck.' The floods of error and persecution can never reach the church's Head: and while the head is above water the body is safe.

IV. Christ exercises mediatorial rule over the church for the accomplishment of the most important ends.

Of course the grand ultimate end, contemplated in the existence of the church, is *the glory of God*. This is the end, indeed, of every thing that exists. 'The Lord hath made all things for himself.' Such being the case, it follows, of course, that this must be the object of what holds so prominent and important a place as the church. All the perfections of Deity are in this way glorified; and glory is reflected on each of the persons of the Godhead:—on the Father by whom the members of the church are chosen to eternal life, on the Son by whose blood they are redeemed, and on the Holy Spirit by whose influences they are renewed and sanctified. But it is the sovereign grace of God as a covenant God, that is pre-eminently and peculiarly displayed by the church. Other views of his character are elsewhere exhibited; it is in this connexion alone that he is magnified and made known as a God of grace. The gracious purpose of God is recognised in the church's existence; the gracious authority of God, in the voluntary submission of men to its laws and institutions; and the gracious power, and exuberant goodness, and immaculate purity of God, in the qualifications of its members, in the exercise of its discipline, and in its prayers, praises, and other acts of worship. 'This people have I formed for myself; *they shall shew forth my praise.*' 'Having predestinated us, unto the adoption of children by Jesus Christ *to himself,* according to the good pleasure of his will, *to the praise of the glory of his grace.*' 'But ye are a chosen generation, a royal priesthood, an holy nation, a peculiar people: that ye should *shew forth the praises of him* who hath called you out of darkness into his marvellous light.' [20]

But this great object is secured by the accomplishment of certain proximate ends, prominent among which stand *the exhibition and maintenance of divine truth.* Divine truth—comprehending the true character of God; the true view of man; the true way of salvation; the true method of sanctification; and the true state of future glory—is a sacred deposit committed to the church. The church is intrusted with this awful charge, for the purpose at once of diffusion and preservation. Without the church, the truth could be neither extensively made known, nor safely kept from extinction. It is contained, to be sure, in the Scriptures; but, without some such institution as the church, the Word of God would be sure to be overlooked by the great mass of mankind, and to fall a prey in the end to the wicked devices of those who are enemies to the truth as it is in Jesus. It is the duty and business of the church, both office-bearers and private members, to watch over the existence and interests of gospel truth, to keep it clear from the obscurations of error, to defend it from the assaults of adversaries who seek its destruction, and to

[20] Isa. xliii. 21; Eph. i. 5, 6; 1 Pet. ii. 9.

hold it up bright and attractive to the notice and attention of all. To the Jews of old were 'committed the oracles of God,' and from them the precious custody has descended to the church in later times. All the members and ministers may be accounted as, in some sense, 'stewards of the mysteries of God,' and bound, according as every man hath received the gift, 'to minister the same one to another as good stewards of the manifold grace of God.' It is required of stewards that they be found faithful; and fidelity, in the instance before us, consists, not in an exclusive personal appropriation and use of the invaluable gift, but in a cheerful, liberal, and universal diffusion of divine truth amongst others, in the spirit of the authoritative canon, *Freely ye have received, freely give;* and in protecting it, with true fortitude and at all hazards, from the assaults of those who would tread under foot or annihilate it. It is for this reason that the church is described as *the pillar and ground of the truth*,[21] a noble column on whose sides the lines of sacred truth are so deeply engraven as to defy the obliterating hand of time, and so highly raised that the mutilating hand of man cannot reach them, while from its lofty summit the heaven-lit lamp sheds afar its cheering and life-giving rays. As expressive of the same sentiment, individual churches are compared to 'golden candlesticks,'—suspended on high by the hand of God, to dispense spiritual illumination to a benighted world, and to preserve alive that holy fire from which all the nations of the earth are yet to receive light and warmth. What a glorious and benign end this which

[21] 1 Tim. iii. 15.

the Saviour subserves by means of his church! Nor shall the benevolent purpose be defeated, by any or all of the insidious attempts that are made, by men who love darkness rather than light, because their deeds are evil. They may seek to undermine the sacred pillar; but the event will shew, that it is built upon a rock and is not to be overthrown. They may try, by heaping around it the rubbish of their errors, to hide from view its glorious inscription; but their attempts shall all prove abortive. They may flatter themselves that, by the mists and noxious exhalations of their false systems, the pure and blessed light of truth shall be hid, but all these obscurations shall be finally scattered as by a whirlwind, and the lamp of Gospel illumination shall continue to burn brighter and brighter till every quarter of the world has been gladdened with its beams. The cause of truth is subject, no doubt, to many vicissitudes; and circumstances may occur to make its timid and anxious friends bewail 'that truth is fallen in the streets.' But while the Saviour has a church in the world, it shall never be wholly trodden down; and that 'Lord, whose eyes are upon the truth,' by pouring out 'the Spirit of truth' on the reading and preaching of 'the word of truth,' will see to it that to the end of time 'Jerusalem shall be called *a city of truth.*'

By setting up a church in the world the Mediator has provided for *the public celebration of Divine worship.* It is every way proper that some acts of public homage should be paid to the God of the whole earth. The private adoration of individuals would seem not to be all the honour that is due to Him whose claims are so universal and transcendent. He is certainly entitled to acknowledgment in the most public and open manner possible. This is secured by the existence of a visible church, in which his being, perfections, purposes, and works, are publicly discussed; in which his praises are publicly sung, and in which united and public supplications are offered at his throne of grace. Even supposing that, for this end, secret acts of worship might suffice, it may fairly be questioned whether the spirit of such could be kept up, without the influence arising from public institutions. The devotions of the sanctuary, doubtless, exert, and are designed to exert, no small influence on those of the closet and the family. The lamp of personal or domestic piety will send forth but a dim and sickly ray, unless trimmed and replenished by frequent visits to the house of the Lord. When the believer feels those fervent emotions that are represented by his soul thirsting for God, and under the impulse of which he is stirred up to seek the Lord with great earnestness, it is that he may 'see the power and glory of the Lord as he had seen them before in the sanctuary.' If the psalmist David poured forth the sweetest and warmest strains of devotion in the wilderness of Judea and in the forest of Hareth, we must go back, for the secret of his high and holy inspiration, to the days when he trod the courts of the temple,—days which not merely exerted a reflex influence on his solitary exercises, but which, so far from making him contented with these, caused his soul still to long, yea even faint, for the courts of the Lord, and to count a day in God's house better than a thousand. If we would rise to true elevation of heart in the closet, we must 'lift up our hands in the sanctuary.' So necessary is the church to the proper worship of God.

The church is designed for *the salvation of men.* It is an asylum, to which destitute and needy sinners may betake, to have all their wants supplied; a city of refuge, whither the guilty and justice-pursued may flee for protection; an ark, in which safety is provided from the threatened judgment about to come on a wicked and ungodly world. Here, whatever a lost and fallen sinner of the human family can require, is provided,—pardon, sanctification, peace, happiness, eternal life; and, by betaking to it in time, all these benefits may be infallibly secured. It is the means by which the grand benevolent purpose of the divine will, respecting our lapsed race, is carried into full effect. It is the nursery of saints, not less than the refuge of sinners. By its doctrine and discipline, by the spiritual instruction and vigilant superintendence it provides, the edification of its members in knowledge, holiness, comfort, and social duty, is promoted. The ordinances to which it gives access, and the interest it secures in the prayers of those who have power with God, cannot fail to render the fellowship of the church a distinguished means of extending knowledge, strengthening faith, confirming love, deepening humility, increasing joy, and cherishing every devout and holy affection. The whole work of grace in the soul is thus progressively advanced, and the individual is ultimately trained for the exalted exercises and enjoyments of the heavenly kingdom. The church, in this way, becomes the joyous parent of a numerous spiritual progeny. She is the bride, the Lamb's wife, by whom the free-born sons and daughters of the Almighty are nursed and reared, till such time as they are made fully meet to be partakers of the inheritance of the saints in light. She is 'the joyful mother of children,'—'the Jerusalem from above, which is free, and the mother of us all.' It has pleased God, for the purpose of bringing many sons into glory, to set up a visible church in the world, where these sons should be born again; supplied as new-born babes with the sincere milk of the Word, that they might grow thereby; fed with the strong meat of the covenant; and thus nurtured and disciplined into the vigour of spiritual manhood,—the fulness of the stature of perfect men in Christ Jesus. It is, by being instrumental in the salvation of souls, that the church promotes the glory, and secures the worship, of Jehovah. Divine worship can be celebrated, and the praise of the glory of divine grace can be shewn forth, only by those who are 'saved and called with an holy calling, not according to their works, but according to his own purpose and grace, which was given us in Christ Jesus, before the world began:' and this work of salvation is carried on in and by the church. The church, by subjecting the conscience to the authority of Christ, by maintaining wholesome discipline, and by affording opportunity of communion with God and with his saints, tends powerfully to enlighten the understanding, to enliven the affections, to restrain the passions, to promote

Gospel morality, and to advance the divine life in the soul. 'The Lord added to the church such as should be saved.' 'He gave some, apostles; and some, prophets; and some, evangelists; and some, pastors and teachers: for the perfecting of the saints, for the work of the ministry, for the edifying of the body of Christ.'

Such are the ends subserved by the existence of a church in the world. And it is carefully to be observed, that all these ends are brought about by the mediatorial administration of the Saviour. He it is who sends forth his light and his truth to gladden and direct an ignorant and benighted world; who prompts and enables men to celebrate the ordinances of God's worship; and who carries forward the work of salvation in the souls of believers.

V. All the ordinances of the church are instituted by Christ, the Mediator.

The ends above enumerated, are accomplished by means of ordinances, whose existence in the church is to be ascribed to the authority of Prince Messiah. He alone could determine what were fit to be instituted, or could give them the sanction of universal obligation. For such purposes, neither the wisdom nor the will of man could avail; the one being destitute of sufficient depth, and the other of adequate power. Nothing is, of course, left to man, but all is the work of the Mediator, whose skill is infinite, and whose authority is supreme.

He has given to the church a clear, authoritative, and

perfect *law*. The church, like every other society, must have regulations. These are contained in the Scriptures. Some of them may be viewed as proceeding originally from God, as the moral governor of the universe; others, as issuing immediately and directly from Christ. The ten commandments, and the natural duties of prayer and praise, are instances of the former; the peculiar ordinances of New Testament worship, are examples of the latter. But, as regards their administration to our fallen race, both classes must be looked upon as emanating from the Mediator. While not without law to God, we are under law to Christ. The promulgation of even the moral law itself was preceded by an exhibition of God's covenant character, and so might be said, not less than the Jewish law, to be ordained of God in the hands of a Mediator. The Lord is our Lawgiver, as well as our King and our Judge. The revelations given to Adam, to Noah, to Abraham, and to the other patriarchs, must be regarded as communicated to the church through Christ. The disclosures that were made at Sinai, we are assured, proceeded from him. 'This is he,' says Stephen, speaking of the Prophet predicted by Moses, 'that was in the church in the wilderness, with the angel which spake to him in the mount Sinai, and with our fathers, who received the lively oracles to give unto us.'[22] It was he, too, who, by his Spirit, enabled the evangelists and apostles to complete the volume of inspiration. The whole of revealed truth, comprehending the Scriptures of the Old and New Testaments, may thus be looked upon as the code of laws given to the church

[22] Acts vii. 38.

by the Messiah. The sacred volume is often expressly designated 'the law,' 'the law of the Lord,' &c.; and, in communicating it to men, Christ acts, not merely as a *prophet* making known the will of another, but as a *king* issuing his own authoritative regulations to his subjects which they are bound to obey. 'Come ye, and let us go up to the mountain of the Lord, to the house of the God of Jacob; and he will teach us of his ways, and we will walk in his paths: for out of Zion shall go forth the law, and the word of the Lord from Jerusalem.'[23] The law, thus promulgated, is authoritative. It is not at men's option whether they shall receive and obey it. It is supremely obligatory on all. It is clear and explicit; not expressed in such ambiguous terms that the reader may put upon it what construction he pleases. Men, it is true, may frequently misapprehend it, and may experience some difficulty in ascertaining its meaning; but this arises rather from the want of diligence, application, humility, holiness, perseverance, or prayer, on their part, than from any thing equivocal in the law itself. Nor is this law, in any respect, incomplete. The law of the Lord is perfect. It neither requires, nor admits of any addition being made to it by the ingenuity or authority of man. No individual, however gifted, no council, however solemnly constituted, may assume a strictly legislative power in the church of Christ. Men can only legitimately make known the laws of the Redeemer; and dare not, under pain of a fearful malediction, venture to take from, or to add to, the complete promulgation of his will contained in the

[23] Isa. ii. 3.

Bible. It is of itself sufficient to make the man of God perfect, thoroughly furnished unto all good works.

Christ has instituted in the church ordinances of divine *worship* and ecclesiastical *fellowship*. Public prayer, praise, reading the Scriptures, preaching the Word, baptism, and the Lord's supper, are sanctioned, either by his express institution or his administrative example. In the presence of his disciples, he lifted his eyes to heaven in solemn supplication to the Father. He sung with them a hymn, before going out to the Mount of Olives. When he went into the synagogue on the Sabbath day, 'he stood up for to read.' 'Go ye into all the world and preach the gospel to every creature,' was among his last directions to the apostles and their successors. He commanded them also to 'baptize in the name of the Father, and of the Son, and of the Holy Ghost.' In reference to the ordinance of the supper, he said, 'Do this in remembrance of me.' And, as for that portion of time which is consecrated to the peculiar observance of all these institutions, it is written, 'The Son of man is the Lord of the Sabbath.' There is not an institution of divine worship, by which the devotional feelings of the church are expressed, or the edification of the body promoted, which bears not the stamp of the Saviour's authority; and, in observing them all, the true saint has the satisfaction to know that he is 'serving the Lord Christ.'

The same is the case with respect to the *government* of the church. In every social body, order is essential to edification, and government is essential to order. This itself would seem to furnish a presumptive argument in favour of the sentiment that Christ has given to the church a regular form of government, in opposition to the opinion of those who contend that this matter has been left to be regulated by the wisdom of men, and to be modified agreeably to the various circumstances of those among whom the ordinances of religion happen to be set up. According to this view, there is no form of church government which may be said to possess divine authority. To a sentiment so vague and loose, it may be sufficient to reply, that, when it is considered how important a thing government is to every society, it is perfectly incredible that Christ should have left his church without any specific directions on this point: the more so that human wisdom, so liable to err at all times, is incompetent to determine a matter on which so much depends: to which it may be added that, on the above supposition, there would be no room whatever for submission to the authority of Christ in the point in question. It seems much more reasonable, therefore, *a priori*, to conclude that the grand principles of ecclesiastical government are laid down in the Scriptures, to which, and not to the ever-shifting ground of expediency, the appeal is to be made. It is true, those who advocate the opinion, that the Scriptures contain a regular prescribed plan, are not all agreed as to what that plan is. But this is no argument against the principle for which we contend, inasmuch as, at least equal diversity of sentiment prevails with regard to the doctrines of the Gospel, among those who hold that the Bible is the only standard of doctrinal truth. It cannot be expected that we should enter now into the discussion of what that form of government is which Christ has prescribed in his Word; although, in other circumstances, we should not shrink from the task of attempting to make it appear that, if not direct statement, at least fair Scripture inference, and the example of the primitive Christians, warrant us to adopt the presbyterial model, or that form in which different individual churches are regarded as parts of a grand whole, and the office-bearers as representatives of the people, forming a gradation of church courts, by which all controversies are to be settled, with a right of appeal from the lower to the higher. It is enough, in present circumstances, in proof of the fact that Christ has instituted in his church some form of government, to refer to those passages of Scripture in which ecclesiastical officers are represented as invested with the power of rule. 'We beseech you, brethren, to know them which labour among you, and are *over you* in the Lord. Let the elders that *rule* well, be counted worthy of double honour. Obey them that have the *rule* over you, and submit yourselves, for they watch for your souls, as they that must give account.'[24]

Closely connected with its government, is the *discipline* of the church. By this we understand the provision Christ has made for admitting persons to the fellowship of the church; for exercising a salutary vigilance over its members; and for administering censure in case of offences. The term has, perhaps, been too much restricted to the last of these objects; but a little reflection will be sufficient to convince that the

[24] 1 Thess. v. 12; 1 Tim. v. 17; Heb. xiii. 17.

others also ought to be included. The purity, peace, and order of the church, depend much on this institution of Christ being properly administered in all its legitimate objects. That he has made provision for these, appears from the power with which he has invested office-bearers in the church, to receive qualified persons into communion; to exercise a watchful inspection; to take cognizance of offences against the laws of Christ's house; to cite and examine offenders; to administer censure according to the nature and degree of the offence; and either to restore to, or finally eject from, the fellowship of the body, as the person may appear to have profited or not by the censure administered. The authority of Christ in this, as in the other institutions of his house, is a merciful authority. It is a proof of his love, designed to promote the best interests of the offenders themselves, as well as of the body at large to which they belong, and, if rightly improved, a manifest and decided blessing. 'If he shall neglect to hear them, tell it unto the church; but if he neglect to hear the church, let him be unto thee as an heathen man and a publican. Them that sin rebuke before all, that others may fear. A man that is an heretic, after the first and second admonition, reject.'[25]

VI. The Lord Jesus Christ, in virtue of the mediatorial dominion with which he is invested, prescribes the qualifications of the members of the church.

He has a right to say who they are that shall enjoy the privileges of his kingdom. The church is a peculiar

---

[25] Matt. xviii. 17; 1 Tim. v. 20; Tit. iii. 10.

society; those who belong to it are, of course, a peculiar people; and it is the prerogative of Him who is its Head to determine the character of such as shall be admitted into its fellowship.

What the qualifications of church members should be, is a point of equal importance and difficulty. With respect to the invisible church, it cannot be questioned that actual regeneration and true faith in Christ are indispensable. Nor can it be doubted, even with respect to the visible church, that the possession of true and vital religion can alone qualify for fully promoting the objects of ecclesiastical communion. But, as this is a thing of which the office-bearers of the church are incompetent to judge, it would seem that the utmost they can require is *a credible profession of true religion.* Of this, intelligence and orthodoxy constitute essential elements. Philip required of the Ethiopian eunuch an avowal of his belief in the doctrine of Christ, before administering to him the initiatory rite of baptism. 'See here is water, what doth hinder me to be baptized? If thou believest with all thine heart thou mayest. I believe that Jesus Christ is the Son of God.'[26] Paul instructed Titus, after a suitable trial and admonition, to reject 'a man that is an heretic.' Peter speaks of 'heresies' as being 'damnable,' and denounces, with merited severity, those false teachers who bring such into the church. From all this it appears that soundness in the faith is a requisite qualification. But the soundness required is not that which springs from implicit belief in the church or its ministers, as is contended for by the church of Rome.

[26] Acts viii. 36, 37.

It is intelligent orthodoxy; arising from an enlightened understanding, and a careful study of the Holy Scriptures. There is a spurious knowledge of sound doctrine which may be acquired by being taught to repeat certain set phrases by rote. This consists, rather in the memory of words than the comprehension of ideas. Words, instead of being the vehicles, are, in such a case, the substitutes of thoughts. There is reason to fear that much of the orthodoxy that exists in our churches is of this description; for it is too much the case with many, when taken off the favourite and accustomed phraseology into which they have been initiated, to display, instead of an enlightened acquaintance with Christian truth, a most deplorable and disgraceful ignorance. Such can never be regarded as intelligent church members. Their attachment to the church cannot be styled 'a reasonable service;' nor can they be said to be 'always ready to give a reason of the hope which is in them to any man who asks them.' Their knowledge is, at best, but a *'form* of knowledge, and of the truth.' However worthless mere speculative knowledge is in itself, it must not be forgotten that a certain degree—we presume not to fix the extent—is indispensable; for God, who will have all men to be saved, will have all men also to come to *the knowledge of the truth;* and the apostles did not cease to pray for their people that they might be *filled with the knowledge of God's will, in all wisdom and spiritual understanding.* The ignorant then, as well as the heterodox, are unfit for the communion of the church.

Full *submission to the ordinances* of Christ is another

qualification of the members of the church. The disciples of Christ are required to observe all things whatsoever he has commanded; and such as refuse to follow him in this cannot claim to be regarded as his disciples. It is by the observance of these that the fellowship of the visible church is expressed; and such as refuse all or any of them are practically disqualified for membership. It is not uncommon for persons who profess religion to live in the neglect of some one ordinance;—family worship, or the Lord's supper, for example; and yet they would fain be regarded as members of the church. But how can they? The authority which attaches to one, attaches to all; so that a refusal to submit, in any one case, is a virtual denial of the authority which sanctions the whole. A member of the church must be one who submits to all the laws and institutions of Christ's house, not one who obeys only what is agreeable or convenient; the principle of observance being submission to the authority of Christ, and not convenience, expediency, or caprice.

Apparent *religious experience* is also indispensable. *Apparent*, we say, because of the reality man is incompetent to judge; appearances are all that is within the sphere of his cognizance. Whoever seeks admission to the fellowship of the Christian church, professes to have experienced something of the power of religion on his heart. And, although the rulers in the church may not be able to determine whether this profession be real, they are entitled to demand that it be made, and to apply to it certain criteria of judgment. They may not be fit, in any case, to pronounce absolutely on the presence of true religion in the soul, nor, in every case, to decide on its absence; yet the appearances of its being present or absent may be in general so marked as to form a sufficient guide in receiving or refusing persons applying for admission. An individual who knows nothing of the nature of Christian experience, or of the marks by which it is distinguished, is, of course, inadmissible. Nor is it a bare pretension to religious experiences, or every plausible story of feelings and ecstasies, that can form a sufficient ground for admitting to ecclesiastical privileges. Credible evidences of the experimental power of religion are to be required, and nothing but what is rational, sober, consistent, and holy, can ever constitute credible evidence. 'We know that we have passed from death to life, because we love the brethren. And hereby we know that we are of the truth, and shall assure our hearts before him. For if our heart condemn us, God is greater than our heart, and knoweth all things. Beloved, if our heart condemn us not, then have we confidence toward God.'[27]

To these qualifications must be added *consistent behaviour*. The rule of judging is thus explicitly laid down by the Saviour himself:—' By their fruits ye shall know them. Not every one that saith unto me, Lord, Lord, shall enter into the kingdom of heaven; but *he that doeth the will* of my Father which is in heaven.' To the same purpose is his expostulation—' And why call ye me Lord, Lord, and *do not* the things which I say? It is not enough that men 'repent and turn to God;' they must also ' do works meet for repentance.'

[27] 1 John iii. 14, 19-21.

They must be 'zealous of good works.' 'Whosoever abideth in Christ sinneth not: whosoever sinneth hath not seen him, neither known him. He that saith he abideth in him ought himself so to walk even as he walked.' 'Lord, who shall abide in thy tabernacle? who shall dwell in thy holy hill? *He that walketh uprightly, and worketh righteousness, and speaketh the truth in his heart.*'

Such are the ingredients of a credible profession of true religion,— the elements of a visible Christian character, the possession of which is necessary to qualify for admission to the church. And let it be carefully observed, that all the qualifications specified are essential. The profession in question does not exist where any one of them is wanting. Suppose a person to pretend to have felt religious experiences, to observe all the institutions of Christ, and to maintain outward regularity of conduct, at the same time that he is either ignorant of, or entertains sentiments at variance with, the grand principles of the Gospel, such a person is utterly disqualified for church membership. The same may be said of those in whom intelligent orthodoxy, submission to ordinances, and pretended experience, exist apart from consistency of outward life and conversation; or of those in whom intelligence, orthodoxy, observance of ordinances, and an umblamable moral reputation are combined, while there is a want of all evidence of the spiritual power of the Gospel. While we decidedly object to making actual saintship a term of admission to the visible church, we must at the same time contend for the appearance of it, and for the right of ecclesiastical rulers to judge of the evidences of its existence, the presence of some such evidences being requisite to a credible profession. We deny that the office-bearers of religion have either the power or the right to judge men's hearts: but it were strange, indeed, if they were not warranted to require that those who are professing to believe the Gospel shall give some signs that it is exerting its proper influence on their hearts, and to inquire whether it has taught them to abjure self-righteousness, to renounce the practice of sin, and to live by faith on the Lord Jesus Christ; whether, in short, it has taught them to deny ungodliness and worldly lusts, and to live soberly, righteously, and godly in the world. Yet, their making these inquiries, and insisting on these qualifications, are not to be considered as supposing that they are infallible judges of the signs of grace in the heart. The Lord only can search the heart and try the reins. But where such evidences as we have spoken of exist, though not infallible proofs of true Christian character, they are to be regarded as sufficient to banish suspicion, and to warrant rulers to admit to the privileges of the church. We are to conclude, in the spirit of charity, that men really *are* what they so plainly *appear* to be.

That such things as constitute a credible profession, and not actual saintship or a positive spiritual change, are the qualifications required by Christ, may be argued on various grounds. It is visible qualifications alone that can properly be required to constitute visible membership in a visible church. It is absurd and unreasonable to require invisible qualities as essential prerequisites to visible fellowship. To the communion of the invisible church such are indispensable, but not to that of which we are speaking. Analogy may serve to throw light on this subject. In every society of whatever kind, be it scientific, or literary, or benevolent, all that is required to membership is a professed approbation of its constitution, and an apparent conformity to its rules. It is never thought necessary to scrutinize the heart, with a view to ascertain whether the person be sincere. He may not be sincere; but so long as he gives no evidence of insincerity, so long as he continues to act as if he were sincere, that is to say, so long as he makes a credible profession, he is considered as entitled to all the privileges of membership. Man, as we said before, has neither the ability nor the right to judge the heart. 'I am he,' saith the faithful and true Witness, 'who searcheth the reins and hearts.' To do so is a divine prerogative, and no man or set of men may presume to exercise it. Nay, even the most penetrating angelic intellect is incompetent to discover, excepting by outward manifestations, what is passing within the human breast. It is well that it is so; as, were rulers in the church invested with the right to pronounce infallibly on the spiritual condition of their fellow-men, it is not difficult to see what an engine of tyranny and oppression such a power might become; besides superseding the exercise of self-examination, and making way for the most unprincipled, unfounded, arrogant, and provoking pretensions. Indeed, the principle that actual saintship is indispensable, is at variance with the exercise of that discipline which we have before seen is one of the institutions of the church. When a church member is suspended or excluded from the enjoyment of privileges for misconduct, it is not because he is considered not to be a saint, but because he has acted inconsistently with his profession. He may be a saint; in the spirit of charity it may be hoped that he is such; nay, there may be very good reasons for entertaining a favourable view of his state. But a real saint may act so as to incur the discipline of the church. This is supposed in the very institution of discipline, which is designed to promote the edification of the godly. David, while his sin was unrepented of, was unfit for the fellowship of a holy society. A person who departs for a time from the right path is not to be 'counted as an *enemy*, but admonished as a *brother*.' But if a saint may be lawfully excluded from the fellowship of the visible church, even for a time, it is plain that something else than saintship is the qualification for communion.

Both Christ and his apostles appear to have acted on the principle for which we contend. Judas, who had a devil, and was known by Christ to be unconverted, was recognised and treated as a disciple, until he proved the hollowness of his profession by his conduct. Simon Magus, on a credible profession of religion, received the ordinance of baptism, although he was afterwards pronounced to be in the gall of bitterness and bond of iniquity. And, in short, there might have been less dispute on this subject, had due attention been given to the figures under which the church is represented. It is spoken of as a vine, some of the branches of which are barren, while others are fruitful; as a floor, on which there is found chaff as well as grain; as a field, in which are tares as well as wheat; as a net, which incloses bad as well as good fishes; and as a house, in which there are vessels to dishonour as well as to honour;—figures which could, with no propriety, be employed to represent the church, were actual saintship essential to her communion.

But does not this suppose that there may be hypocrites in the communion of the church? It does: but what then? The same admission will fall to be made on the supposition that actual regeneration is the qualification for church membership, as of this man can judge only by appearances, and it must be admitted that appearances may sometimes deceive. Nor is it destructive of the character of the church, as a spiritual society and the body of Christ, to suppose, that it may comprehend within it persons who are not real saints. Let it be recollected that it is of the visible church of Christ we are now speaking; and if there be only visible saintship, it is all that can be strictly required, as it is all that can be judged of by man, to the visible fellowship of such a community. Analogy may here aid our conceptions. The world is God's world, notwithstanding that there are sinful men in it. The heart of a believer is a renewed heart, notwithstanding that it is infested with manifold corruptions. Why then may not the church of Christ be supposed to contain in it some who are not real Christians, without destroying its character?

Nay, it might even be shewn that such a mixed state as we have supposed, is turned to good account in the providence of God. The quantity of moral evil in the world is thus diminished; inasmuch as the nominal members of the church are necessitated to conform to the laws of morality more strictly than they would otherwise do, in order to keep up the consistency of their assumed character. The persons themselves may not be in a whit better state, as regards God, than the openly profligate and abandoned : but, as respects their fellow-men, it is not to be doubted that it is better they should repress than that they should give full scope to their enmity of heart; better surely that they should treat the name of God with reverence than that they should blaspheme it; better that they should maintain a show of truth, probity, and respect for the ordinances of religion, than that they should lie, steal, and pour contempt on all the institutions of Christ; better, in short, that they should maintain before their families and others the common decencies of life, than that they should set before them the example of open profligacy and vice. If so, the state of things by which they are constrained to do so is not without its use. Besides, it is calculated to lessen the sum of human misery, by averting public judgments. Facts warrant us to believe, that open judgments may be restrained, where the souls of men are not saved, out of respect to the restraints laid upon open sin : so that whatever tends to promote the latter, goes also to secure the former. Moreover, it would not be very difficult to shew that the arrangement in question is overruled for extending the resources, increasing the numbers, and promoting the protection of the church.

Not less unfortunate is the objection that the principle in question leads to the prostitution of sealing ordinances. For it must be obvious to all, that, unless the friends of the opposite scheme can pretend with infallible accuracy to judge the heart, the objection applies as much to them as to us. And, it may be added, that it overlooks the relation of the sacraments to the visible church. They have a special relation, it is true, to the church invisible; and, as signs of spiritual blessings, can be participated of with individual profit only by true believers. But they have also a relation to the visible church; and viewed as signs of the covenant character of God, certifying the doctrine of salvation by the blood of Christ, and affirming the necessity of being interested in the mediation of the Lord Jesus, the public administration of them, even where some who outwardly partake are unbelievers, may serve many important purposes to both the church and the world.

This view of the matter, if properly understood, can have no tendency to retard the exertions of the office-bearers and friends of the church in promoting her purity. It can have no effect in inducing them to receive into communion known unbelievers, or in warranting them to administer to such the sacred privileges of Christ's house. By no means. That God glorifies himself by a state of things in which good and evil are mingled together, is no reason why we should be indifferent to the existence of evil, much less why we should give encouragement to its existence. It is the prerogative of infinite wisdom, power, and grace, to bring good out of evil. But we are not warranted, on that account, to attempt any thing but what is good; we must not do evil that good may come. The existence of evil in the world, as before remarked, does not destroy its relation to God; yet we are not, on this account, at liberty to encourage vice in the world, but bound to use every effort for its suppression and extirpation. The existence of depravity in the heart of a saint does not destroy his renewed character; yet is he bound to resist every known sin, to repress every evil principle, and to make no provision for the flesh to fulfil the lusts thereof. In like manner, although the existence of nominal Christians in its communion does not destroy the character of the church, this is no reason why the doors of ecclesiastical fellowship should be thrown open, and the seals of the covenant administered, to known unbelievers, or why every effort should not be made to exclude such from her membership.

VII. Christ, in virtue of his mediatorial dominion, appoints, qualifies, and invests with power, the office-bearers in the church.

Laws, institutions, and ordinances, suppose the existence of an order of men by whom they are administered. They cannot administer themselves; nor can it be regarded as any thing short of fanaticism to maintain, as is done by some, that everyone is to be guided in the worship of God merely by the fluctuating impulse of his own feelings, or 'the light' within, as it is called. The Scriptures give no countenance to any such wild idea. On the contrary, they give us good reason to believe that, from the beginning, the heads of families were authorized by God to act both as priests and as prophets. During the Mosaic economy, we know that a regular order of office-bearers existed; for there were laws for regulating their preparatory qualifications, their administration, and their succession. At the New Testament period, also, there existed a regular lawful ministry, some of the offices connected with which were certainly of a permanent nature, while others, of an obviously temporary kind, after serving the purpose for which they were introduced, were suffered to die away. Of this latter description were the offices held by those who were called apostles, prophets, and evangelists, the peculiarities of whose functions we wait not to delineate. But there is no reason for supposing that with these the existence of a standing ministry in the church was to cease. The very reverse is the inference we should seem warranted to draw. For if, even in an age which was blessed with extraordinary communications of the divine Spirit, teachers and rulers were deemed requisite, it is not reasonable to expect that, when these extraordinary gifts are withdrawn, the church should be able to do without office-bearers altogether. This view of the subject is confirmed by much that is found in the history and writings of the apostles themselves. To this purpose are these express statements of Paul:—'And he gave some, apostles; and some, prophets; and some, evangelists; and some, pastors and teachers; for the perfecting of the saints, for the work of the ministry, for the edifying of the body of Christ: till we all come in the unity of the faith, and of the knowledge of the Son of God, unto a perfect man, unto the measure of the stature of the fulness of Christ. And God hath set some in the church: first, apostles; secondly, prophets; thirdly, teachers; after that, miracles; then, gifts of healing, helps, governments, diversities of tongues.'[28] The apostles, accordingly, were careful to 'commit the form of sound words to faithful men, able to teach others also.' They ordained them elders in every city. The author of the Epistle to the Hebrews, by reminding the persons to whom he wrote of those who had *had* the rule over them, whose faith they were required to follow after their decease, and at the same time exhorting them to obey those that *have* the rule over them, distinctly recognises the existence of not merely one but two sets of teachers after the apostles. When John wrote his Apocalypse there were *angels*, that is to say, office-bearers, to whom the epistles to the Asiatic churches were addressed. Add to these considerations, the circumstance that the promise made by the Head of the church himself to his apostles proceeded on the supposition that there should be a standing ministry to the end of time, and is utterly irreconcilable with the notion that such was to expire with the apostles. *Lo, I am with you* ALWAY, EVEN UNTO THE END OF THE WORLD.

The permanent and ordinary office-bearers in the church are presbyters and deacons. Presbyters are of two kinds, namely, such as teach as well as rule, and such as rule only. The former are commonly known by the names of pastors, teachers, or ministers, and the latter by that of ruling elders. Presbyters of the former

---

[28] Eph. iv. 11, 12; 1 Cor. xii. 28.

class appear to be the only description of bishops authorized by the Scriptures or by the practice of the primitive churches. The word commonly translated *bishop* signifies an *overseer*, and is so rendered in several instances in the common version. By a comparison of texts, we are led to conclude, that, in the early Christian church, the bishop and the presbyter were synonymous terms, denoting the very same office. In the twentieth chapter of the Acts, those called in the seventeenth verse 'elders,' πρεσβυτερους, are called 'overseers,' or bishops, επισκοπους, in the twenty-eighth. In the Epistle to Titus, first chapter, the qualifications of 'elders,' πρεσβυτερους, and of a 'bishop,' επισκοπος, are the same. In the first Epistle of Peter, the verb from which the word translated *bishop* is derived, is employed in describing the duties of elders:—'The elders, πρεσβυτερους, which are among you I exhort.—Feed the flock of God which is among you, taking the over-sight thereof,' επισκοπουντες. It is not, then, from any thing in the Scripture usage of the terms, that the inference can be drawn, that the one term describes a different and a higher office than that which is pointed out by the other. Neither is there any thing in the original signification of the terms themselves to warrant this conclusion; but rather the contrary. *Overseer* and *presbyter*, while they are used indiscriminately to designate persons holding the same office, differ from one another in their primitive meaning so as to point out, indeed, the one the activity of service, the other the dignity of rule: but it so happens that the former idea is suggested by the term which Episcopalians understand to designate the office which is superior, and the latter idea attaches to the term which they regard as expressive of the office that is inferior. So far, indeed, from *presbyter* being, either in its primitive import or its current use in Scripture, expressive of inferiority, presbyters are described as exercising the very highest official acts—acts which, according to Episcopalians, belong only to bishops. Presbyters are described as *ruling*. The *elders* of Ephesus are required to '*take heed* to the flock.' We read of 'the *elders* that *rule* well.' Presbyters are spoken of as ordaining: 'Neglect not the gift which is in thee, which was given thee by prophecy, with the *laying on of the hands of the presbytery*.' When to these considerations it is added that there is but one ministerial commission, and that the preaching of the Word is spoken of in Scripture as a more dignified function than that of ruling, and as entitling to more abundant honour,[29] the evidence adduced appears sufficient to warrant the opinion that overseer and presbyter describe the same office, and that the one supposes no sort of superiority over the other, but on the contrary a clear and perfect equality.

As to the presbyters of the second class—those who rule only—their existence is plainly enough intimated in the plurality of elders which existed in the primitive churches, it being highly improbable that there should be more than one teacher who required to be supported by the members; in the distinction made betwixt 'him that exhorteth' and 'him that ruleth,' and betwixt 'teachers' and 'helps and governments;' and

[29] 1 Tim. v. 17.

in the very clear line of demarcation drawn betwixt the elders that merely rule, and those who also labour in the word and doctrine. [30]

But it is not so much our object, to shew what offices Christ has appointed in his church, as to speak of the exercise of his mediatorial authority in appointing, qualifying, and investing with power, the men by whom these offices are held.

Appointment to office in the church is essential to the regular discharge of the functions belonging to office. 'I sent them not, nor commanded them : therefore they shall not profit this people at all, saith the Lord.' 'How shall they preach except they be sent ?' 'No man taketh this honour unto himself, but he that is called of God as was Aaron. So also Christ glorified not himself to be made a High Priest; but He that said unto him, Thou art my Son, to-day have I begotten thee.' [31] It must surely be presumptuous, in any mere servant of Christ to dispense with what was requisite to give validity to the office of his Master. But what constitutes a sufficient and valid appointment ? An *inward impulse* of the divine Spirit, inclining an individual to serve the church in a public capacity, is not enough, as it can be of use only to the person himself. An *immediate* commission requires to be substantiated by miracles, and is not now to be expected. The only appointment, then, that can now be looked for, would seem to be that which consists in solemn and regular investiture with office by persons previously

---

[30] Acts xiv. 23 ; Rom. xii. 8 ; 1 Cor. xii. 28 ; 1 Tim. v. 17.
[31] Jer. xxiii. 32 ; Rom. x. 15 ; Heb. v. 4, 5.

qualified and authorized; in other words, presbyterian ordination, or ecclesiastical designation.

Now, ordination derives its authority and validity from the institution of Christ as King and Head of his church. The custom of ordination existed in the primitive church. The apostles could not have practised it, nor could the inspired writers have given directions with regard to the performance of it, unless they had been authorized so to do; and by whom could they be so authorized but by Christ himself? The 'laying on of hands,' we are taught to consider as a part of Christianity as much as 'repentance from dead works, or faith toward God, or the resurrection of the dead, or eternal judgment.'[32]

Ordination consists in the transmission of ecclesiastical power, by the solemn and appropriate form of the laying on of the hands of presbyters. The laying on of hands in ordination, is not a mere unauthorized ceremony. It is distinctly recognised both by apostolical example and precept. 'The gift that is in thee, with the laying on of the hands of the presbytery' (1 Tim. iv. 14). 'Lay hands suddenly on no man' (1 Tim. v. 22). Not that any thing is actually conveyed, by the mere imposition of hands, from the persons engaged in the act to the person who is the object of it. It is properly the *sign* rather than the *medium* of conveyance; just as sprinkling with water is significant of the application of the blood of Christ and the regenerating influence of the Spirit to the soul of the person baptized. Sprink-

[32] Heb. vi. 1, 2.

ling with water does not convey these spiritual benefits; yet it is not an empty unmeaning ceremony, but an appropriately significant act. In like manner, the imposition of hands in ordination is not a useless form, but the appropriate mode by which it has pleased the Head of the church to express the communication of official power, to those by whom it is to be exercised. It were well that this view of the subject were more attended to than it is.

The act of ordination belongs to persons previously ordained. If it is significant of the conveyance of office-power, it can only be performed by those who possess such power. The power, it is true, is not *derived from* men but from Christ, the fountain-head of all authority. But it is *transmitted through* men; and there is an obvious propriety, if not necessity, that the medium of transmission should be such as to bring to view the thing transmitted. It follows, that the act of ordination belongs not to the people. It is of great importance to observe that the existence of the ministerial office is in no way dependent on the members of the church. Some have identified ordination and the call of the people. Others have considered the call of the people to be an indispensable prerequisite to ordination, an essential preparatory step to investiture with power and authority in the church. It does not appear to us that either of these opinions is correct. Not that we are indifferent to the right of the Christian people to call such as shall be placed over them in the Lord. The call of the people, we hold to be essential to the formation of the *pastoral relation;* and every attempt to deprive them of this right, or to cripple them in the exercise of it, we regard as a scandalous interference with the prerogative of Christ the church's Head, and a daring invasion of the privileges of the church's members. We hold that, in the formation of the interesting, and solemn, and important relation in question, the people should have a *choice;* it is mockery to put them off with a *veto.* But, then, there is a distinction betwixt *the pastoral relation* and *the ministerial office*—a distinction which is not sufficiently understood, but one, the correct understanding of which would go far to prevent many mistakes, and to remove many prejudices, on subjects connected with the office-bearers of the church.

The *ministerial office* is necessary to the full exercise of the functions arising out of the *pastoral relation.* Accordingly, the former is usually conferred at the time when the latter is formed; and hence may have arisen the misconception by which they are identified or confounded. But, although the pastoral relation supposes the existence of the ministerial office, the ministerial office may, and often does, exist without the pastoral relation.* This being the case, the choice of the people may be essential to the latter, and yet in no way necessary to the former. On the one hand, the pastoral relation, springing from the choice of the people, and supposing the mutual consent of the parties betwixt whom it exists,

---

* The church is now happily familiar with this in the case of missionaries to the heathen. It is to be remembered that this was written in 1837, the middle of the Ten Years' Conflict.—ED.

is necessarily restricted and exclusive. On the other hand, the ministerial office, derived from the church's office-bearers, is wide as the wide world itself in the sphere over which it extends, and is altogether independent of the will of the people. The pastor, as such, cannot properly discharge the functions of the pastoral relation, without the consent of the people; and even this he can do only within the limited bounds of his own parish or congregation: but the minister of Christ as such, is, in virtue of his office, entitled to traverse the bounds of the habitable globe, and to proclaim the message of salvation in the ears of all those with whom he meets, whether they will hear, or whether they will forbear. No magic circle circumscribes the bounds of *his* ministrations. The laying on of the hands of the presbytery has given him a relation to the church universal, has invested him with authority to exercise his ministry, wherever God in his providence may call him, or may give him an opportunity. Wherever his voice can reach, wherever his feet can carry him, wherever, by land or by water, he can have his person transported, there has he a full and unquestionable right to unfold the message with which he is entrusted as a minister, and to beseech sinners of every clime, in Christ's stead, to be reconciled to God. In this he needs not to wait for the call of the people. The exercise of his office is not suspended on the invitation of men. The people can neither impart nor remove the right to exercise it. It descends from Christ the fountain of all authority, through a regular and divinely-appointed ordination.

It is scarcely necessary to add, after this, that the power of ordination does not lie with a bishop,—a diocesan bishop. Paul and Barnabas, indeed, ordained elders in every city; but they did so, not as bishops, but as apostles—an extraordinary office, whose functions included those of the ordinary. Timothy and Titus ordained; but it will require stronger proof than we have yet seen, to convince us that they were *diocesan* bishops. Timothy himself was ordained by the laying on of *the hands of the presbytery*. *Supernatural* gifts he appears to have received by the putting on of *Paul's* hands; but the *ministerial* gift was conferred on him by the laying on of the hands of the *presbytery*.

By means of ordination, provision is made for the regular and orderly transmission of official power in the church, throughout all ages. We do not contend for an uninterrupted succession from the apostles as essential to the validity of official ministrations. The value of the Christian ministry is suspended on no such contingency. Extraordinary circumstances, we fully admit, may warrant extraordinary measures; and there is no form or rite in being in the church which may not lawfully be dispensed with on particular occasions. The letter must ever be held to be subordinate to the spirit; and when both cannot be had, the former must yield to the latter. So it is in the case of ordination. The importance and propriety of installing men into office, in all ordinary cases, by the imposition of the hands of presbyters, may be maintained, in perfect consistency with the admission that cases may occur in which, at the call of the people, persons may warrantably and validly exercise the functions of the ministry, without having undergone the solemnity in question. Still, in all common cases, the regular and orderly way is that of which we have been speaking. It thus appears that ordination, while it confers authority of boundless extent as regards the sphere within which it may be exercised, provides for the perpetuation of it to the end of time. It possesses the property of indefinite and endless reproduction, and is in this way adapted to the conveyance of powers for which the necessity is both universal and perpetual.

And what, it is time now to ask, are these *powers* with which the Head of the church invests her officebearers? In general, the authority with which ministers are invested, is authority to dispense all the laws and ordinances of the church; and by adverting to what we have previously said regarding these, we may come to form a tolerably correct idea of the nature and extent of office-power in the church of Christ. This power, let it be distinctly marked, is, in no shape or degree whatever, absolute and unlimited. As it is derived from the Lord Jesus Christ, it is to be exercised within such limitations as he, in the exercise of his sovereignty, has seen fit to appoint. In short, it is not sovereign but delegated power; and this necessarily supposes restriction and accountability.

Church power has usually been distributed into three kinds. (1) The first is called *dogmatic power* (potestas δογματικη), and refers to dogmas or articles of faith. This may be viewed as comprehending whatever is connected with instruction. It concerns what men are to believe; and consists in the right, not, as is claimed by the church of Rome, of determining what man is to believe, but of explaining and enforcing the truths of religion, either by circulating the Scriptures, or preaching the Gospel, or exhibiting summaries of Christian truth; the ultimate appeal being in every case to the word of God. (2) The second is called *ordaining power* (potestas διατακτικη), and refers to the government of the church. This comprehends, again, whatever is connected with rule; and consists, not in the power to institute a form of church government, or to make laws for regulating the conduct of men, or to appoint rites and ceremonies, but in the power to take such steps, and devise such measures, as may be requisite for administering the laws and ordinances which Christ has instituted. It is not legislative, but ministerial; it supposes an authority, not to make laws, but to administer them, and of course to pass such enactments or regulations, on points of external order, as may be necessary to give full effect to the institutions of Christ. (3) The third is called the *power of discipline* (potestas διακριτικη), and refers to admission to, or exclusion from, the communion of the church. The existence of such a power has been formerly proved. Its nature is entirely spiritual; extending to the souls of men, and not to their bodies, property, or lives. The highest censures which the office-bearers of the church, in virtue of this power, are entitled to inflict, are addressed to the conscience, and have for their object 'the destruction of the flesh, that the spirit may be saved in the day of the Lord.' Civil pains, whether fines, confiscation, imprisonment, exile, or death, belong not to ecclesiastical office-bearers; and the church which has recourse to these, in whatever degree, so far identifies itself with the Romish usurpation, which claims dominion alike over the bodies and the souls of men.

Such is the power possessed by the ministers of religion; with which they are invested, not by the people over whom it is exercised, nor by the civil magistrate, but solely by the Lord Jesus Christ himself; and which is conveyed in the manner formerly described.

The exercise of such varied and solemn powers, presupposes certain necessary *qualifications*, for which also the office-bearers in the church are indebted to him from whom the powers themselves are derived. The extraordinary endowments possessed in the primitive age, have long since been suspended; and their place must now be made up by a competent share of natural talents, educational acquirements, and spiritual gifts. Without a portion of such qualifications, there can be no regular call to ministerial office. The Head of the church sends none a warfare on their own charges. He fits his servants for the work he requires of them. Where he has not given the qualification, he does not require the work. And if the functions of office are of so arduous and responsible a nature as to make all who have right feelings, to exclaim, in the prospect of undertaking them, 'Who is sufficient for these things?'

the promised assistance is also such as to permit them to add, 'Not that we are sufficient of ourselves to think any thing as of ourselves, but our sufficiency is of God, who also hath made us able ministers of the New Testament.' To qualify for public instruction, there must be not only an extensive knowledge of the Scriptures, but an acquaintance with literature in general, and particularly with sacred literature. To fit for government and discipline, much knowledge of human nature, a large share of natural sagacity, and no small degree of gravity, patience, and prudence, are requisite. These and similar qualifications are derived from Christ himself, with whom is the residue of the Spirit, and whose it is so to clothe his ministers with salvation that his people may, through their successful labours, have reason to shout for joy. 'To every one is given grace, according to the measure of the gift of Christ.' Nor are those intrusted with the transmission of official power at liberty to confer it on any who are found, on proper trial, to be deficient in gifts and attainments. 'The things that thou hast heard of me among many witnesses, the same commit to faithful men, who shall be *able* to teach others also.' No greater injury can be done to the church, and we may add to the persons themselves, than to admit to office men who are not qualified to discharge its functions with ability. The office is in this way exposed to contempt; the members of the church who happen to be placed under the care of such persons are not edified; and the persons themselves become a laughing-stock to the profane. Most mistaken policy it is, therefore, in every point of view, from motives of commiseration and pity, to make a farce of preparatory trials, and to

> 'Lay careless hands
> On skulls that cannot teach and will not learn.'

VIII. Christ's power over the church is, farther, apparent in rendering the administration of ordinances, by her proper office-bearers, effectual to the salvation of her members.

The laws, worship, government, and discipline, instituted by the Redeemer, are designed to promote the spiritual welfare of souls. Their efficacy for this purpose, is derived from Christ himself. In one point of view, indeed, this efficacy is to be ascribed to the Spirit. But the Spirit, it should never be forgotten, is the Spirit of Christ; is sent by Christ; and acts in every case under the commission of Christ. Thus it is that the whole honour of man's redemption is secured to the Mediator, as well the renovation of man's nature and character as the removal of his guilt. Agreeably to this, Christ is represented as He with whom is the residue of the Spirit; as sending the Comforter to reprove the world of sin, of righteousness, and of judgment; and as having, when he ascended on high, received gifts for men, yea, for the rebellious, that the Lord God might dwell among them. The precious oil, which goes down to the skirts of the garments, is first poured on the Head.

The whole world being, by nature, in a state of rebellion against the Lord and his Anointed, the Redeemer can have no friends among men until he makes them such; can have no spiritual subjects until he subdues them to himself; can have no obedient children, until, by the rod of his strength sent forth out of Sion, he has made a willing people in the day of his power. The renewed heart is Satan's seat. To dethrone the tyrant, and lead the rebel captive, is the prerogative of Him who is king in Sion, the Faithful and True, who in righteousness doth judge and make war. The rescue of fallen man from sin and Satan, is effected, not by the strength of the evidence by which the gospel is supported; not by any inherent power in the truth itself; not by the clearness, and faithfulness, and eloquence with which it is propounded; not by mere moral suasion: but by the naked energy of the Saviour himself. Where the word of this king is, there is power; and nowhere else. It is by his omnific power, convincing of sin, enlightening the mind in the knowledge of Christ, and renewing the will, that any are persuaded and enabled to embrace the Saviour as he is offered to them in the gospel. This it is alone that can open men's eyes, and turn them from darkness to light, and from the power of Satan unto God. The kingdom of God is within men. It cometh not with observation. The arrow which pierces the heart and brings down its enmity, which inflicts the wound that nothing but a Saviour's blood can heal, is selected, is fitted to the string, is propelled with unerring aim, and guided with infallible certainty, by the skill and power of the Redeemer himself. 'Gird thy sword upon thy thigh, O most Mighty, with thy glory and thy majesty. And in thy majesty ride prosperously, because of truth, and meekness, and righteousness; and thy right hand shall teach thee terrible things. Thine arrows are sharp in the hearts of the king's enemies; whereby the people fall under thee.'[33]

To such as are thus subdued by the power of his grace, he imparts the comforting sense of pardon and the honourable title of children. Their justification and adoption are legal acts for which they are indebted to Christ as a Priest; but the comforting sense of safety derived from the one, and of dignity derived from the other, they owe to his power as a King conveying it to their hearts. If it is true that by his sacerdotal blood they are justified from all things from which they could not be justified by the law of Moses, it is no less true that 'he is exalted a *Prince* and a Saviour, *to give* repentance to Israel and *forgiveness of sin.*' Nor is it less explicitly made known that 'to as many as receive him, He gives power to become the sons of God;' sending forth his Spirit into their hearts, enabling them to cry 'Abba, Father.' Now, all this is brought about by his giving efficacy to the ordinances.

In the same way it is that He rules and reigns in the hearts of his people. He asserts his authority over the conscience, the will, the life; and prescribes his law as the rule of their obedience. They recognise him as their master; cheerfully acknowledge his supremacy; and delight in the law of the Lord after the inward man. He puts his law into their minds, and writes it in their hearts. They yield themselves up to him as his willing

[33] Ps. xlv. 3-5.

servants; and every principle that is within them, every affection, volition, desire, proclaims him King and Lord.

The members of the church have many enemies. The devil, the world, and the flesh, are in league against them. They wrestle not only against flesh and blood, but against principalities, against powers, against the rulers of the darkness of this world, against spiritual wickednesses in high places. They are required to assume the character, equipments, and attitude of soldiers. They must put on the whole armour of God, that they may be able to stand; having their loins girt about with truth; having on the breastplate of righteousness; having their feet shod with the preparation of the gospel; and taking the shield of faith, the helmet of salvation, and the sword of the Spirit, which is the word of God. Satan, the chief and leader of these enemies, exasperated at his overthrow, makes a desperate effort to regain his lost dominion over them; and, although he cannot succeed, he does much to annoy such as have been rescued from his grasp. They are in themselves too feeble and powerless to sustain the shock of this unequal combat. But they have an omnipotent King, whose wisdom and might are exerted to assist and protect them. By the instructions of his Word, by the influence of his example, by the moral power of his ordinances, as well as by the positive strength which he imparts by his Spirit, he teaches their hands to war and their fingers to fight; he girds them with strength unto the battle, subdues under them those that rise up against them, and gives them the necks of their enemies. Sin, indwelling sin, has no longer dominion over them: by faith they overcome the world: and God bruises Satan under their feet. Yes; ye good soldiers of Jesus Christ! your King not only witnesses from his throne in the heavens the contest in which you are engaged, but cheers you on with his presence, encourages you by his example, animates you by his promises, stretches over you the impenetrable shield of his righteousness, and by his grace insures your final conquest. Well, then, may you exclaim with the Jewish prophet, 'Rejoice not against me, O mine enemy; when I fall I shall arise; when I sit in darkness the Lord shall be a light unto me:'[34] or break forth into the exulting language of the apostle, 'Who shall separate us from the love of Christ? Shall tribulation, or distress, or persecution, or famine, or nakedness, or peril, or sword? Nay, in all these things we are more than conquerors, through him that loved us.'[35]

Nor will their glorious Captain and Leader rest satisfied, until he has rendered the administration of Gospel ordinances effectual, in conducting forward the work of grace in the souls of his people to its final consummation in eternal glory. The honour of having brought the struggle with their enemies to a successful issue, shall be followed by the enjoyment of an everlasting reward. And the Saviour himself, as King of saints and King of glory, shall adorn them with their white robes, put the palms of victory into their hands, place upon their heads their crowns of gold, invite them to sit with him on his great high throne, and fill their mouths with unceasing Alleluias.

[34] Mic. vii. 8.   [35] Rom. viii. 35, 37.

IX. The mediatorial dominion of Christ may be seen in the provision he has made for the diffusion and perpetuation of the visible church;—its diffusion over the habitable globe; and its perpetuation to the end of time.

We have already specified universality among the attributes of the visible church. Its nature is such as to admit of universal extension; and its divine Head will so order the affairs of providence, as to secure for it a diffusion proportioned to the catholicity of its character. Of this the Scriptures give positive and direct assurance. 'The stone cut out without hands became a great mountain, and filled the whole earth. He shall have dominion from sea to sea, and from the river unto the ends of the earth. All nations shall serve him. All nations shall call him blessed. The whole earth shall be filled with his glory. The mountain of the Lord's house shall be established in the top of the mountains, and shall be exalted above the hills; and all nations shall flow into it. The earth shall be full of the knowledge of the Lord, as the waters cover the sea.'[36] It is lamentable to think how small a portion of the earth has hitherto been blessed with the ordinances of true religion. Taking a survey of the world, and bearing in mind such predictions and promises as those above cited, we cannot help feeling that 'there remaineth yet very much land to be possessed.' The field of Messiah's operations is the world; nor will he cease to put forth his power for the extension of his church, till he has made the wilderness and the solitary place to be glad,

---

[36] Dan. ii. 35; Ps. lxxii. 8, 11, 17, 19; Isa. ii. 2; xi. 9.

and the desert to rejoice and blossom as the rose. The outward ordinances of visible Christianity shall be universally spread abroad; efficacy shall be given to the means of grace, by the outpouring of the Spirit; and every obstruction to the triumphant progress of the chariot of salvation shall be effectually removed. Ignorance shall be dispelled before the spreading beams of gospel light. The evidences of divine truth shall compel infidelity, which now rears its unblushing front, to hide its head. The delusions of the false prophet shall be dissipated by the drying up of the river Euphrates, that a way may be prepared for the kings of the East. Jewish obstinacy and unbelief shall be broken, and the veil taken from the eyes of that interesting people in reading Moses and the prophets. All the hideous forms of polytheistic paganism shall give way to the one religion of Jesus. That monstrous corruption of Christianity, which has so long usurped the place and claimed the honour of the true faith, shall be cast into the lake of fire. The anti-Christian leaven, which has been so extensively diffused, shall be purged out of both the churches and the nations. Every usurper of the rights and prerogatives of Sion's King shall be pushed from his seat. Every rival kingdom shall be overthrown. The civil and ecclesiastical constitutions of the earth shall be regulated by the infallible standard of God's word; their office-bearers, of every kind, shall acknowledge the authority of Messiah the Prince; and the greatest kings on earth shall cast their crowns at his feet. All enemies shall be put under his feet; and such as resist the melting influence of his grace, shall be crushed beneath the iron rod of his power. By spiritual conversion or judicial destruction, he shall effect the entire subjugation of the globe. And, at the last, there shall not be a spot on the face of the habitable earth where the true church of Christ shall not have effected a footing, nor a single tribe of the vast family of man which shall not have felt the meliorating and blissful influence of Christian laws and institutions. Europe, Asia, Africa, and America, shall then be united in one vast brotherhood,—ranged under one standard : the bond of their union, the holy cement of the Gospel, the emblem of their banner, the Cross.

The church, thus universally diffused, shall be effectually perpetuated. The government of Messiah shall not only increase, but it shall have 'no end.' It shall be 'established with judgment and with justice from henceforth even for ever.' We have seen the provision Christ has made for a succession of ministers. Not less carefully has he provided for a succession of members throughout all generations. Even after all other enemies have been subdued, death, it is true, shall be perpetually removing to another world those who have held both public and private stations in the church; but even death cannot bring about the extinction of the church of Christ. Instead of the fathers, he takes the children. He sends forth his Spirit to accompany the ordinances with power, and thus secures a succession of spiritual men to occupy the places of those who are taken to a higher sphere of existence. The ravages that are daily made in the ranks of the disciples, by the fell destroyer, are thus repaired, and his covenant people preserved from extermination. Till the end of time, there shall be 'daily added to the church such as shall be saved.' 'A seed shall serve him; it shall be accounted to the Lord for a generation. They shall come and shall declare his righteousness unto a people that shall be born.' Families which take great pride in their antiquity, and look back with pleasure on a long unbroken line of ancestry, have their names at length blotted from the earth. Societies which, for a length of time, make a conspicuous figure in the world, fall at last into decay, and finally disappear. Empires which have flourished for ages, and borne sway over a large portion of the earth, are destined to sink into everlasting oblivion. But the church of Christ, notwithstanding the combined assaults of which she is the object, shall continue to flourish and to exist while sun and moon endure; nay, when the sun has been changed into darkness, and the moon into blood. Christians are apt to feel discouraged when they reflect on the extensive prevalence of error compared with the limited success of the true religion, and despondingly to inquire, 'By whom shall Jacob arise? for he is small.' But if they can only have faith in the mediatorial dominion, they may dismiss their fears, and confidently rely in, not merely the preservation, but the triumphant success and universal establishment, of the church. The Lord reigns: and the children of Sion may well be joyful in their King.

What, then, must be the unspeakable happiness of those who are true members of Christ's church;—a society founded, organized, and incorporated by the

Redeemer himself; purchased with his precious blood; possessed of the most interesting properties; subservient to the most important ends; whose ordinances, members, office-bearers, and administration, are all so illustrious; and which is destined to attain to such permanency and extent? The honour and advantage of being connected with such a community cannot be small. It is a lamentable evidence of the extent of human depravity, that these should be appreciated by so few. The church of Christ is even now but a little flock.

In reflecting on the mediatorial dominion over the church and the many things which it involves, one cannot help being struck with the glory which it reflects on the character of the Mediator himself. *Head of the church, King of Sion, and King of saints*, are illustrious titles; they bespeak majesty and splendour; and are well fitted to preclude all unworthy conceptions of him to whom they belong. They are calculated to prevent any false inference being drawn from the more humiliating points of his history. Were we only to look at him lying in the manger of Bethlehem's inn, sitting at the well of Jacob, standing at Pilate's judgment-seat, hanging on the cross, or sleeping a lifeless corpse in Joseph's tomb, we might be induced to regard him as, indeed, a root out of a dry ground. But, when we think of him giving existence to such a society as the church, instituting her ordinances, authorizing and qualifying her ministers, giving efficacy to her laws, and protecting her from destruction; when we think on the wisdom of his government, the bountifulness of his gifts, the resistless energy and gracious influence of his administration, we are filled with high and elevated views of his character. Instead of supposing him to have no form nor comeliness, no beauty for which we should desire him, we feel drawn towards him with the admiration and respect due to one who is crowned with glory and honour.

To interfere, in any degree, with the Redeemer's prerogatives as Head of the church, is conduct the criminality of which cannot well be over-estimated. Such wickedness it might well be supposed none would be found sufficiently abandoned to perpetrate. It is not to be wondered at, therefore, that men should disclaim, in words, all participation in such aggravated guilt. But let us look at the testimony of facts.—In the church of Rome, the Pope claims a universal spiritual power; while professing to act only as the vicegerent of Christ on earth, he blasphemously assumes the title of *head of the church;* and, that it may not be conceived to be an empty title, he sacrilegiously presumes to alter, add to, and dispense with, the ordinances which Christ himself has appointed.— Supremacy over the church is claimed also by the British crown. It is expressly provided for by law, that the imperial power in these realms shall have annexed to it the dignity of supreme head of the church, in virtue of which authority the monarch ' convenes, prorogues, restrains, regulates, and dissolves all ecclesiastical synods and convocations—has the right of nomination to vacant bishoprics and certain other ecclesiastical preferments — and, as head of the church, is the *dernier* resort in all ecclesiastical causes; an appeal lying ultimately to him in chancery from the sentence of every ecclesiastical judge.'[37] Nor is the exercise of this supremacy confined to the Episcopal church of England. It is deserving of consideration whether, by prescribing the form of church government which is established in Scotland; by the right of patronage claimed and exercised by the state in the appointment of ministers; by enjoining the observance of days of fasting and thanksgiving without consultation with the church; and by authoritatively convening and dissolving the supreme court, the state is not guilty of such encroachments on the liberties even of the Scottish church as imply an invasion of the sole headship of the Lord Jesus Christ.

It is truly appalling to think, in how many instances the crown rights and royal prerogatives of Sion's King have been invaded by men, taking upon them to legislate in and for the church; to model her government and worship, in order to meet the ends of a pitiful expediency; to settle articles of faith; and even to brandish the sword of civil power over the heads of such as refused to submit to an arbitrary and unrighteous dictation. Nor is it greatly less grieving to reflect, that so many should tamely submit to these sinful encroachments, and shew so little regard for the honour of the Redeemer, as not to stand up at all hazards for his inalienable rights. The arrogance

---

[37] Black. Com., Book 1, chap. vii. sec. 6.

of these pretensions on the one hand, and the unfaithfulness of such compliance on the other, are alike to be reprobated. With regard to the one and to the other, the friend of the Redeemer may well feel disposed to say, 'Tell it not in Gath;' and be stirred up to use every means in his power to prevent the dear-bought and exclusive rights of Emmanuel from being infringed upon by any power upon earth. And as all such encroachments are as unsafe as they are sinful, such as lift their warning voice against them, and refuse to submit to them, certainly manifest more true regard for the welfare of their fellow-men, as well as more laudable zeal for the glory of their Lord and King, than those who regard them with cowardly silence or spiritless acquiescence.

CHAPTER VIII.

THE MEDIATORIAL DOMINION OVER THE NATIONS.

It was before remarked that under the universal dominion of Messiah are comprehended two grand associations, the peculiar importance of which seemed to render necessary a more full and separate discussion of each. These are, the church and civil society. To the former some attention has been given in the preceding chapter. We now take up the latter.

The matter, here, is the headship of Jesus, as Mediator, over the nations of the world, or the political associations of men. Besides its own intrinsic importance, this branch of our subject demands attention, from the neglect with which it has long been treated, from the opposition it has had to encounter, and from its intimate connexion with questions which are fiercely agitated from time to time.

I. Let us first of all look at the EVIDENCE in support of Christ's right of dominion, as Mediator, over the nations of the earth.

His mediatorial authority over the *church* is readily conceded. Nor is there any hesitation to admit that Christ, *as God,* exercises a sovereign control over the civil affairs of men. But that he does so in his *mediatorial* capacity seems not to approve itself so directly to the minds of many. Yet a candid consideration of the proof which we have it in our power to bring forward, cannot fail, we think, to remove every shadow of doubt on this subject.

Indeed, the point in question might be argued on other than direct Scripture testimony. It might be argued on the ground that Christ's investiture with mediatorial dominion does not suppose the abrogation of his necessary right of dominion as God. As before remarked, in assuming the office of Mediator, he did not divest himself of any thing belonging to him as divine. His moral authority over all creatures being essential to his very existence and character, never was, and never indeed could be, laid aside.—His moral fitness to exercise such dominion, might also be insisted on.— The terms of absolute universality, as formerly shewn, in which the mediatorial dominion is spoken of in the word of God, further imply what we have now in view. For if all things are delivered to him of his Father, if all power is given to him in heaven and in earth, if all things are put under his feet, it is not easy to see on what principle any thing so vast and important as the civil associations of mankind could be excepted.—Nay, the necessity of such an extent of mediatorial power as includes the nations of the world, to his performing with efficiency the functions which belong to him as Head of the church, is enough to set this question for ever at rest. Without such extent of power, he could never open up a way for the diffusion of his gospel among the nations of the earth; could never, either subordinate their administration, or overrule their rebellion, so as to bring about the period when the kingdoms of this world shall become the kingdoms of our Lord and of his Christ. But, without insisting on these points, in regard to which the evidence is of an inferential nature, let us give our attention to the direct proof by which the dominion of Christ as Mediator over the nations is supported. By nations, of course, we mean civil associations; men existing in civil or political institutions; including the office-bearers by whom the laws are administered, as well as the people at large for whose good they are appointed to govern.

First. In looking into the Word of God, we find subjection to Jesus Christ as Mediator directly enjoined upon civil rulers. 'Be wise now, therefore, O ye kings; be instructed, ye judges of the earth. Serve the Lord with fear, and rejoice with trembling. Kiss the Son, lest he be angry, and ye perish from the way, when his wrath is kindled but a little.'[1] The person to whom subjection is here enjoined, is doubtless the Messiah. 'The Son' is a title by which the Redeemer is often designated, both in the Old and New Testaments. If Solomon, the son of David, is referred to at all, it can only be in a very subordinate sense. We are at no loss to shew that a greater than Solomon is here, even He who was at once David's Son and David's Lord,—the Son of David according to the flesh, but the Son of God by a high, necessary, and ineffable relationship. Again and again, throughout the New Testament, do we find

[1] Ps. ii. 10–12.

passages from this psalm referred to Christ.[2] One may here suffice for the establishment of this point. 'And when they heard that, they lifted up their voice to God with one accord, and said, Lord, thou art God which hast made heaven and earth, and the sea, and all that in them is; who, by the mouth of thy servant David, hast said, Why did the heathen rage, and the people imagine vain things? The kings of the earth stood up, and the rulers were gathered together, against the Lord and against his Christ. For of a truth against thy holy child Jesus, whom thou hast anointed, both Herod and Pontius Pilate, with the Gentiles and the people of Israel, were gathered together for to do whatsoever thy hand and thy counsel determined before to be done' (Acts iv. 24-27).

The psalm, then, refers to Christ; but does it refer to him in his mediatorial capacity? There can be as little doubt, we think, on this point, if only the scope of the psalm itself, and the purposes for which it is elsewhere quoted, are considered. The opposition of which it speaks, is opposition made to him as Mediator; as the Lord's Anointed; as He whom the Father hath set King upon his holy hill of Sion; in the same capacity, in short, in which he is to have the heathen given him for his inheritance, and the uttermost parts of the earth for his possession.

And on whom is it that this psalm enjoins subjection to the Mediator-King? On 'kings,' and 'judges;' that is to say, civil rulers, supreme and subordinate. But is it civil rulers in their personal, or in their official,

[2] Acts iv. 25; 'xiii. 33; Heb. i. 5—v. 5; Rev. ii. 27.

capacity? There are some who evade the force of this passage by alleging that it is only in their private character that they are here addressed. But this is contrary alike to the whole scope and design of the psalm, and to the concurrent testimony of the most judicious commentators. Indeed we have only to consider in what capacity it was that the opposition spoken of was offered to the Son by civil rulers. It was in their public character, undoubtedly, that Herod and Pontius Pilate conspired against the holy child Jesus; and we are only acting on the plain principles of fair interpretation, when we conclude that it is in their public and official character also that civil rulers are here commanded to do homage to the Redeemer;—that kings and judges are required as such to serve the Lord with fear, and to kiss the Son lest he be angry.

Nor can there be a doubt that the *duties*, to which the terms in which these injunctions are expressed refer, involve the idea of complete moral subjection,—the subjection that inferiors owe to a superior, that subjects owe to a king. Such is the common meaning of the verb to 'serve,' as well as the sense in which it is often used in Scripture. And one passage will be sufficient to show that to 'kiss' is expressive of loyal subjection to a reigning prince:—'Then Samuel took a vial of oil, and poured it upon his (Saul's) head, and *kissed* him, and said, Is it not because the Lord hath anointed thee to be captain over his inheritance?'[3]

Here, then, we have a most decided, unequivocal proof of the right of dominion over the nations of the

[3] 1 Sam. x. 1.

earth which is possessed by the Mediator; for, had not such been his right, it is inconceivable that the Spirit of God should have enjoined subjection to him upon all civil rulers without exception, whether supreme or subordinate, whether belonging to Old or to New Testament times. We have here a command of universal and permanent obligation; and, while it retains its place in the Word of God, it will be impossible to deny the dominion which Jesus as Mediator possesses over the nations of the earth and their rulers.

Secondly. Predictions respecting the kingdom of the Mediator, conduct us to the same conclusion. Predictions in general unfold the purposes and appointments of God. Whatever, therefore, we find predicted regarding Christ, must be included in the grant of the Father to the Son. Now, dominion over the nations is matter of frequent announcement in prophecy.

The forty-seventh psalm is understood to refer to the Messiah. His exaltation to glory, the gathering of the Gentiles, and the ultimate establishment of his kingdom of righteousness and peace, form the subject of this beautiful ode. The ascension of the Redeemer is plainly referred to in the expression, 'God is gone up with a shout, the Lord with the sound of a trumpet.' Nor can it be doubted, from this circumstance itself, that it is in his official, and not his personal, character that he is spoken of throughout the psalm. Now, mark the expressions which are employed with regard to his dominion. He is described as 'a great king over all the earth;' as He who 'shall subdue the people under us, and the *nations* under our feet;' as He who 'reigneth over the *heathen;*' as He to whom 'the *princes* of the people are gathered together, even the people of the God of Abraham;' as He 'to whom belong the *shields* of the earth.'[4] These are not equivocal expressions. The nations and their princes are distinctly specified as brought under his control, and as doing him homage, which certainly imply a right of dominion over them; while magistrates who are set for the defence of the people, are undoubtedly meant by the shields of the earth, which are said to be his property.

The seventy-second psalm is, by universal consent, referred to Christ. In only a very inferior or subordinate sense can it be understood of Solomon. To whom but David's greater Son can its lofty descriptions be applicable? Of whom but the Messiah can it be affirmed that his name shall endure for ever; that men shall be blessed in him; and that all nations shall call him blessed? We may rest assured that the psalm celebrates the majesty, benignity, and dominion of Jesus as Mediator, with the glory, peacefulness, extent, and duration of his kingdom. Now, observe how many things are contained in it bearing on our present subject. 'The kings of Tarshish and of the Isles shall bring presents: the kings of Sheba and Seba shall offer gifts. Yea all kings shall fall down before him; all nations shall serve him. All nations shall call him blessed.'[5] No language can more directly assert the doctrine for which we are contending. The Mediator, as such, is spoken of. Kings and nations are expressly introduced in their

[4] Ps. xlvii. 2, 3, 8, 9.   [5] Ps. lxxii. 10, 11, 17.

civil capacity as recognising his dominion. And the acts of homage in which they are represented as engaging, are such as necessarily involve the idea of distinct moral subjection;—namely, bringing presents, offering gifts, falling down before him, serving him, and calling him blessed. He who is the legitimate object of such acts must possess a rightful dominion over the nations and kings of the earth.

'Thus saith the Lord God, Behold, I will lift up mine hand to the Gentiles, and set up my standard to the people: and they shall bring thy sons in their arms, and thy daughters shall be carried upon their shoulders. And kings shall be thy nursing-fathers, and their queens thy nursing-mothers: they shall bow down to thee with their face toward the earth, and shall lick up the dust of thy feet.'[6] This is a very decisive passage. The prophecy refers to New Testament times, when the Gentiles are to be gathered unto the Redeemer. A prominent feature of these times shall be the subserviency of civil rulers to the church, which surely supposes their subjection to Christ her Head. *Kings shall be thy nursing-fathers* is a similitude which imports the most tender care, the most endearing solicitude; not mere protection, but active and unwearied nourishment and support. If, according to the opinions of some, the best thing the state can do for the church, is to let her alone, to leave her to herself, to take no interest in her concerns, it is difficult to see how this view can be reconciled with the figure of a nurse, the duties of whose office would certainly be ill discharged

[6] Isa. xlix. 22, 23.

by such a treatment of her feeble charge. But to neutralise the force of this beautiful passage, it has been alleged that rulers are here spoken of, not in their public or official, but in their private or personal, capacity. It is supposed to mean nothing more, than that persons of exalted station shall become the devoted servants of Messiah, and take a deep and pious interest in the concerns of his kingdom. And this view is understood to be confirmed by the pronoun '*their*' occurring before the word 'queens,' denoting, as is alleged, that they are spoken of, not as queens *regnant*, but as queens *consort*. It is, however, far from being self-evident that queens are spoken of here in the latter capacity; for every candid person will admit, that the very same phraseology might as naturally be employed in speaking of queens-regnant in relation to their husbands, as of kings-regnant in relation to their wives. It is, therefore, not by any means clear that queens are here to be understood as consorts only. Nor, even admitting this, will the inference follow from it legitimately, that the kings are to be understood merely in their private domestic capacity as consorts of the queens. When in countries where there is a married king the subjects pray for the blessing of God on their king and *his* queen, as they are in the habit of doing, the queen is of course queen-consort; but it surely cannot be supposed that because his partner can only be viewed as associated with him in her private capacity, they do not refer to the monarch himself in his official capacity. Even admitting, then, for the sake of argument, the interpretation proposed with regard to queens—that they are only referred to as consorts—the inference drawn with regard to kings does not follow. It does not follow that kings are referred to only in their private capacity. The kings may still, after all, be kings-regnant: and the utmost that the passage can be made to bear is, that both kings and queens, whether regnant or consort, are bound to exert all the influence they possess, in their own proper spheres, to aid and foster the interests of Christ's kingdom in the world. Because queens-consort can do this, only in their own proper sphere, it surely does not follow that kings-regnant, in their proper sphere, are not also bound to do the same. On the contrary, the prediction before us leads us to conclude, that, in the times of the gospel, persons of the most exalted public stations shall exert their influence on behalf of the church of Christ; and this certainly supposes the subjection of such to Christ himself.

The same view is strongly corroborated by another passage in this prophecy. 'Therefore thy gates shall be open continually; they shall not be shut day nor night; that men may bring unto thee the forces of the Gentiles, and that their kings may be brought. For the nation and kingdom that will not serve thee shall perish; yea, those nations shall be utterly wasted. Thou shalt also suck the milk of the Gentiles, and shalt suck the breasts of kings.'[7] Here there cannot be the shadow of a doubt about the sense in which kings are spoken of. The pronoun '*their*,' in this instance at least, is decidedly in favour of the view that they are

[7] Isa. lx. 11, 12, 16.

to be regarded in their public capacity; they are spoken of as the people's kings, or kings in the possession and exercise of official power and influence. In this capacity, they are represented as ministers to the church of Christ in various ways. Nor is the passage less decisive, that it comprehends a threat of awful judgment denounced on such nations and rulers as shall refuse to yield the service required. Surely, unless civil society had been placed under the dominion of the Mediator, there could have been no room for supposing, either that such duties are obligatory, or that such consequences shall follow the neglect of them.

'And it shall be the prince's part to give burnt-offerings, and meat-offerings, and drink-offerings, in the feasts, and in the new moons, and in the sabbaths, in all solemnities of the house of Israel.'[8] The remarkable prophetic vision, with which these words are connected, is, we believe, held by all judicious commentators to refer to the church in New Testament times. Without pretending minutely to explain the import of all the figurative allusions, the words we have quoted would seem plainly enough to carry in them the idea, that the civil ruler is to give public support to the institutions of the church of Christ, which, as in the case of the passages above quoted, necessarily implies that magistrates, as such, are under the authority of the Mediator.

'And I saw in the night visions, and, behold, one like the Son of Man came with the clouds of heaven, and came to the Ancient of Days, and they brought him near before him. And there was given him dominion,

[8] Ezek. xlv. 17.

and glory, and a kingdom, that all people, *nations*, and languages should serve him.'[9] The reference of this passage to Christ will not be doubted. The eternal Son of God, viewed with regard to his human nature and mediatorial character, is he who is called 'the Son of Man.' The power spoken of is clearly mediatorial, as it is said to be 'given' him. It is also universal, including 'all nations,' of whom it is predicted that they should 'serve him,' which certainly supposes the possession of rightful authority over them.

'And the seventh angel sounded; and there were great voices in heaven, saying, The kingdoms of this world are become the kingdoms of our Lord and of his Christ.'[10] The phrase, *the kingdoms of this world*, necessarily suggests the idea of social relations and civil rights—all those public interests and immunities, in short, which distinguish a compact civil body from a loose assemblage of private persons living in a disconnected state or individual capacity. All know that such is the idea attached to a *kingdom*. But the kingdoms of this world are to become the kingdoms of Christ. It must, therefore, be, in the same sense in which they are kingdoms in the one case, that they are to become kingdoms in the other. Now it is not the private sentiments or individual conduct of the inhabitants of a land, which gives character to a kingdom of this world, as such; neither are the adoption of Christian principles and practices, by the great bulk of a people, sufficient to constitute the nation a kingdom of Christ. The nations of the world have, in their national

[9] Dan. vii. 13, 14. [10] Rev. xi. 15.

capacity, too plainly acknowledged and served the god of this world. They have also, in too many instances, proclaimed themselves kingdoms of antichrist, giving their power and support directly to the beast, in their public social character. When the happy state of things announced in this prediction shall have been introduced, it is impossible to believe otherwise than that these kingdoms shall, in the same public social capacity, become the kingdoms of Christ. And what does their becoming the kingdoms of Christ import? Certainly, at the very least, that for which we are now contending; namely, that, in token of their subjection to him, they shall recognise his authority, and subordinate their interests to the advancement of his glory.

'And the nations of them which are saved shall walk in the light of it: and the kings of the earth do bring their glory and honour into it. And they shall bring the glory and honour of the nations into it.'[11] It is the church which is here spoken of as receiving the attention in question. Whether in its millennial or celestial state, commentators are not agreed. But whichever of these views is taken, the passage must be understood as describing a course of preparation that takes place on earth, as it is only in this world that national and official distinctions exist. Now, if nations, as such, are to walk in the light of the New Jerusalem, that is to say, are to derive distinguished honour and privileges from the church of Christ, they must surely be regarded as under the dominion of the church's Head. And if kings, as such, are to bring their glory and honour into

[11] Rev. xxi. 24, 26.

it, that is to say, are to subordinate their authority, power, revenues, and whole administration to the interests of Christ's kingdom, they also must be regarded as under the dominion of the Mediator.

Such is the voice of prophecy on this interesting subject. Every unprejudiced mind must admit that it bears decided testimony to the doctrine we are now attempting to establish. Many more passages might have been quoted. Indeed, the whole tenor of Old Testament prediction speaks the same language. No one, therefore, who has any respect for the word of God, can hesitate to admit that Christ possesses mediatorial dominion over the nations of the earth.[12]

Thirdly. Another set of proofs will be found in numerous designations, implying dominion over the nations, which are given to Christ in the Scriptures. Such are the following:—'For the kingdom is the

---

[12] 'God addresses the nations in a collective capacity, reproves them for their idolatry, and calls them to his worship (Isa. xxxiv. 1; xli. 1, 21-29). He proposes Christ, as his anointed servant, to them (chap. xlii. 1); declares that he has given him the nations for his inheritance, and that he shall inherit them all (Ps. ii. 8; lxxxii. 8; Isa. lii. 15; lv. 5). Christ addresses himself, not only to individuals, but to whole islands (Isa. xliv. 1); nations join themselves to him (Isa. ii. 2; Micah iv. 1, 2; Zech. ii. 11; viii. 20-22), bless themselves, and glory in him (Jer. iv. 2); all nations and dominions serve him (Dan. vii. 14, 27). They consecrate all things in them, and employ them in his service (Isa. lx. 6-12; Zech. xiv. 20, 21); he owns these nations as his, and blesses them, while he breaks in pieces and wastes others (Ps. xxxiii. 12; cxlv. 15; Isa. xix. 25; Ps. ii. 9, 12; Isa. lx. 12). The force of the argument arising from these and similar predictions, is such that Mr. Edward Williams, although an independent, acknowledges that they imply a national profession and establishment of Christianity. In answer to the objection, "If the above prophecies refer to *national conversions*, does not that lead to *national churches?*" he replies, "That a national establishment, if WELL ORDERED, appears more agreeable to the prophetic passages we have been considering than the antipædobaptist plan; nay, more agreeable to the general tenor of revelation."'—*M'Crie.*

Lord's, and he is GOVERNOR AMONG THE NATIONS.'[13] That the psalm in which this occurs refers to Christ, we need not wait to prove; and that it refers to him as Mediator, is evinced by the whole tenor of the composition itself. His being called in the verse *Lord* or *Jehovah*, is not inconsistent with this view, as the same high appellation is applied to him in other parts of Scripture. It cannot be doubted that the preceding verse foretells the extension of the church of Christ. 'All the ends of the world shall remember and turn unto the Lord; and all the kindreds of the nations shall worship before thee.' What immediately follows being introduced as accounting for the universal spread of the kingdom of Messiah, it must be considered as referring to the same illustrious personage. 'For the kingdom is the Lord's; and he is the governor among the nations.' Here, then, is a glorious title, distinctly recognising the dominion of the Mediator over the nations of men—a title which the nations may, indeed, overlook, but which they cannot disregard with impunity, and which shall one day be as fully acknowledged by them as it has been hitherto shamefully neglected and despised.

The eighty-ninth psalm refers to Messiah. He is the chosen of the Father, with whom he has made a covenant, whose seed he will establish for ever, and whose throne he will build up to all generations. Now, mark what he says of him in the course of this psalm:—'I will make him my first-born, HIGHER THAN THE KINGS OF THE EARTH.'[14] Here is another glorious title. His being to be *made* what the title imports, determines in

[13] Ps. xxii. 28.   [14] Ps. lxxxix. 27.

what character it belongs to him. It must be as Mediator that the Son of God is here described as *'made* higher than the kings of the earth.' In the sense of natural superiority he *is* 'higher,' and needs not to be *made:* in the sense of official supremacy only, then, can this phrase be understood. Besides, the words might have been rendered *most high* or *supreme over the kings of the earth.* The very same term is often used to express the supremacy of God, and is translated 'Most High.' The dominion of Messiah over civil rulers on the one hand, and the subjection of such to him on the other, are thus clearly imported in this title.

In the prophecy of Jeremiah, there occurs the following passage: 'Forasmuch as there is none like unto thee, O Lord; thou art great, and thy name is great in might. Who would not fear thee, O KING OF NATIONS?'[15] *Nations* here mean organised civil bodies. *King* is a title of office, expressive of supreme rule or government. He to whom this title belongs is the true and living God, the God of Israel as distinguished from heathen idols. But as the God of Israel is God in Christ, the title may be regarded as equally applicable to the Redeemer.

Should any hesitate, however, to admit this inference, the excuse for doing so cannot be urged in respect to the next proof we have to adduce. The exile of Patmos, while introducing his apocalyptic vision under the influence of the Spirit, speaks of Jesus Christ as 'THE PRINCE OF THE KINGS OF THE EARTH.'[16] The whole context, not to speak of the very verse in which the title occurs, determines the reference to the mediatorial character

[15] Jer. x. 6, 7.   [16] Rev. i. 5.

of our Redeemer,—that character, namely, in which he bore faithful witness as a prophet, rose from the dead, and washed us from our sins in his blood. There is no room to doubt for a moment that it is Christ as Mediator who is spoken of as ὁ ἀρχων των βασιλεων της γης. The persons who are here supposed to be subject to Christ, are kings, civil rulers, supreme and subordinate, all in civil authority, whether in the legislative, judicial, or executive branches of government. Of such Jesus Christ is Prince;—ὁ ἀρχων, ruler, lord, chief, the first in power, authority, and dominion.

The most splendid title of all remains to be noticed. It occurs twice in the Revelation of John. 'These shall make war with the Lamb, and the Lamb shall overcome them: for he is LORD OF LORDS, AND KING OF KINGS.' 'His name is called the Word of God—and he hath on his vesture and on his thigh a name written, KING OF KINGS, AND LORD OF LORDS'[17]—Κυριος κυριων και Βασιλευς βασιλεων. The whole book of Revelation relates to Christ as Mediator. The sublime predictions, in which this resplendent title is ascribed to him, treat of the last struggle betwixt Christ and his enemies, in which these enemies are to be finally subdued, and their opposition to him to be buried in oblivion. He, by whom the victory is to be secured, is the same who is spoken of, in the forty-fifth psalm, as 'girding his sword upon his thigh, and in his majesty riding prosperously, because of truth and meekness and righteousness!' and, in the prophecy of Isaiah, as 'coming up with dyed garments from Bozrah, red in his apparel, and his garments like

[17] Rev. xvii. 14; xix. 16.

him that treadeth in the wine fat.' It is 'the Faithful and True, who in righteousness doth judge and make war.' He is represented as Head of the Church, sitting on 'a white horse;' while, as Head over all things to the Church, he is described as 'having on his head many crowns, as clothed with a vesture dipped in blood, as smiting the nations with a sharp sword, ruling them with a rod of iron, treading the wine-press of the fierceness and wrath of Almighty God, and having on his vesture and on his thigh the name written King of kings and Lord of lords.' There is nothing equivocal here. The Mediator is exhibited as waging war with the kings of the earth, who oppose his reign: and his right so to do is plainly involved in the title conspicuously inscribed on his vestment—a title not more fraught with terror to those who oppose his dominion, than confirmatory of his official supremacy over civil rulers of every description.

The proof of the mediatorial dominion over the nations, derived from these sources—from commands, predictions, and designations—is so abundant, varied, direct, complete, that we cannot but express our surprise the doctrine in question should ever have been denied or overlooked. After what has been said, there may be few who will venture formally to impugn this precious truth; but it cannot escape observation, that there are many, very many, who are in the habit of constantly neglecting it. This is the case to a mournful extent, not only with the nations and their rulers, whom it greatly concerns to recognise and act upon it; but with private Christians, who profess to be concerned for the mediatorial honours of their Redeemer. That it should be so, is much to be deplored, and is, to a considerable extent, unaccountable. How dishonouring to Christ thus to attempt to tear from his head the crown of the nations! And how blind, even to their own true interests, are those who thus provoke the Lord to anger, and expose themselves to the withering frown of his sovereign displeasure!

To the doctrine thus established, no solid objection can be made. Standing as it does on such a basis of Scripture evidence, it bids defiance to every argument which prejudice, or self-interest, or perverted reason can muster against it. It has been violently assailed in some quarters, notwithstanding. The grounds on which this opposition has proceeded have, for the most part, been already overturned.

It has been supposed, for example, to exclude Jehovah, essentially considered, from the government of the nations. This objection is just a branch of the common objection which is brought against the mediatorial dominion altogether, and which has already been sufficiently answered. We repeat, that delegation does not involve the surrender of power; and Messiah's dominion over the nations being of a delegated character, it does not at all follow that when the Father committed this power to the Son he parted with it himself. Indeed, it is with the mediatorial power over the nations as it is with that over the Church; and as the latter certainly does not interfere with the essential dominion of God, no more does the former.

Equally vain is it to object that the doctrine in question is at variance with the opinion that civil society originates with God as the God of nature. True, civil society is founded in nature, and not in grace: but its subjection to Christ is not the least inconsistent with this. The objection will be found to carry farther than, perhaps, its friends were aware of; for, if everything that springs from the law of nature is to be excluded from the dominion of the Mediator, many things must be excepted which they have been accustomed to admit as under that dominion. Marriage originates in a law of nature: does it follow that parties united in this relation are to have no regard to the authority and honour of the Redeemer, that they are not to be guided by his law, or to act under the influence of his grace? 'Let him that marrieth, marry only *in the Lord.*'—The domestic relation has its foundation in the law of nature: are parents and children, masters and servants, at liberty to regard themselves as not under subjection to the Redeemer? What, then, are we to make of those commands which require parents to 'bring up their children in the nurture and admonition of *the Lord;*' children to 'obey their parents *in the Lord;*' and servants to be obedient to them that are their masters '*as unto Christ*'? Nay, are there not even some prominent parts of religion, such as prayer and praise, which have their foundation in nature, and in which we are certainly not at liberty, much less bound, to have no respect to Christ as Mediator? On the same principle, then, it by no means follows, because nations originate in nature, which we freely admit that they do, that they are not placed under

Christ: or, in other words, it is no objection to the dominion of Christ over the nations, that civil society springs from God as the God of nature.

But the most specious objection, perhaps, is derived from what is matter of fact. The nations do not acknowledge Christ. They are, many of them at least, in a state of open rebellion against him. Not a few of them hath given their power to the Beast,—to the avowed enemy of the Messiah. 'The kings of the earth set themselves, and the rulers take counsel together against the Lord and against his Anointed, saying, Let us break their bands asunder and cast away their cords from us.' But, as before remarked, right and acknowledgment are different things; and the former is not dependent on the latter. On the one hand, an unlawful usurper may be acknowledged, but this can never confer on him the right to rule. On the other hand, acknowledgment may be refused to one whose right of dominion rests on the most solid foundation. It is easy to see that if acknowledgment were necessary to establish right, neither the Messiah's dominion over the *Church*, nor Jehovah's moral government of *the world*, could be established, as there are many, who not only refuse to recognise, but pointedly dispute, both the one and the other. Because, 'we see not yet all things put under him,' as respects active moral subjection, we are not to consider the statement as invalidated, that the Father 'hath put all things in subjection under his feet,' as respects his right of sovereignty.

II. The fact, of the mediatorial rule over the nations having been considered, we proceed to the ACTS of Christ's regal administration towards this class of his subjects.

First. Although civil society originates with God as the God of nature, nations may be said, in a certain sense, to derive even their existence from Christ. The origin of civil society and political government has given rise to much speculation. Whether they originate with God or with man, and in what sense they can be said to originate with either or with both, are topics that admit of extensive discussion, but into which we do not feel ourselves called at present to enter. The Scriptures, it may be remarked, represent civil government as at once an ordinance of *God* and an ordinance of man.[18] In as far as it is the right of the people to fix the constitution, to elect the rulers, and to revise and amend the system under which they live, civil government may be regarded as an ordinance of *man*. But it is not to be inferred from this, that it depends solely on the will of man whether civil institution should be set up in a country at all, that civil society originates wholly in voluntary compact, or that whatever is sanctioned by the public will is necessarily right, and consequently obligatory. The most frightful results would follow from admitting such an absolute sovereignty of the people as this. There are too many instances on record, of the great body of the people having gone egregiously astray, ever to permit us to give our unqualified assent to such a principle. Indeed, it is manifestly absurd,

[18] Rom. xiii. 2; 1 Pet. ii 13.

to suppose that the majority of a nation should be free from the moral control of the law and authority of God, in the formation of their civil institutions. This were to ascribe to an aggregate body, composed of moral subjects who are individually responsible, a proud, irreligious, irresponsible independence of the will of the great moral Governor himself;—a supposition so monstrous that, however much overlooked in practice, every one must shrink from it in theory. It is admitted that God has invested the people with power in political matters, and that the people of course have a right to the exercise of this power; but it is at the same time to be attentively observed that *he has given them a law* by which they are to be regulated in the use of this power, and it is only when they act according to the law given them that their determinations and institutions possess the sanction and obligation of righteousness.

Civil government can be the ordinance of *man* in no sense that is inconsistent with its being strictly and properly the ordinance of *God*. Now, it is not merely in regard to his overruling providence that it is the ordinance of God. In this respect, indeed, 'the Most High ruleth in the kingdom of men, and giveth it to whomsoever he will, and setteth up over it the basest of men: he removeth kings and setteth up kings' (Dan. iv. 17). But, in this sense, the grossest tyranny and misrule might also be regarded as the ordinance of God. Civil government originates with him *morally* not less than *providentially*. It is the *moral ordinance* of God. It is a *divine institution*. The principles, by which its formation and management are to be regulated, are laid down in the Bible. Lawful magistrates, whether supreme or subordinate, are consequently 'the ministers of God;' not the mere creatures and servants of men, but the authorised vicegerents of heaven.

Nor, in saying that the nations derive their existence from Christ, do we say anything at variance with what has just been laid down. This is perfectly consistent with maintaining, as we do, that civil government proceeds from God, not as the God of grace, but as the God of nature. We admit that it springs from him as the supreme moral Governor of the universe, having its foundation in natural principles which belong to the constitution of man. National society, political government, magistratical authority, all originate in the moral government of God as the God of nature, and not in the mediatorial system. These might all have existed, had there never been a mediatorial economy; nay, they do often exist where the economy of grace is quite unknown. We are anxious not to be misunderstood on this point.

At the same time, it must not be forgotten that, as we have already shewn, God has placed the affairs of the moral universe in the hands of his Son as Mediator. The dispensations of providence in general are put under his feet; in consequence of which, such dispensations as give rise to the existence of nations, or regulate their political aspects and interests, may be viewed as managed and directed by him. And not only so; but civil government, as a moral ordinance of God, is put under the Redeemer's feet;

and, in as far also as this is the case, may not nations be regarded as deriving their being from Christ? It is not enough to say that nations owe their existence to God. This is true: but it is not the whole truth. They originate in the will, authority, and appointment of the Messiah. We find it, indeed, said, 'There is no power but of God: the powers that be are ordained of God;' but we also find issuing from the Mediator this proclamation, 'By ME kings reign, and princes decree justice: by ME princes rule, and nobles, even all the judges of the earth.' [19]

Nations are thus invested with a high and noble character. They are the moral subjects of the Redeemer. Their rulers are not the mere servants of men, the creatures of popular choice, but the ministers of God, the moral deputies of heaven, the servants, the representatives, the vicegerents of the Prince of the kings of the earth. This gives them a peculiar elevation and dignity; throws around them a moral grandeur; lays them under obligations to attend to moral qualifications and conduct; and entitles them to be treated by the people with esteem, veneration, and honour.

Secondly. Messiah watches over and directs all occurrences connected with nations. National concerns are numerous and diversified. The origin of national associations, whether it be warlike aggression, internal revolution, arbitrary usurpation, or voluntary compact, involves a vast variety of interest and events. So also the progress of nations, whether this is con-

[19] Prov. viii. 15, 16.

nected with the management of internal and foreign relations, the counsels of statesmen, the conduct of generals, or the prowess of armies. Nor is it less so with the circumstances which occasion the dissolution of states. Yet these, in all their aspects and bearings, are ordered and controlled by the Mediator. They form prominent parts of that universal providence which, as before shewn, is placed under Messiah. The wheels of providence, in all their intricacy, are propelled by the God-man, Mediator. And, as for that department of providential arrangements which respects nations, the control of Messiah is fully illustrated and confirmed in the Apocalypse. The events unfolded in this book have respect to the nations of the earth in general, and more especially to such as are connected with the Roman empire, the fourth great monarchy, in whose decline and fall are involved the interests of the principal European powers. But these events are represented as developed by the Lion of the tribe of Judah, the root of David, the divine Mediator, who opens the sealed book of God's purposes respecting the nations, blows the trumpets of divine warning, and pours forth the vials of Jehovah's wrath;—thus carrying forward the scheme of predetermined decrees, till Babylon the great is overthrown, till all thrones of iniquity are overturned in its downfall, and the kingdoms of this world become the kingdoms of our Lord and his Christ.

Thirdly. Jesus, as king of nations, exacts obedience to his commands. The moral law and all the precepts of Scripture are administered by Christ. Communities, as well as individuals, are under the divine law. Such commands, therefore, as are found in the Word of God, applicable to nations and their rulers, are to be regarded as issuing from the divine Mediator, who is invested with all possible sovereignty and power;—with not merely physical control, but moral dominion. It follows that wherever we find nations commanded to serve the Lord, and civil rulers required to promote the public good—to restrain evil—to administer the laws with equity, impartiality, and benevolence—to set a good example in intelligence, morality, and religion—and to give countenance, protection, and aid to the Church, we are to recognise the authority of the Redeemer. The duties of subjects are, perhaps, more frequently inculcated in Scripture than those of rulers; yet are not either the qualifications or the duties of rulers entirely overlooked. And if rulers are, as we have shewn, under moral subjection to Messiah, in those passages of Scripture which prescribe their qualifications and duties they are addressed by the Redeemer. Such are the following:—'Hear the causes between your brethren, and judge righteously between every man and his brother, and the stranger that is with him. Ye shall not respect persons in judgment: but ye shall hear the small as well as the great; ye shall not be afraid of the face of man: for the judgment is God's. Judges and officers shalt thou make thee in all thy gates, and they shall judge the people with just judgment. He that ruleth over men must be just, ruling in the fear of God. Be wise now, O ye kings: be instructed, ye judges of the earth. Serve the Lord with fear. How long will ye judge unjustly, and accept the persons of the wicked? Defend the poor and fatherless: do justice to the afflicted and needy. Deliver the poor and needy: rid them out of the hand of the wicked. For rulers are not a terror to good works, but to the evil. He is the minister of God to thee for good. He beareth not the sword in vain: for he is the minister of God, a revenger to execute wrath upon him that doeth evil.'[20] These and similar precepts and prescriptions, if all power is given to Christ, must be regarded as emanating from the mediatorial throne, and as enforced by the gracious but sovereign authority of the Redeemer. It follows that national communities and civil office-bearers, who disregard or neglect them, are guilty, not only of a contravention of the people's rights, but of rebellion against Jesus, the King of nations.

Fourthly. And here we have another act of Christ's regal administration, for this rebellion he overrules for good. The nations ofttimes refuse to serve him. 'The kings of the earth have set themselves, and the rulers take counsel together, against the Lord and against his Anointed, saying, Let us break their bands asunder, and cast away their cords from us.' Jeroboam, the son of Nebat, is not the only king who has made his people to sin; Herod and Pontius Pilate are not the only rulers who have 'of a truth conspired' against Jesus of Nazareth. National honour and personal aggrandisement are more commonly the objects they pursue than the glory of God, the honour of Christ, or the good of his

---

[20] Deut. i. 16, 17; xvi. 18; 2 Sam. xxiii. 3; Ps. ii. 10, 11; lxxxii. 2-4; Rom. xiii. 3, 4.

people. His prescribed qualifications are not seldom contemptuously disregarded, and his commands trampled under foot. The power with which they are invested is too often employed to persecute and oppress his Church, and to support his enemies. 'The ten horns which thou sawest are ten kings. These have one mind, and shall give their power and strength unto the beast.'[21] But all this is overruled for the accomplishment of ultimate good by the Divine Mediator. He makes the wrath of man to praise him. The nations and their rulers may refuse to serve him, but they cannot prevent him from serving himself by them. By their counsels and treaties, their ambitious wars and lawless' transactions, he fulfils his own sovereign purposes. Their conspiracy against his rights he causes to issue in the development of the weight of his arm; their persecution of his Church, in her purification; and the countenance they afford to his enemies, in the chastisement and overthrow of his impenitent foes. The Assyrian is the rod of his anger; and when he meaneth not so, neither doth his heart think so, Christ executes by him his own righteous decrees. But for this comforting assurance, what friend of the Redeemer could look abroad, without the most gloomy forebodings, on the tyranny, oppression, blasphemy, and iniquity of every sort and degree, which are practised among the nations of the world, under the convenient cloak of civil power. 'The Lord, Jehovah-Jesus, reigneth. He rules in the midst of his enemies. Therefore will not we fear, though the earth be removed, and though the mountains be

---

[21] Rev. xvii. 12, 13.

cast into the midst of the sea : though the waters thereof roar and be troubled, though the mountains shake with the swelling thereof.'

Fifthly. Christ, as Mediator, executes the righteous judgments of God on wicked nations and rulers. 'The Father judgeth no man, but hath committed all judgment to the Son. The Father hath given him authority to execute judgment also, because he is the Son of man.' The treasures of wrath, as well as those of grace, are at his disposal. We read not only of 'the wrath of *God*,' but of 'the wrath of the *Lamb*.' Nor is it merely the solemnities of the final judgment that are administered by him, but those judicial dispensations which are unfolded in the providential occurrences of the present state. Among these, the judgments inflicted on civil communities stand conspicuous. The moral character of nations, and the moral responsibility of rulers, shew the possibility of national and official sins. By cherishing a spirit of pride, self-confidence, and independence of God; by practising tyranny, cruelty, and oppression; by indulging a perverse, ungrateful, and turbulent temper; by prostituting their power and influence to the encouragement and support of irreligion, blasphemy, and immorality; or by employing the sceptre and the sword in hostile opposition to the tenets and institutions of true religion; —civil communities may be guilty of such heinous iniquity as to call forth the retributive judgments of God. National crime, when carried to a height, operates as a conductor to draw down the lightning of vengeance from the eternal throne. And what we here wish to be remarked is, that it is the province of the King of nations to execute these judgments. He is the mediatorial Angel, described in the Apocalypse, as 'taking the censer, and filling it with fire of the altar, and casting it upon the earth,' causing 'voices, and thunderings, and lightnings, and an earthquake.'[22] These judgments, whether they consist in a dark and confounding infatuation, seizing hold of the thoughts and counsels of men in power; or in a sudden paralysing of the hearts of the people, by which they are disarmed of all their wonted fortitude, and reduced to a state of the most cowardly and effeminate timidity; or in the pressure and succession of those fearful calamities which induce ignominy, disorganisation, and ruin; or in those terrible things in righteousness, by which the Almighty speaks to the guilty and makes bare his holy arm against the workers of iniquity:— whether they be brought about by the whirlwind of war, by the blast of famine, by the withering breath of pestilence, or by the earthquake of popular commotion:—in whatsoever they consist, by what means soever they are effected, they are the doings of Him who is Governor among the nations. In general, we are assured, with regard to rebellious princes, that 'He shall speak to them in wrath, and vex them in his sore displeasure; shall break them with a rod of iron, and shall dash them in pieces like a potter's vessel.' 'The Lord shall strike through kings in the day of his wrath; he shall fill the places with dead bodies; he shall wound the heads over many countries.'[23] 'The

---

[22] Rev. viii. 5.   [23] Ps. ii. 5; cx. 5, 6.

nation and kingdom that will not serve thee shall perish; yea, those nations shall be utterly wasted.' By whom this sentence is carried into execution, we are not left to conjecture. 'Who is this that cometh from Edom, with dyed garments from Bozrah? this that is glorious in his apparel, travelling in the greatness of his strength? I that speak in righteousness, *mighty to save.* Wherefore art thou red in thine apparel, and thy garments like him that treadeth in the wine-fat? I have trodden the wine-press alone; and of the people there was none with me: for I will tread them in mine anger, and trample them in my fury; and their blood shall be sprinkled upon my garments, and I will stain all my raiment. For the day of vengeance is in mine heart, and the year of my redeemed is come.'[24] Here we have the almighty Saviour executing the most awful judgments on his enemies. With regard, in particular, to those great empires, prefigured in Nebuchadnezzar's image, the Chaldean, the Medo-Persian, the Grecian, and the Roman, we know that it is the kingdom of the Messiah, under the government, of course, of its glorious Head and Prince, that 'shall break in pieces and consume all these kingdoms.'[25] While, with respect to the judgments already executed, or yet to be executed, on the kingdoms of the Roman empire, the nations of the Latin earth, we find them directly and unequivocally ascribed to the same source. 'He that overcometh,' saith the Son of God, 'and keepeth my words unto the end, to him will I give power over the *nations* (and he shall rule them with

[24] Is. lx. 12; lxiii. 1-4.   [25] Dan. ii. 44.

a rod of iron, as the vessels of a potter shall they be broken to shivers), even as I received of my Father. The kings of the earth hid themselves from the wrath of the *Lamb*. And out of his mouth goeth a sharp two-edged sword, that with it he should smite the *nations:* and he shall rule them with a rod of iron; and he treadeth the wine-press of the fierceness and wrath of Almighty God.'[26] We are thus bound to believe that those occurrences by which guilty nations are scourged and chastised for their sins, are not merely brought about in providence, but ordered and directed by the Mediator. And whether, therefore, we behold the desolating sword cutting off the inhabitants, or the blasting mildew destroying the crops, or commercial stagnation obstructing the sources of wealth, or wasting disease stalking with ghastly power over a land, or the upheavings of popular commotion overturning the foundations of social order, we recognise the wisdom, and might, and righteous retribution of Prince Messiah, carrying into execution the divine decree, *The nation and kingdom that will not serve thee shall perish: yea, those nations shall be utterly wasted.*

Sixthly. The Prince of the kings of the earth opens up a way for the universal dissemination and success of his Gospel among the nations. The religion of the Cross is to be universally diffused. This supposes that the ministers of Christ are to circulate throughout the nations, making overtures of reconciliation to their inhabitants, and urging upon them the claims of their divine Sovereign. 'Go ye and teach *all nations*, baptiz-

[26] Rev. ii. 26, 27; vi. 15, 16; xix. 15.

ing them,' &c., is the command of the Redeemer to his ministering servants. But it is only in virtue of his sovereignty over the nations, that he could issue such a mandate: and in this way only could those invested with his commission be warranted to demand admission for themselves and reception for their message by the nations of the earth. When the ambassadors of Jesus visit foreign lands to disseminate the knowledge of the Gospel, however exclusive the laws and strict the prohibitions of these lands against foreign intrusion, they are not to be regarded as lawless aggressors. Jealous potentates may refuse to acknowledge the King in whose name they come; the subservient functionaries of these potentates may use all means to shut them out from their dominions: but they have a right to enter, and as faithful and authorised ambassadors, have a right to negotiate with the inhabitants of all lands in behalf of their Sovereign Lord. It may be their duty to use caution, and exercise prudence, in introducing themselves into heathen kingdoms; but still they are to regard themselves as fully entitled to be heard, in the name of him by whom they are sent. The sovereignty of their Lord spares them the moral degradation of feeling that they are doing what is illegal,—that they are violating the principles of international law,—that they are acting the part of contraband traders. What they are doing may be unauthorised by man, may be contrary even to the will and command of the rulers of those regions of the earth into which they have gone: but they proceed in the name of One whose authority extends over all nations, who claims all the kings of the earth as his subjects, and whose commands cannot, without rebellion, be disputed. *He* has said to them, 'Go and teach all nations:' and, when the jealousy of heathen princes interferes to impede them in the execution of this commission, by arresting them on the confines of their territory, and commanding them to 'depart from their coasts,' they are entitled to refuse, and to plead as an excuse for so doing the obligation to obey God rather than man. Without the supremacy of Christ over the nations, however, the missionaries of the Cross could have no right thus to penetrate into all lands;—the apostolic commission could not, indeed, be lawfully executed. In consequence of this supremacy, however, they may circumnavigate the globe, may touch at every island that studs the ocean, may make a descent on every coast, may pass every boundary, may knock at the gates of every palace, may address every crowned head, may pervade the length and breadth of every kingdom, and ask admission, in name of the King of kings, for themselves and for their message.

Nor is the right of his ambassadors to proceed, the only thing that is secured by the Messiah's headship over the nations. Provision is thus made for the opening up of a way, for the success of their cause, and the protection of their persons. There may be much in the prejudices, the opinions, the habits, and the manners of the inhabitants, much in their legal institutions and superstitious rites, to present barriers to the introduction of the pure and self-denying religion of Jesus: but, notwithstanding all, the Prince of the kings of the earth can open a way for his own cause in the midst of all obstructions. Nothing can baffle his counsel; nothing withstand his might. Difficulties disappear at his approach: before him mountains become a plain. 'He hath the key of David; he openeth, and no man shutteth; and shutteth, and no man openeth. Behold,' says he, 'I have set before thee an open door, and no man can shut it.'[27] Yes; the herald of salvation in foreign lands may have numerous discouragements, and may often find reason to say with the great apostle of the Gentiles, 'there are many adversaries;' but, believing in the dominion of Christ over the nations, he need not despair of being enabled to add, 'a great door and effectual is opened unto me.'[28]

Seventhly. It is thus easy to see how the mediatorial dominion over the nations is connected with the gathering of a Church, and the setting up of a spiritual kingdom in the midst of them. The preservation of this Church, the protection of this kingdom, is another purpose for which Christ wields the mediatorial sceptre. There is much, very much, in the nature and spirit of the civil institutions set up among men, which tends to endanger the Redeemer's covenant-society. The indifference with which her interests are regarded, and the seductive attempts made to induce her to barter away her spiritual liberties, and to permit herself to be degraded into a political engine, not to speak of the positive hostility with which she may be directly assailed, are evils against which she requires to be guarded, and into which, if left to herself, she would be sure to fall a prey. There is much, in the doctrines and precepts of

[27] Rev. iii. 7, 8. [28] 1 Cor. xvi. 9.

the Christian religion, that is opposed to the immoral principles and practices, patronised and acted upon by the nations of the world in general; so that she could not continue to exist among them uncorrupted and independent, unless protected by One who can control, modify, and overrule all their counsels and doings. Without this, the Church would not long be tolerated pure and unfettered; but would either be crushed beneath the iron rod of despotic power, or be extirpated by the flames of persecution. To her blessed and glorious King, who is Governor among the nations, is she indebted for so overruling the hearts and conduct of men in power, as to throw around her a shield of safety. Considering the dangers of the Church, and the character of the nations, we could have no hope of her continuing to subsist, were it not for the feature of mediatorial dominion now under review.

Eighthly. It only here remains to notice, that, in this capacity, the Mediator will ultimately bring about an entire change in the character and constitution of the nations of the world. To the fulfilment of Scripture prophecy, such a change is indispensable. At present, the nations are all, more or less, in a state of hostility to the Redeemer; either sunk in criminal apathy, or extensively pervaded with pagan and anti-christian leaven. A numerous and influential class have given their power and strength to the Beast. The authority and law of the Redeemer are not regarded; his glory is not contemplated; the true interests of his Church are opposed or forgotten. It will be otherwise, however, in the end. When 'kings shall be nursing fathers and their queens nursing mothers' to the Church ; when 'the Zion of the Holy One of Israel shall suck the breasts of kings ;' when 'the kingdoms of this world shall become the kingdoms of our Lord and of his Christ ; ' the nations of this earth will assume an aspect very different from the present. The basis of their organisation will then be the Word of God, and the aim of their administration, the glory of Christ: their officers shall be peace and their exactors righteousness ; and the spirit which shall pervade all their actions, shall be the pure spirit of the Gospel. But by whom is this change to be effected ? How is this marvellous revolution to be brought about ? By the overruling providence and gracious energy of Him who is Governor among the nations. He will shake all nations with the thunder of his power, till everything connected with them that is opposed to his cause is overthrown, and they are led to hail himself 'as the Desire of all nations.' He will purge out the leaven of infidelity and antichristianism with searching scrutiny, and liberally infuse the opposite principles till they leaven the whole lump. He will overturn, overturn, overturn, till he come whose right it is ; and he will give it him. The secular tyrannies of the Latin Earth shall be broken to pieces, shall become like the chaff of the summer thrashing floor, and be carried away by the wind till no place be found for them ; and the kingdoms that shall succeed will be actuated with the spirit of that kingdom which is represented by the stone cut out without hands, which is to become a great mountain and fill the whole earth. Thus to purify, sanctify, revolutionise, nay, Christianise, the nations of the world, is what none but he could perform ; and were it not that he is Head of the nations, as well as Head of the Church, we should have to despair of these glorious anticipations being ever realised.

III. If it is admitted that the Messiah is invested with dominion over the nations, towards which, in consequence of such investment, he performs the acts of administration, of which we have been speaking, it follows as a natural and unavoidable inference, that there are DUTIES which the nations owe to the Mediator.

If the Mediator is the King of nations, nations are the subjects of the Mediator, and all the duties which subjects owe to their prince must be due by them to him. It is vain to plead exemption from moral responsibility for bodies politic, or civil office-bearers, as such. Associations, composed of such as are individually, morally responsible, must be morally responsible collectively. An aggregate of moral subjects must itself possess a moral character. Every society of moral beings is itself a moral being or subject. That a nation is not a responsible moral subject, is a sentiment monstrously inconsistent in itself, and fraught with consequences of the most hideous description. By means of its laws and its rulers, a nation is capable of putting forth acts as strictly of a moral character as those of any individual. This view of the matter is not more consonant with sound reason than with Scripture : for we there read, in express terms, of 'an ungodly nation ; ' 'an hypocritical nation ;' 'a rebellious nation.'[29] The same principle is admitted

[29] Ps. xliii. 1 ; Isa. x. 6 ; Ezek. ii. 3.

in the common language of mankind. We are accustomed every day to speak of national virtue, national honour, national faith, national sin;—phraseology which distinctly recognises the moral character and obligation of nations, as such. Nor is at all difficult to conceive, how every precept of the decalogue may be as expressly kept or violated by a body politic as by a private individual. Such being the case, we can be at no loss to perceive, either that nations are under moral obligations to Christ, or what are the specific duties they owe to him.

First. It is the duty of nations and their rulers, to have respect to the glory of Christ in all their institutions and transactions. No principle can less admit of dispute than that it is the duty of subjects to honour their king: and if Christ is King of nations and magistrates subjects of the Messiah, they must be held bound, in virtue of their relative characters, to pay all possible respect to his honour and glory. The spirit of the divine command—'Honour the king,' carries in it thus much. Indeed, from the relation in which we all stand to God, we are bound to have respect to his honour in everything as the grand end of our being. ' Whether ye eat or drink, or whatsoever ye do, do all to the glory of God.' On the same principle, kingdoms and civil rulers, from the relation in which they stand to the Redeemer, are bound to subordinate all that belongs to them to *his* honour. It is not enough that they have respect to the public good, to the promotion of social order and happiness among men; such is, doubtless, the grand immediate end they are to contemplate; but, as moral and responsible subjects, they are, in seeking this end, to look higher, and to have an ultimate regard to the honour of him to whom they owe their being, preservation, and powers. Like all other moral creatures, they are to have respect to the highest possible end in all that they do; and certainly no end can they ever propose to themselves, at all so dignified and illustrious as the display of the glorious excellency of the Prince of the kings of the earth, who possesses undisputed sovereignty over all. This object, therefore, they are bound to keep distinctly before them, in the formation of their constitution; in the establishment of their various institutions; in the shaping of their policy, whether domestic or foreign; in the selection and appointment of their functionaries, whether supreme or subordinate; in their legislative enactments; and in all their separate acts of administration. Not an establishment are they at liberty to set up; not a law are they entitled to pass; not a step are they free to take; not an alliance are they permitted to form, without having supreme regard to this high and glorious end. Hostility, or even indifference, to this, partakes of the very essence of rebellion against their sovereign Lord. The true feeling of loyal subjection to a lawful prince, requires more than a mere selfish regard to the subject's own immediate interests. A devoted regard to the prince's honour, and a willingness to maintain his dignity against every infringement, enter essentially into the nature of loyalty. For disregard of this, Nebuchadnezzar of old was subjected to the fearful punishment by which he was driven from among men, and had his dwelling with the beasts of the field, until seven times passed over him.

'The king spake and said, Is not this great Babylon that I have built for the house of the kingdom, by the might of my power and for the honour of my majesty? While the word was in the king's mouth, there fell a voice from heaven, saying, O king Nebuchadnezzar, to thee it is spoken, Thy kingdom is departed from thee; and they shall make thee to eat grass as oxen, until *thou know that the Most High ruleth in the kingdom of men, and giveth it to whomsoever he will*' (Dan. iv. 32). And what was the crime for which the impious Belshazzar had the ominous sentence so miraculously inscribed against him? 'Thou hast praised the gods of silver and gold, of brass, iron, wood, and stone, which see not, nor hear, nor know; and the God in whose hand thy breath is, and whose are all thy ways, *hast thou not glorified*' (Dan. v. 23). These are cases which it well becomes civil communities and their office-bearers deeply to ponder, as not only involving by implication the duty of nations to consult the glory of the Messiah in all things, but as holding out a solemn warning of the danger to which the neglect or violation of this duty necessarily exposes. And, oh! when we reflect, how little reason we have to suppose, that, in the great majority of national concerns and transactions, this end is at all regarded by civil communities, we may well tremble at the fearful retribution that awaits them, if they repent not. How few, alas! of those who conduct public affairs in the political world, give evidence of being actuated by the high motive in question. A patriotic regard to the good of the community, is the highest object to which, in general, any ever pretend to have respect; and there is reason to fear that not seldom they come far short even of this: while a regard for the glory of the Mediatorial king is neither thought of nor professed.

Secondly. It is the duty of nations, as the subjects of Christ, to take his law as their rule. They are apt to think it enough that they take, as their standard of legislation and administration, human reason, natural conscience, public opinion, or political expediency. None of these, however, nor indeed all of them together, can supply a sufficient guide in affairs of state. Of course, heathen nations, who are not in possession of the revealed will of God, must be regulated by the law of nature: but this is no good reason why those who have a revelation of the divine will should be restricted to the use of a more imperfect rule. It is absurd to contend that, because civil society is founded in nature, men are to be guided, in directing its affairs and consulting its interests, solely by the light of nature. Might not the same be said with as much propriety, of many other relations of human life, such as parents and children, husbands and wives, masters and servants,— the duties of which we never think of exempting from the control of a preternatural revelation? Nay, might it not, with equal propriety, be maintained, as was formerly hinted, that as certain religious duties, such as prayer and praise, are founded in nature, we are in the performance of them to have no respect either to the authority or directions of the Holy Scriptures? The truth is, that revelation is given to man to supply the imperfections of the law of nature; and to restrict ourselves to the latter, and renounce the former, in any case in which it is competent to guide us, is at once to condemn God's gift and to defeat the end for which it was given. We contend, then, that the Bible is to be our rule, not only in matters of a purely religious nature, in matters connected with conscience and the worship of God, but in matters of a civil or political nature. To say that in such matters we have nothing to do with the Bible, is to maintain what is manifestly untenable. To require nations, who possess the sacred volume, to confine themselves, in their political affairs, to the dim light of nature, is not more absurd than it would be to require men, when the sun is in the heavens, to shut out its full blaze and go about their ordinary duties by the feeble rays of a taper. Indeed, if nations are moral subjects, they are bound to regulate their conduct by whatever laws their moral Governor has been pleased to give them; and as they are the subjects of the Mediator, they must be under the law of the Mediator as contained in the scriptures. He has not placed his moral subjects in ignorance of his will, nor left them to search for it amid the obscurities and imperfections of a law which sin has effaced and well nigh obliterated. In the Holy Scriptures of truth, he has given them a fairer and more complete exhibition of the principles of immutable and eternal justice, than that which is to be found in the law of nature.

We have only to look into the volume of revelation itself, to have these reasonings confirmed. The people of Israel were instructed to regulate their national concerns by a revealed standard, and were taught to regard the possession of God's revealed statutes and judgments as a national distinction for which they were bound to be grateful. Nor is there anything said, which would warrant us to conclude that this was to be regarded as peculiar to that people. 'Behold,' says Moses, 'I have taught you statutes and judgments, even as the Lord my God commanded me, that ye should do so in the land whither ye go to possess it: keep therefore and do them; for this is your wisdom and your understanding in the sight of the nations. And what nation is so great that hath statutes and judgments so righteous as all this law which I set before you this day?'[30] In strict conformity with this, the chief magistrate was to have a copy of the law, according to which he should act in the discharge of his official duties. 'And it shall be, when he sitteth upon the throne of his kingdom, that he shall write him a copy of this law in a book out of that which is before the priests the Levites. And it shall be with him, and he shall read therein all the days of his life, that he may learn to fear the Lord his God, to keep all the words of this law, and these statutes, to do them: that his heart be not lifted up above his brethren, and that he turn not aside from the commandment, to the right hand or to the left: to the end that he may prolong his days in his kingdom, he and his children in the midst of Israel.'[31] The same principle is illustrated in the instructions given to the rulers, judges and kings of Israel. To Joshua it was said, 'This book of the law shall not depart out of thy mouth; but thou shalt meditate therein day and night, that thou mayest

[30] Deut. iv. 5, 6, 8. [31] Deut. xvii. 18-20.

observe to do according to all that is written therein: for then thou shalt make thy way prosperous, and then thou shalt have good success.'[32] When the days of David drew nigh that he should die, he charged Solomon, his successor on the throne, thus: 'Be thou strong and shew thyself a man; and keep the charge of the Lord thy God, to walk in his ways, to keep his statutes, and his commandments, and his judgments, and his testimonies, as it is written in the law of Moses, that thou mayest prosper in all that thou doest, and whithersoever thou turnest thyself.'[33]

We wait not to quote those passages, in which nations and their rulers are encouraged to obey the law of God by the promise of suitable rewards; are cautioned against disobedience by appropriate threats; and are spoken of as actually punished for their transgression of this rule. What has been already adduced is sufficient to shew that the Jews, at least, were bound to regulate their national concerns by the revealed will of Jehovah: and the inference from this is neither obscure nor illegitimate, that nations, like them in possession of revealed truth, are still bound to take it as their supreme rule, standard, and guide, in all their civil affairs. Neither do we wait to inquire what parts of the judicial law given to the Jews, are binding upon Christian states. We build at present upon the broad and undeniable *fact* that nations as such, and civil magistrates in their official capacity, when the matter of revelation was less extensive than it is now, were bound to make it their rule of duty; and from this we deduce the natural and reasonable inference,

[32] Josh. i. 8.   [33] 1 Kings ii. 1-3.

that civil communities blessed by God with the perfect revelation of his will, are under obligation, at all times, to shape and model their political conduct by the dictates of this infallible standard. The principle on which they were at any time bound to do so being a moral principle, they must be held bound to do the same at all times: what is moral is neither of local nor of temporary obligation. If nations are not bound by the Word of God, they are not responsible or punishable for acting contrary to it, but may, at pleasure, revel with impunity in the violation of every branch of revealed truth;—a degree of licentious indulgence which, however agreeable to the taste of the infidel, cannot fail to shock the mind of every Christian.

When we look into the New Testament, we find even in it many things respecting the nature, origin, and ends of civil government; the qualifications, duties, and claims of civil rulers; and the obligations of subjects towards magistrates, both supreme and subordinate. For what purpose, we ask, are these placed in the sacred volume? Surely not to be overlooked, but to be read, pondered and obeyed. They are certainly designed to be of use; but this they cannot be, if nations as such, and men in their civil capacity, are not under their authority as parts of revealed truth. When, therefore, we find civil rulers, king and judges, commanded to *be wise* and to *be instructed*, must we not understand them as required to go to the Bible for the instruction they need, and to extract from this sacred repository their lessons of political wisdom? It thus appears satisfactorily established, that nations are under the obligation of the revealed will of Christ in general, and bound to regulate their transactions by it, in as far as it contains what is applicable to such, whether in the form of principle, precept, or example.

And if this is the case with regard to revelation as a whole, it will not be denied to be so with regard to the moral law in particular. Nations, as such, are under the obligation of the moral law; they are bound to regulate their affairs by the principles and precepts of the decalogue. Every precept of that law they are bound to obey. It is, we are aware, maintained that only the precepts of the second table are obligatory on civil communities. As an individual standing in a particular relation and circumstances is not under obligation to obey those parts of revelation which have respect to persons placed in other relations and circumstances, so it is contended that nations are only under the obligation of such parts of the moral law as can be shewn to apply to them. We frankly admit the fairness of this reasoning. But then we are prepared to maintain that every part of the moral law is applicable to nations. If nations in their national capacity, and magistrates in their official character, are admitted to be moral subjects, it will not be easy to shew that they are exempt from the obligation of any part of the moral law. If it could be shewn that there are some requirements in that law which nations are incompetent to fulfil, it would follow, of course, that from these they are exempted. If, however, it can be shewn that nations are capable of obeying every precept—those of the first as well as those of the second table—it will be difficult to persuade an unprejudiced mind that they are free from the obligation of any one of them. With regard to the second table, there is, of course, no dispute; yet the last precept of this department reaches farther than many of those who contend against all national religion can consistently go; it respects the state of the heart. But it may easily be shewn, that nations are as capable of obeying the precepts of the first as those of the second table. How is it, we ask, that nations can obey even the fifth, sixth, seventh, eighth, and ninth commandments, but just by passing laws obliging men to perform their respective relative duties; by protecting the life and property of individuals; by discouraging licentiousness; and by promoting truth between man and man, by the sanctity of an oath? And may they not, in like manner, manifest their obedience to the first, second, third, and fourth precepts, by embodying into their constitution an acknowledgment of the being and character of the one living and true God; by providing for the ordinances of divine worship being maintained and observed in the land; by enacting laws calculated to restrain all blasphemous abuse of God's sacred name; and by making provision for the sanctification of the Sabbath? And if nations are thus capable of obeying the whole moral law, who will contend that they are not under obligation so to do? We allow that the Scriptures of truth are necessary to guide them in yielding this obedience: but is not this true of the one table as much as of the other? The kingdoms of the world require, indeed, much direction from the Word of God, in performing the solemn and delicate duties obligatory upon them by the first table of the moral law: but do they require no such direction with regard to those of the second? They do. The law of marriage belongs to the fifth precept; but how, without having recourse to other portions of the Scriptures, can any Christian nation legislate against polygamy? The law of murder is founded on the sixth; and how, without betaking to some other part of revealed truth, can it be shewn that the murderer should be punished with death? It thus appears that nations, as such, are bound to recognise the obligation of the Word of God as a whole; to make it their rule in all their transactions, and their standard of appeal in all circumstances; and, in this way, to shew their dutiful subjection to that divine Mediator, who is at once the author of revelation, and the Governor among the nations.

Thirdly. It is a duty which nations owe to Messiah the Prince, to have respect to moral and religious qualifications in those whom they appoint over them. We wait not to agitate the question of the people's right to elect their own office-bearers. Whatever diversity of opinion may prevail regarding the first magistrate, there is now no dispute, at least in these lands, with regard to the right of election in the legislative and executive departments of government. The general practice of the nations unites with Scripture and common sense in support of a representative system of government. Rulers as the representatives of the people are understood to be elected by and responsible to the people, according to the constitution and laws of the land. Even under the Old Testament dispensation, when kings were designated to office by immediate revelation, the consent of the people was deemed indispensable to their lawful authority; and they were liable to removal from office, by the people, for abuse of their trust. With regard to subordinate office-bearers, also, such directions were given as clearly imply that the right of election belonged to the community. 'Take ye wise men, and understanding, and known among your tribes, and I will make them rulers over you. When thou art come into the land which the Lord thy God giveth thee, and shalt possess it, and shalt dwell therein, and shalt say, I will set a king over me, like as all the nations that are about me; thou shalt in any wise set him over thee, whom the Lord thy God shall choose; one from among thy brethren shalt thou set king over thee; thou mayest not set a stranger over thee, which is not thy brother.' [34]

But is it to be supposed that the people, who are invested with the right of election, are left without all control in the exercise of this right; that they are at liberty, acting from mere prejudice, self-interest, or caprice, to choose whom they will; and that the objects of their choice are forthwith, in consequence of being so chosen, invested with lawful and indisputable authority? So far from this being the case, the people are bound to use their elective power discreetly and wisely; they are under obligation to fix upon men possessed of qualifications fitting them for office; nor are they themselves

[34] Deut. i. 13; xvii. 14, 15.

constituted the sole judges of what these qualifications may be. God has given them in his Word a supreme rule of direction, in which the character of civil rulers is described, and only such as seem to them to be possessed of this character are they at liberty to appoint. If the people were under no restriction of this nature, it is fearful to think of the consequences that would ensue. As the power of the magistrate is not an absolute power which he is at liberty to employ as he chooses, so neither is the right of the elector an absolute right which he is at liberty to exercise as he chooses. Both the one and the other are placed under the limiting control of the Divine Law; and it is only when they are used according to this law that they are used aright.

It is not every individual who is qualified to hold office in a nation. Good natural talents, a cultivated mind, and a due share of acquaintance with the principles of government and with the constitution and laws of the country, seem indispensable. Scripture, not less than common sense, discountenances the practice of setting persons of feeble intellect to bear rule. 'Wo unto thee, O land, when thy king is a *child!* Thou shalt provide out of all the people *able* men. Take ye *wise* men and *understanding*, and I will make them rulers over you.'[35]—Not less essential are *moral* qualifications. High and incorruptible integrity, well regulated mercy, strict veracity, and exemplary temperance, are all specified with approbation in the Word of God. 'Moreover, thou shalt provide out of all the people men of *truth*, hating *covetousness*. He that ruleth over men

[35] Eccl. x. 16; Exod. xviii. 21; Deut. i. 13.

must be *just*. *Mercy* and truth preserve the king, and his throne is upholden by *mercy*. If a ruler hearken to *lies*, all his servants are wicked. It is not for kings, O Lemuel, it is not for kings to drink wine, nor for princes strong drink; lest they drink and forget the law, and pervert the judgment of any of the afflicted.'[36]—Nay, more than this, *religious* qualifications are required in the Scriptures. A profession of religion would seem to be implied in the canon: 'One *from among thy brethren* shalt thou set over thee; thou mayest not set a *stranger* over thee, who is not thy brother.'[37] But true religion in the soul is also specified. 'Thou shalt provide out of all the people such as *fear God*. He that ruleth over men must be just, ruling in the *fear of God*.'[38] It is needless to say, that the fear of God is spoken of in Scripture as the very essence and sum of true piety. 'The fear of the Lord, that is wisdom. Fear God and keep his commandments, for this is the whole duty of man. I will put my fear in their hearts, and they shall not depart from me.'

Thus it appears that three distinct classes of qualifications are necessary in civil rulers:—natural, moral, and religious. They are required to be men of good abilities, of unimpeachable character, and of sound piety. Weak and ignorant men; drunkards, libertines, sabbath-breakers, profane swearers; papists, socinians, infidels, are, accordingly, disqualified for exercising government in a country which is blessed with the volume of revelation. Such the people are not at liberty to appoint to

---

[36] Exod. xviii. 21; 2 Sam. xxiii. 3; Prov. xx. 28, xxxi. 4, 5.
[37] Deut. xvii. 15.   [38] Exod. xviii. 21; 2 Sam. xxiii. 3.

places of power and trust. As regards the two former classes of qualifications, namely, such as are natural and moral, this statement will not perhaps be disputed by many who will demur to it as regards the third, that is, religious qualifications. The Word of God, however, is as explicit on this point as on the others: and if it is asked, 'Of what use is religion to a civil ruler?' it might be deemed enough, in reply, to refer the objector to the Bible, where such qualifications are expressly required. But no one who candidly reflects that civil magistrates are denominated 'ministers of God;' that they are required to administer oaths; that they exert a mighty influence by their example; and that decided personal piety adds greatly to the lustre and power even of natural and moral qualities; can be at a loss to perceive the importance of religion to one who is invested with civil power.

It will be allowed then that the nations owe it, as a duty to Messiah their Prince, to appoint over them rulers possessed of such qualifications as his Word prescribes. What these qualifications are we have already seen. And it requires but a slight glance at the state of things, even among those nations which are in possession of the inspired volume, to perceive how utterly and how extensively this duty is disregarded. It is a too common maxim with many in our day, that magistrates as such have nothing to do with religion,—nothing to do with it, it would seem, not only as an object of legislation, but even as a qualification for office. How often does it happen that men of *any* religion, or of *no* religion at all, are unblushingly preferred to those who have justly acquired a reputation for godliness? How dishonouring to Christ thus to set up, as his ministers, his open and avowed enemies —men who deny his divinity, who blaspheme his name, who deride his worship, and who openly profane his sacred day! Such conduct is attempted to be justified on a principle which is alike pernicious and fallacious, namely, that we have nothing to do with the private character of public men. Away with the treacherous maxim.

> 'For when was public virtue to be found
> Where private was not? Can he love the whole
> Who loves no part? he be a nation's friend
> Who is in truth the friend of no man there?
> Can he be strenuous in his country's cause,
> Who slights the charities for whose dear sake
> That country, if at all, must be beloved?'*

Apart from the divinely authorised maxim, that 'the wicked walk on every side when the vilest men are exalted,'—a maxim which all history illustrates,—if rulers are required, as we have shewn, to respect the glory of Christ, and to take his law as their rule, it is impossible that their moral and religious qualifications can be a matter of indifference, for without such qualifications, they cannot perform any one of these duties. However the force of circumstances, and the overruling providence of God may compel men of no private worth to devise and execute measures of public utility, there can be no security for either the existence or efficient execution of such measures, when the public offices are filled with worthless men. And, even if there were, this would not prove it to be the duty of Christians to

* *The Task*, v. 502-508.

confer the highest honours of state on persons of this description, and that, too, in preference to men of distinguished private worth. How differently did the patriotic Nehemiah feel and act in this matter. 'I gave,' says he, 'Hananiah, ruler of the palace, charge over Jerusalem; *for he was a faithful man and feared God above many.*'[39] The senseless outcry of *measures not men*, may serve the purpose of the slavish adherents of a profligate ministry, but it is a maxim that is essentially base, unmanly, irrational, and unchristian. It overlooks the necessary connexion subsisting betwixt cause and effect; it pours contempt on those parts of revelation in which the qualifications of rulers are prescribed; and it manifests an utter disregard of the honour and glory of the Saviour. The maxim *measures not men*, is not more deserving of respect than its converse, *men not measures*. Indeed, if we were under an absolute necessity of choosing either the one or the other, we should not hesitate to prefer the latter, there being, in our opinion, a much greater likelihood of good men correcting the evils of bad measures, than of good measures restraining the evils of bad men. But there is no need for adopting either. With the Bible in our hands, we are entitled to insist on both. *Measures* AND *men*, or rather *men* AND *measures*, is the maxim on which Christian nations should proceed. And every people, duly alive to their obligations, by making it an unalterable and fundamental law that they shall set over them only 'able men, such as fear God, men of truth, hating covetousness, a terror to evil-doers and a

[39] Neh. vii. 2.

praise to them that do well,' will take care so to frame their constitution and regulate their practice, that the openly vicious and ungodly shall not have it in their power to thrust themselves into the sanctuaries of law and justice.

Nor is it only to the qualifications of the rulers whom they choose, that, out of respect to the will and glory of Christ, men are bound to attend, but also to their own qualifications as electors. This point is too apt to be forgotten. It is, however, one of great importance. Where the elective franchise is liberally enjoyed, everything may be said to depend upon the manner in which it is exercised. Electors, who are themselves irreligious and immoral, are not likely to set a high value on the existence of proper qualifications in those whom they choose to represent them. To such, the absence of these qualities is apt rather to prove a recommendation. But the choice of a representative, it should be borne in mind, is a civil right, the exercise of which involves, to a great extent, the welfare of the nation. It is not the individual himself alone that suffers from an improper use of this privilege, but the community at large. It is, consequently, of immense moment, that he exercise it, not from passion, fancy, or prejudice, but under the guidance of sound Christian principle. He is bound to subject his judgment and inclinations in this matter to the control of God's Word. Hence the vast importance of having the public mind deeply imbued with pure moral sentiments, and correct religious principles. Never should the professing Christian suffer himself to forget that he is bound to act in character at all times. Never can the circumstance occur which will warrant him to say, Now I may drop the Christian and act the civilian or the man. It is not in matters of an ecclesiastical nature merely that he is to act as a Christian. He must conduct himself as a Christian at all times; when acting as a member of the state, not less than as a member of the church; in the workshop, as well as in the sanctuary; at the hustings, as well as at the table of the Lord.

Fourthly. The nations ought to have respect to Christ, in their subjection to those who rule over them by his authority. Scripturally-qualified and lawfully constituted magistrates are entitled to conscientious submission. Whatever are the specific duties to which such are entitled, whether respect, or tribute, or prayer, the duties are to be performed, not from slavish dread or selfish motives, but from respect to the authority and honour of the Redeemer. The law of Christ, on this point, is very fully and explicitly laid down in an oft-quoted but ill-understood part of New Testament Scripture. 'Let every soul be subject unto the higher powers. For there is no power but of God : the powers that be are ordained of God. Whosoever, therefore, resisteth the power, resisteth the ordinance of God : and they that resist shall receive to themselves damnation. For rulers are not a terror to good works, but to the evil. Wilt thou, then, not be afraid of the power? Do that which is good, and thou shalt have praise of the same : for he is the minister of God to thee for good. But if thou do that which is evil, be afraid; for he beareth not the sword in vain: for he is the minister of God, a revenger to execute wrath upon him that doeth evil. Wherefore ye must needs be subject, *not only for wrath, but also for conscience' sake*. For, *for this cause*, pay ye tribute also: for they are God's ministers, attending continually upon this very thing. Render, therefore, to all their dues; tribute to whom tribute is due; custom to whom custom; fear to whom fear; honour to whom honour.'[40] We say nothing at present of the character of the powers to which subjection is here enjoined. The nature of the subjection is that to which we would first call attention. It is conscientious subjection that is spoken of; free, willing, hearty; not forced or constrained. It is such as supposes the lawfulness of the authorities to which it is paid, and such as recognises the will of him by whom they act. It is to proceed from respect to the authority enjoining obedience, and not from a mere dread of the consequences of disobedience. In this way are the inhabitants of the nations bound to yield to their rulers;—'*fear*,' not a slavish involuntary dread, but an affectionate, respectful, and confident veneration;—'*well-doing*,' in the diligent performance of the duties of their station, and constant fulfilment of the laws;—'*tribute*,' the pecuniary support which is requisite for internal improvements, national defences, and the maintenance of such functionaries as devote their whole time to the public good, and which is to be paid cheerfully, not merely as a return for

[40] Rom. xiii. 1-7.

privileges enjoyed, but as a mark of submission to, and approbation of, God's ordinance;—'*custom*,' that particular form of taxation which falls not directly on persons or landed property, but on goods imported or exported;—and '*honour*,' in the use of respectful language and demeanour, avoiding, on the one hand, all scurrilous vilification, and, on the other, all idolatrous adulation, of men in power. These duties are to be performed from a principle of conscience; and the refusal to perform them is denounced and threatened with danger. 'Whosoever resisteth the power, resisteth the ordinance of God; and they that resist, shall receive to themselves damnation.' The resistance of lawful authority is thus stigmatised as rebellion against God, and, according to the views formerly laid down, must be regarded as peculiarly offensive to the Messiah.

It is obvious, however, that it cannot be to every power, without exception, that subjection, under these lawful sanctions, is inculcated. Such a supposition is anything but honouring to Christ. Some, indeed, have maintained this, and, the better to support their views, have regarded the apostle, in the above passage, as having immediate respect to the then existing government. This opinion they found on the words, 'The powers that *be*,' 'There *is* no power.' But they overlook the circumstance that similar phraseology is employed, in laying down general principles applicable to every age. For example:—'There *is* no man that hath left house, &c., but he shall receive an hundredfold.' Here the phrase is the same as when it is said, in the passage in question, 'There *is* no power but of

God:' and if the latter is restricted to the then existing authorities, ought not the former to be explained as applying exclusively to the men of the then existing generation? Again, we read:—'There *be* just men to whom it happeneth according to the work of the wicked;' where the mode of expression is the same as in the phrase, 'The powers that *be:*' yet who ever thought of regarding the sentiment expressed in this passage as peculiar to the time when Solomon wrote? Besides the laws of impartial criticism require us to explain the character of the powers spoken of by the context, where they are described as 'not a terror to good works, but to evil—ministers of God for good—bearing not the sword in vain—revengers to execute wrath upon him that doeth evil.' It is only necessary to compare, or rather contrast, these expressions with the character of the then existing powers, to be convinced that the whole passage is descriptive of the duties of Christians, towards, not any magistrates who may happen to be possessed of power, but such as are what they ought to be. Nero, who at that time wore the purple, was in every respect the opposite of what is here described. He was one of the most wicked monsters that ever occupied a throne;—a terror, not to evil works, but to good;—bearing the sword in opposition to everything that deserved protection and support;—and executing wrath only on such as did good and shunned evil. *Do that which is good, and thou shalt have praise of the same.* Let Nero be tried by this test.* The

---

* The author has made a reference to Birk's *Christian State* in support of his argument. The following are some of the sentences:—

'It is objected that the words of St. Paul apply immediately to the

primitive Christians, who lived during his reign, it will be allowed, did that which was good. They professed and maintained the religion of the cross; they worshipped and served the Saviour of the world; they waited on the ordinances of religion with exemplary diligence; they faithfully discharged the relative duties of life, and conducted themselves in an orderly and inoffensive manner as members of civil society. And what was the 'praise' they received in return? Why, they were charged with every crime: were treated with every indignity; were tortured by every infernal device; were crucified, and their bodies either thrown to the dogs, or converted into torches with which to illuminate the capital! So far from the apostle's language referring to the existing governors, then, it is more natural to regard it as framed on purpose to reprove them, by presenting a striking contrast. Indeed, it would be difficult to conceive a more cutting sarcasm on Nero and his associates in power, than is here furnished. None but the most blinded devotee to the exploded doctrine of passive obedience and non-resistance, would ever think of interpreting this passage of the then existing government. Nor is it easy to conceive a greater insult that could be

Emperor Nero, of whom it is unutterably absurd to suppose that the Apostle meant to invest him with any authority in religion. Hence the application, which is untrue in this case, must be untrue in every other, and no reference to religious authority can possibly be designed.

'This objection would be forcible and conclusive if the Apostle were merely asserting a fact; but if he is defining the real duty of the ruler, which is evidently the case, it becomes quite powerless. Viewed in the former light, the words would scarcely be true, even when limited to secular affairs; for Nero was often a terror to good works, and sometimes more than to evil. St. Paul is clearly stating the true *design* of God's ordinance.' Pp. 288, 289. Edition of 1847.

offered to the Holy One of Israel, by whom kings reign, than to represent such a monster as Nero as 'the minister of God for good,' or his government as 'the ordinance of God' which could not be resisted on pain of damnation.

Without confounding all moral distinctions, it is impossible to suppose that the lawfulness of a power depends solely on the fact of its existence. The distinction betwixt a preceptive and a providential power, is not more consonant with reason and common sense than with Scripture. And if it is a breach of the obligation due to the Messiah, to set up, as his representatives and vicegerents, persons devoid of every requisite qualification for office, equally at variance with the duty we owe to him must it be to honour and acknowledge such persons when set up. Those to whom conscientious submission is due in the name of Christ, should certainly possess some measure of the qualifications which Christ himself has prescribed. It is absurd to suppose that nations, who are the moral subjects of the Redeemer, are bound, in obedience to his authority, to recognise and approve of, as his ministers, those who overlook and despise his authority, who employ their influence in opposition to his interests, and conduct their government on principles that are immoral. It is, doubtless, the duty of Christians living under a government of this description, to submit to it; but they are to submit to it as a chastisement sent them by God, and to conform, for the sake of peace, to the general order of society; while they take care, at the same time, to bear a full and honest testimony against its evils, and to avoid whatever is calculated to involve them in a participation of its guilt.

Under immoral systems of government it is, happily, possible for Christians to do many things, in compliance with the principles of social order, and for the good of the commonwealth, as well as of individuals, without giving the sanction of their approbation to such systems as the ordinance of God. These things may be done, from regard to their own intrinsic obligation, as things moral in themselves and required by God. There is an obvious distinction betwixt doing *what* is enjoined, and doing the same thing *because* it is enjoined. Lawful authority is for the most part, though not always, to be obeyed; unlawful authority, never. Lawful authority may be employed to enjoin what is not lawful; and in this case it is not to be obeyed. Unlawful authority may be employed to enjoin what is lawful; and, in this case also, it is not to be obeyed. What, it may be said, not to be obeyed even when requiring what is right! Certainly not. The thing enjoined is to be done; not, however, *because* enjoined, but from respect to its own intrinsic obligation springing from the law and will of God. A wicked neighbour, usurping an authority which does not belong to him, intrudes into my dwelling and *commands* me to worship God, to love my wife, and to bring up my children in the fear of the Lord. These are lawful commands; and it is at my peril that I neglect them; but in doing them I am not, surely, obeying the intruder. This distinction, betwixt obedience to lawful commands out of respect to the authority enjoining them, and obedience to them out of respect to their own intrinsic obligation, is a most important one, in a practical point of view. It enables Christians, living under iniquitous and anti-christian powers, to do much that is calculated to promote the good of the community, and their own civil interests, without giving the sanction of their approbation to those who renounce the authority and disregard the law of Christ, and thus violating their oath of allegiance to the Prince of the kings of the earth.

Fifthly. Nations, as the moral subjects of Messiah the Prince, are under obligation to recognise his rightful authority over them, by swearing allegiance to him. It is the duty of a subject to swear allegiance to his lawful sovereign; at least he must stand prepared to do so when required. So is it with nations. Not only are the inhabitants of a nation, as occasion calls for it, to enter into sacred confederation with one another in order to secure and defend their valued rights and privileges, but the nation, as such, through the medium of its authorised functionaries and by its usual forms of legal enactment, ought publicly to avow its attachment to the Lord Jesus Christ as its King and Prince, to recognise his legal authority, and to bind itself to his service by an oath. It is not supposed that the formal act of swearing allegiance is to be gone into lightly, or on all occasions. But, certainly, in times of deep distress, as a means of animation and comfort; in times of backsliding and danger, for the purpose of promoting stability; as calculated to promote and maintain steps of reformation; and also as a fit mode of expressing gratitude for public blessings, a nation may warrantably and dutifully engage in such an exercise. The example of the nation of Israel, of old, might be easily adduced in circumstances such as these.[41] From time to time, that people publicly and solemnly recognised their allegiance to the Lord their Redeemer.

The transaction at Sinai partook distinctly of a federal character. The children of Israel were then put in possession of a complete body of laws, for the regulation of their national concerns. Stipulations and restipulations were mutually passed. On the one hand, the Messiah, amid a display of awful majesty, offered them a civil constitution and moral organisation. On the other, by the repeated declaration, 'All that the Lord hath said, we will do,' the people formally accepted the gracious offer, promised obedience to it, and solemnly avowed their allegiance to him by whom it was given. Possessing the nature, this transaction received the name, of a *covenant*. From the gracious covenant relation in which the people of Israel stood to God, it is plain that, in this whole transaction, they had to do with the Son of God as Mediator. In no other character, could any of the guilty race of man receive blessings from him, or promise him obedience. Nor was there anything in the circumstances of that people which rendered the duty in question peculiar to them. What was adapted to promote national prosperity in their case, is calculated to do the same in all cases. It is more reasonable to regard their political

---

[41] The reader may consult at his leisure the following passages :—Neh. ix. 1-13. ; Deut. xxix. 10-15 ; Josh. xxiv. 25 ; 2 Kings xi. 17, 20 ; Ps. lxxvi. 11 ; 2 Kings xxiii. 1-3 ; Isa. xliv. 3-5.

R

organisation as a *model* to future nations, than as an *exception* from all others. The faculties, powers, passions, rights, and interests, of men are the same at all times; nor is there anything either local or restricted in those commands by which ancient Israel were enjoined to enter into covenant with God. Indeed, when we look into the predictions which refer to New Testament times, we are at no loss to perceive that the duty of national vowing to the Lord is not limited to the Jews. 'In that day shall five cities in the land of Egypt speak the language of Canaan, and swear to the Lord of hosts. The Egyptians shall know the Lord in that day, and shall do sacrifice and oblation; yea, they shall vow a vow unto the Lord, and shall perform it.'[42] Here it is distinctly made known that, in the days of the Gospel, Gentile countries should copy the example of ancient Canaan, in the matter of vowing allegiance to the Lord. To the same effect we read :—' Thou shalt no more be termed Forsaken; neither shall thy land any more be termed Desolate: but thou shalt be called Hephzi-bah, and thy land Beulah: for the Lord delighteth in thee, and thy land shall be married.'[43] A *land* is just a people in their civil capacity: and its being 'married to the Lord' surely denotes its being bound to him by covenant engagement, as the wife is to her husband.

The principle has been exemplified in more modern times, in France, Germany, Switzerland, and the Netherlands, as well as in our own country. The National Covenant of Scotland, and the Solemn League entered

[42] Isa. xix. 18, 20.   [43] Isa. lxii. 4.

into by Scotland, England, and Ireland, are memorable instances of national oaths of allegiance to the Messiah. These were sworn and approved by the king and his household, and by persons of all ranks in the land. This is not the place to defend the nature of these noble instruments, to shew their obligation on posterity, or to speak at large of the guilt these nations have incurred by their perfidious neglect of them. These are topics, indeed, of no mean importance in themselves, besides being worthy of very serious consideration at the present time, in connection with existing agitations and discussions. But we have to do with them now only as accredited and interesting exemplifications of the national duty of swearing allegiance to the Redeemer. It has been much the practice of a flippant generation to laugh at 'the Covenant' and 'the Solemn League,' as the products and signs of an illiberal and unenlightened age; but it may fairly be questioned, on the authority of the best historians, whether our country ever appeared in a more dignified attitude than during the period in question, or whether a kingdom can ever be more dutifully or appropriately employed than in solemnly and sincerely vowing to him, by whom kings reign and princes decree justice, the Prince of the kings of the earth.

There is still another duty of nations to the Redeemer, to which, from its importance, we shall devote a separate chapter.

It is impossible, in the meantime,* to review what

---

* The remainder of this chapter was added by the author in the second edition.

we have written on the Mediatorial dominion over the nations, without reflecting that this department of the Redeemer's administration and glory has not met with sufficient attention. Its importance it is impossible to deny. Yet it is lamentable to think how inadequately it has been appreciated. By some it is almost entirely overlooked and treated with neglect. By others it is denied and speculatively opposed. It is easier to account for, than to vindicate or excuse, such conduct. What friend of Messiah the Prince but must lament, deeply lament, such a state of things? Oh, that men would throw aside their prejudices, and not suffering themselves to be warped by their supposed temporal interests, would come forward and at all hazards acknowledge the Redeemer as 'Governor among the nations!'

The doctrine in question is entitled to occupy a prominent place in the contending of the witnesses; it forms a chief part of the word of Christ's patience, for which his disciples are to lift up a clear and manly testimony before an ungodly world and rebellious nations. Instead of being passed over altogether, or thrown into obscurity, or treated with a mere passive assent, it ought to stand conspicuously out in the Church's creed, to be frequently brought forward by her ministers, and clearly unfolded in all its grand associations, in all its practical bearings, and in all the fulness of its consoling power. It should be held up to the nations of the earth to reprove them for their past rebellion, and to admonish them regarding their future procedure. It should be urged upon them, as calculated to remind them of the high and sacred duties they owe to the Messiah, of their obligations to respect his glory, to take his law as their rule, to have regard to his authority in the choice of their office-bearers; and in the subjection they yield to them, to swear allegiance to his crown, and to extend countenance and support to his Church upon earth. Nor should it be omitted to remind them of the divine displeasure they incur, and the judicial visitations to which they expose themselves, by pursuing, as too many of them do, a course of unhallowed rebellion against the King of kings.

CHAPTER IX.

MEDIATORIAL DOMINION OVER THE NATIONS, CONTINUED.

Sixthly. It is the duty of nations, as such, to have respect to religion.

This is a point which, from its intimate connection with the Mediatorial dominion, its vast importance in itself, and its being a subject on which the public sentiment at the present time is greatly divided, demands particular consideration.

That civil government has anything to do with religion is by many pointedly denied. Every sort of alliance betwixt Church and State, is condemned as unlawful and unscriptural. Not content with exposing the abuses of existing civil establishments and seeking their reformation, their entire overthrow is demanded, and the very principle on which they are founded held up to unmeasured reprobation. We are not blind to the evils that prevail in the national churches of our land, and should be sorry that anything we might say should have the effect of perpetuating or palliating these in the least. They are too palpable to be overlooked, and too great to admit of being justified. We are not prepared to approve of the *nature* even of the connection subsisting between Church and State in our existing establishments; and, of course, we frankly admit that it is not a reformation of abuses merely, but an entire constitutional change that is needed. Nevertheless, believing as we do that it is the duty of nations to concern themselves about religion, that consequently a union between Church and State, of an unexceptionable kind, is capable of being formed, and, moreover, that the formation of such a union is not only lawful in itself, but dutiful and obligatory, we are anxious that the principle should be distinguished from the corruptions that have been grafted upon it. In lopping off and giving over to merited destruction the excrescences, it is not necessary that the root should be destroyed. In the preservation of the principle, we see involved the glory of the Messiah, the good of his Church, and the best interests of civil society itself. For this reason, and not by any means to uphold or apologise for existing corruptions, in whose maintenance we have no interest, and for whose continuance we have no wish, we are induced to submit the following statements respecting the duty of Christian nations towards the true religion of Jesus.

It is of consequence, in every controversy, that parties have a distinct idea of the point in dispute. The things in which they agree and those in which they differ, ought to be well understood. In the present instance, it may not be easy to give unexceptionable definitions. We beg attention, however, to the following distinctions :—

It is not, whether it be the duty of a Christian nation to establish a *false* religion ;—but whether it be not its duty to establish the *true* religion.

It is not, whether it be the duty of the Church of

Christ to seek alliance with a *heathen, anti-christian,* and *immoral State;*—but whether it may not enter into alliance with a government, possessing the character, and subserving the purposes of *the moral ordinance of God.*

It is not, whether it be the duty of the State merely to afford *legal protection,* or *positive toleration,* to the true religion;—but whether it be not its duty to extend *positive favour, encouragement,* and *support,* to the Church of Christ.

It is not, whether the *Church of Christ may not exist,* and even prosper, without the favour, encouragement, and support, of the State;—but whether it may not be the *duty of the State* to extend such countenance to the true religion.

It is not, whether the State has power *in and over* the Church, so as to interfere in any way with her internal jurisdiction and management;—but whether it be not competent to, and the duty of, a Christian State to frame regulations *about* the Church, or respecting the external interests of religion. Whether, in short, a Christian State be not possessed of power *circa sacra,* although having no authority whatever *in sacris.*

These statements will help to limit and explain the point on which the present discussion turns. And, without adopting any of the definitions of a civil establishment of religion that have been given, either by their friends or by their enemies, or venturing on any definition of our own, the proposition we design to explain, confirm, and defend, is this:—THAT IT IS THE DUTY OF A NATION, AS SUCH, ENJOYING THE LIGHT OF

REVELATION, IN VIRTUE OF ITS MORAL SUBJECTION TO THE MESSIAH, LEGALLY TO RECOGNISE, FAVOUR, AND SUPPORT, THE TRUE RELIGION.

In this discussion when we make use of the term *State*, we mean a civil government possessing the character of the moral ordinance of God; and when we speak of the *Church*, we mean the Church possessing and maintaining the true religion of Christ.

First. This proposition is but a natural and necessary inference from the fact, already established, of national subjection to the Messiah. Nations and their rulers are, as we have seen, the subjects of Christ. They are under, not only his providential control, but his moral authority. Now the religion of Christ, that is to say, his Church or spiritual kingdom, must be to him an object of the deepest interest; it is that, indeed, to which everything else is subordinate. To it, of course, the nations of the world must be subordinate; and if so, is it not utterly inconceivable that they should be freed from all obligation to have respect to the interests of religion? Indeed, it sounds paradoxical or self-contradictory, to say, that nations, which hold so prominent a place among the moral subjects of the Messiah, should be not only exempted, but absolutely prohibited, from taking any concern about that which is dearest to the heart of their Sovereign. The dominion of the Head of the Church over civil society, renders it, not only expedient and safe, but dutiful and obligatory, for nations, as such, to interest themselves about the true religion. The doctrine of the Mediatorial headship over the nations, lays a firm and ample foundation for an alliance between Church and State, which has been rashly pronounced to be in every case unlawful, unchristian, and sinful. While this doctrine is admitted, it will be difficult to refuse the legitimacy of the inference in favour of the alliance in question. If men would only look, without prejudice, at the plain testimony of revelation, there might be less disputing on this point. Does not the apostle Paul speak of God having put all things under the feet of Christ, and 'given him to be Head over all things to the church?' Mark the language. It is not only 'Head over *all* things;' but 'Head over all things *to the Church.*' It is for the sake of the Church that he is invested with universal regal authority: in other words, the *end* of Christ's universal Mediatorial dominion is *the good of the Church.* Thus far, all is clear and undeniable. But *the nations* are among the 'all things,' over which Christ is appointed 'Head.' It follows, then, that Christ is appointed *Head over the nations for the good of the Church.* If so, there must be some way in which the nations are capable of subserving the interests of the Church. Is it possible, then, to conceive that it is not the duty of the nations to promote, by every means in their power, the good of the Church? Is it conceivable that nations are not under obligations to advance the very end for which they are placed in subjection to Christ? Believe this who can. To us it appears that, although there were not another passage on the subject in the whole Bible, that which we have now in view should be sufficient to prevent us from giving our assent to the proposition that the nations have nothing to do with religion.

We are not unaware that an inference of an opposite nature has been drawn from the Mediatorial dominion over the nations. The argument is this:—Christ as Mediator is governor of the nations—he does not govern the nations immediately, but has delegated this to the people—the people, however, are almost universally wicked—it is, therefore, absurd to suppose that the Redeemer should commit the care of his Church to the wicked. But, in this mode of reasoning, there are several fallacious and mistaken assumptions. It is, first of all, assumed that the theory of an establishment supposes that Christ commits his Church to the care of his civil government, whereas all that it implies is that it is the duty of the civil government to extend countenance and protection to the Church of Christ. There is, farther, the unreasonable and pernicious assumption, that organised civil society and the world lying in wickedness are one and the same, whereas the one is the kingdom of Satan, who is the god of this world, and the other a moral ordinance of God. Moreover, while it is admitted that Christ has committed the power of government, in some sense, to the people, it is forgotten that he has, in his Word, both commanded the people to qualify themselves for the right use of this power, and furnished them with an infallible rule to guide them in the exercise of it.

Secondly. The manner in which the object of the magistrate's office is described in the New Testament, confirms and illustrates the preceding observation. He is the minister of God for GOOD, and a terror, not to good works, but to the EVIL. The terms *good* and *evil* are expressed without limitation or restriction; and, without some other information than the passage itself furnishes, we are surely not warranted to conclude either that offences against religion form no part of the *evil* which it is the duty of the ruler to discourage, or that the interests of true religion form no part of the *good* which it becomes him to promote. 'Had it been said,' writes Dr. Willis, '*power* is an ordinance merely to enforce common justice between man and man, or to protect one from another's violence; and had the ideas of *justice* and *protection* been carefully limited according to the modern theory, which, by the way, circumscribes them almost as arbitrarily as the Scripture terms, *good* and *evil* themselves;—had it thus defined the magistrate's province, then our controversy with those who are ever alleging that secular things only fall within his care, were at an end. But let it be observed, no such limitation is introduced. It is not said, indeed, on the other hand, what offences the magistrate is to resent under the head of *evil*, nor how far, and by what means, he is to promote *good*. But we ask, Does not the burden of proving that offences against religion are excluded from the one, or that the positive advancement of that cause is not included in the other, lie upon our opponents? The analogy of the Old Testament entitles us to call for this. But our right to call for it rests on the broader ground of the moral relation in which the ruler, as well as the nation, stands to God;—a moral relation for which the moral law must be the rule. We claim, on this ground, a positive right to interpret the expressions above quoted in a larger sense. We must remind him who would restrict the province of the civil authorities to the second table of the law, that crimes against the first table are not only, at least, equally offensive to the God of nations, but equally injurious to the safety of the State. Outrages on the Majesty of heaven, open contempt of the mysteries and the rites of religion, are more to be dreaded by society than even fraud or oppression, and will more certainly work a nation's ruin. And, on the other hand, the good connected with the encouragement of sound morals, and the diffusion of Christian truth, is more valuable than any resulting from the wisest human policy, acting merely on the selfish principle of man. We do not, then, forget that the more immediate end of civil government is the outward order of the community. But, if every ordinance of God is bound, as it surely is, to seek its end in connection with his glory who ordained it, they who rule may not warrantably regard with indifference the best, because the divinely-appointed means of moralising and civilising the human race. And besides that in this view Christianity comes into the contemplation of a right and wise policy—surely he who is God's minister for good must be bound, as far as secular power may go, to second its higher object.'[44]

Thirdly. The Scriptures of the Old Testament undoubtedly contain divinely-approved examples of such a connection between Church and State as that for which we contend. Under the Patriarchal economy (which, by the way, bore a closer resemblance, in many respects, to the Christian dispensation than did the Jewish), we meet with a striking combination of things civil and

---

[44] National Establishments, &c., page 32.

ecclesiastical in Melchizedec. This remarkable person was both a king and a priest.[45] He was 'king of Salem'—that is, a prince, a monarch, possessed of regal authority, and exercising civil dominion over a particular district more or less extensive and populous. He was also 'priest of the most high God,'—that is, invested with the sacred functions of the sacerdotal office, and appointed to treat with God on behalf of men by means of sacrifice. These offices were real, not figurative merely. His bringing forth bread and wine to Abraham, when returning from the slaughter of the kings, was a regal act; his blessing Abraham, and receiving from him tithes, distinctly recognise his sacerdotal character. Now, the fact of these offices being combined in the same person—whatever design there may have been to point forward by it to him who sits 'a priest upon his throne'—shews that there is no such incompatibility between things civil and sacred as to render all union of them necessarily sinful and improper. It is utterly inconceivable that Melchizedec was required, either, on the one hand, to abstain from any exercise of his regal functions which might subserve the ends of his priesthood, or, on the other, in the discharge of his sacerdotal functions to avoid having any regard to the civil interests of the people over whom he ruled. Such a separation of objects and interests may be pronounced to have been, in the circumstances, impracticable, and, to say the least, unnatural. This is sufficient to convince us that it was not required; and we may safely con-

[45] Gen. xiv. 18; Heb. vii. 1.

clude that Melchizedec, in acting in the double capacity of king of Salem and priest of the Most High God, felt no jarring of claims, no jealousy of interests, but the most perfect harmony and co-operation between the functions of his respective offices. Here, then, we have one example, at least, of the combination of things civil and sacred possessing the authority and approbation of God, as it is spoken of in the Scriptures, not only without censure, but with obvious commendation.*

We have another example, under the Mosaic economy, in the case of the Jewish kings. Into the *nature* or details of the civil establishment of religion under the law, it is not necessary that we should here enter. We have at present to do with the *fact* that legal countenance and support were given, under that dispensation, to the Church. That Moses, and Joshua, and David, and Solomon, and Hezekiah, and Josiah, concerned themselves, in their capacity of civil rulers, about the interests of religion, about the erection of places of worship, the support of the ministers, the removal of obstructions, and the correction of abuses, will not be denied. This is all that we require for our present purpose. It proves, beyond all controversy, that union of Church and State is not *necessarily*, *abstractly*, or *in itself* sinful, else it never could have received the sanction of divine approbation at any time. There may be room for discussion as to the kind of union that happens to exist, or that may be proposed to be formed; or as to the expediency of forming a union

* Inglis's 'Vindication of Ecclesiastical Establishments,' p. 25.

at all in certain given circumstances, but the undeniable fact of its *having once existed and that for a lengthened period with the express approval of heaven*, demonstrates that there is nothing sinful in the thing itself. This, one should think, ought to teach a lesson of moderation to our opponents, in the denunciations in which they are accustomed to indulge.* However unsparing in their censure of abuses, or decided in their opinion of inexpediency, they ought to beware of even seeming to cast a reflection on the wisdom and rectitude of the Almighty, by unceremoniously pronouncing all civil establishments of religion as, in their very nature and tendency, unscriptural, anti-christian, oppressive, unjust, and essentially sinful. *Is there unrighteousness with God? God forbid. Shall not the Judge of all the earth do right?* And, as if to teach us, in the most impressive manner, the perfect compatibility of a friendly alliance between civil and ecclesiastical matters, —as if to make it palpable to all and for ever, that there is nothing incongruous in the union of the king and the priest, the throne and the altar, the sceptre and the censer, the crown and the mitre,—at every stage of the Jewish history we meet with two distinguished characters, the one civil and the other sacred, acting together a conspicuous part, and exhibiting the most perfectly harmonious co-operation. Such were Moses and Aaron, Joshua and Eleazar, David and Abiathar, Solomon and Zadok, Hezekiah and Azariah, Zerubbabel

---

* When this book was written the voluntary controversy was at its height, and language was used on both sides of a kind which has, happily, long ceased to be heard.—ED.

and Joshua. *These are the two anointed ones that stand by the Lord of the whole earth!* [46]

To all this it may be said, in reply, that these are Jewish things, that they belong to a system which has 'vanished away,' and furnish no pattern for the imitation of believers under the New Testament dispensation. It is admitted that there were some things peculiar in the Jewish establishment, which succeeding nations are not bound to imitate. But it will not surely be contended for, that the whole was peculiar; there were certainly some things about it both moral and exemplary; and the question is, whether the duty of the civil ruler to interest himself about religion was not one of these things. 'It is not pleaded that all the actions of rulers among the Jews are imitable by Christian magistrates, or that the latter have exactly the same power which was allotted to and exercised by the former. . . . But it will not follow from this, that we can draw no argument from the conduct of Jewish rulers, to establish the warrantableness and duty of Christian magistrates employing their power in support of religion. Some are ready to conclude that the argument is entirely set aside when it is allowed that there is not an absolute sameness between the two cases. Nothing can, however, be more unfounded than this conclusion. Such a mode of reasoning is of the most dangerous tendency; and, if applied in all the extent to which it will lead, it would cut off the practical use of the greater part of the Old Testament. According to it, no argument could be drawn from the approved examples which it records, of persons of any

[46] Zech. iv. 14.

rank, or in any station, of parents or children, husbands or wives, masters or servants, because many of their actions were peculiar, or clothed with extraordinary circumstances. . . . The apostle argues for the support of a Gospel ministry from that which was given to the Levitical priesthood; but his argument did not imply that they should be supported exactly in the same way (1 Cor. ix. 13, 14). The priestly and prophetical offices were extraordinary and typical, in a sense in which the regal among the Jews was not; yet we do not scruple to illustrate the office, and enforce the duties of ministers of the Gospel, from those of the priests and prophets, especially in their actions with reference to the public state of religion, and in advancing reformation. The judgments inflicted upon the Israelites in the wilderness were in many respects peculiar, yet the apostle holds them out as monitory ensamples to the Corinthians (1 Cor. x.). The prayer of Elijah was extraordinary, yet the apostle James urges it as exemplary to Christians (James v. 16-18). And shall we suppose that the actions of Jewish magistrates form a single exception, and that they were so peculiar, that we cannot reason from them in the way of example or analogy? . . . Persons may affect to talk of the difficulty of ascertaining what is moral and exemplary from what was peculiar; and by dwelling on the more intricate cases, may endeavour to lead away the attention from the subject altogether. But why should it be magnified, and represented as insurmountable, any more than others of a similar kind? The peculiarity of the divine government of Israel, or, as it is commonly called, the theocracy, consisted in general in two things; in a system of laws which was immediately given to that people from heaven; and in the exercise of a peculiar providence in supporting and sanctioning that system, by conferring national mercies and inflicting national judgments, often in an immediate and extraordinary way. Now why are not the difficulties which are started as to the application of the first of these, urged also as to the application of the last? If we cannot apply what is said in the Old Testament, concerning the duty of the rulers and nation of Israel respecting religion unto Christian nations and rulers, because the former were under a peculiar law; then we cannot apply what is said in the Old Testament, respecting the judgments denounced against the nation and rulers of Israel, unto Christian nations and their rulers, because the Israelites, as a people, were under a peculiar providence, which constituted a part of their theocracy. The same distinctions will remove the difficulty in both cases.'[47]

To these extracts from a source of high authority, we beg to add the following judicious remarks by an acute and able writer on the same subject. 'We cannot discern any evidence of the Old Testament example of a church establishment being a ceremonial thing. Nor can we believe that any reader of the Old Testament, unbiassed by system, in reading of the pious care of a David and a Solomon, a Hezekiah, a Josiah, and others, for the building, repairing, and purifying, the house of God, could have reckoned this an exercise of kingly authority, only fitted for the period of the church's

[47] M'Crie's Statement, pp. 121-128.

nonage. There is something in it which recommends it to the best feelings of the heart, as worthy of all times and countries. We are confirmed in this when we recollect that it was not only to be a figure of the church to come, that the Almighty set apart that peculiar people; it was also to be a witness to the nations around, for the one living and true God, in opposition to their universal idolatry. We see that while the ceremonial worship was evidently ordained for one country, and was therefore impracticable for other nations, being in fact as a sort of wall of partition between Jews and Gentiles; yet in the great features of their national policy, it was intended by God that other nations should observe and learn from Israel.[48] If, then, the care of the Jewish princes about the affairs of religion had not been a duty to be imitated by others, it is certain that the polity of that nation, set up as God's witness to mankind, was, throughout its whole duration, fitted to confirm them in a great and prevalent error. The laws of all nations took cognisance of religion. Now, we see that the manners and worship of the Jews in almost all circumstances, were so framed as just to be contrast to the manners and worship of the heathen. Strange, if *this* was so great an error, I mean the principle of a national recognition of a Deity, that the most prominent part of the Israelitish constitution should have been fitted rather to perpetuate than to correct it! What nation, looking on, but must have deemed this one of the very points in which Israel was "an understanding people." How could they look at its religious character

[48] Deut. iv. 7, 8; xxviii. 10; xxix. 24; xxxii. 27.

at all, without being impressed with the lesson, that the acknowledgment of the true God is the first duty of states and highest honour of princes? Why they did not learn of them more to profit, it does not fall to us here to explain. But we are sure it was in the plan of Providence,—even while the typical institutions could not be adopted by them as nations, and the mystery was to be "hid for ages,"—that the great principles of natural religion should be visible in the church and state of the peculiar people, and so far make the heathen inexcusable. Just, then, as the reasons specified in the judicial law itself shew that certain statutes above referred to were of moral and perpetual obligation, so do *these* reasons appear to us conclusive, as proving that the precedent of a national establishment of the church is available as a moral example.'[49]

So much in reply to the objection by which it is attempted to neutralise the argument from Old Testament examples, namely, that these examples are Jewish. But it may not be irrelevant to remind our readers that the Old Testament contains others besides Jewish examples. We have already specified an instance, before the Mosaic economy, in the case of Melchizedek; and we now beg leave simply to remark that several instances are on record of *Gentile* princes who, with marked approbation and distinguished success, employed their influence to promote the welfare of the church. Cyrus, king of Persia, issued a decree respecting the rebuilding of the house of the Lord at Jerusalem, and we are expressly informed that it was the Lord who stirred him

---

[49] Willis on National Establishments, &c., pp. 85-88.

up to do so.[50] Darius afterwards published an edict to the same effect.[51] Another regal enactment of the same nature was passed by Artaxerxes.[52] These are examples the force of which cannot be set aside on the score of being *Jewish*: and yet they were highly approved. 'Blessed be the Lord God of our fathers,' said the pious and patriotic Ezra, in grateful acknowledgment of the divine goodness, 'who hath put such a thing as this in the king's heart, to beautify the house of the Lord which is in Jerusalem.'

Fourthly. From the examples just adverted to, it may be inferred to be agreeable to the light of nature or sound reason, that nations should interest themselves in religion. The cases we have specified may be said to be extraordinary, but the fact that almost all nations, ancient as well as modern, barbarous as well as civilised, have incorporated with their constitutions laws respecting religion, shews that these extraordinary impulses were in accordance with the dictates of nature. We wait not, however, to argue from this fact, but avail ourselves of it only as introductory to some observations on the intimate connection subsisting between religion and civil society. The church and the state, so far from being diametrically opposed, are intimately connected, capable of friendly co-operation, and fitted to exert the most happy mutual influence on each other. On the one hand, there is much that religion can do for a nation; and on the other hand, there is much that a nation can do for religion.*

---

[50] Ezra i. 1-4.   [51] Ezra vi. 8-12.   [52] Ezra vii. 12-20.

* The author has here made a reference to certain pages of Birks's *Christian State* which contain the following sentences:—

'The general laws of Christian duty, when applied to the case of rulers,

Let us, first of all, see what religion can do for a nation. True religion, apart from the influence it is fitted to have on the inhabitants and rulers of a country individually, cannot but affect beneficially its civil institutions and interests. Whether the government be monarchical, aristocratical, democratical, or mixed, it is not difficult to see that religion must have a mighty effect in directing it toward the ends it is designed to subserve, and guarding it against the evils to which it is incident. Religion alone can effectually guard the monarch against an arbitrary abuse of his prerogative, tyrannical oppression, and rapacious aggrandisement; or can teach him to feel and to act as the father of his people, and thus at once enable him to promote their good and merit their affection and confidence. Religion alone can restrain the nobles of a land, from seeking the supposed welfare of their own order, at the expense of that of the humbler classes of society. Nor can any

lead us to infer that his aim ought not to be, as many conceive, barely to secure property and life by motives of compulsion and fear. The wise distribution of wealth and its right improvement should be the objects of his policy, far more than its mere accumulation. Even in his efforts to secure the temporal prosperity of the nation he needs religious truth, and its open confession, to qualify him for the task. . . . What is the true character of a national policy framed on these maxims [those of an entire divorce of religion from the state], and where are they carried out consistently to their natural issue? . . . The whole system, like some chemical mixtures, detonates and explodes when the least gleam of sunlight from eternity breaks in upon its quiet darkness. . . . Wherever the light of Christianity has shone, the nations which have drunk its truths most deeply have risen the most, even in outward greatness; and when it has been quenched in the mere spirit of religious strife or superstitious darkness, their strength has commonly begun to decay. Though a fitful gleam of worldly greatness may be secured where the truths of religion are despised and cast away, the world has never seen a state openly irreligious and profane that has been more than a meteor flashing with a momentary brilliance, and then setting swiftly in darkness.'—Pp. 140-144.

thing but true religion ever prevent the claims of popular liberty and rights from degenerating into licentiousness, and issuing in tumultuary anarchy. Religion is requisite to teach legislators to have respect, in their enactments, to the honour and decrees of the supreme Lawgiver, rather than to the unstable dictates of worldly expediency. In courts of law and justice, religion is well calculated to disengage civil enactments from that embarrassing ambiguity which goes far to defeat their end; to put a stop to the pernicious practice of pleading any cause however bad; to place an effectual barrier to the taking of bribes, which blind the eyes even of the wise; and to inspire with a sacred regard, at all times, to moral rectitude and honesty.

Religion is favourable to liberty. By checking selfishness, inspiring benevolence, and teaching a strict moral equality, it proves itself decidedly friendly to the rights of the people; while, by its opposition to injustice and oppression, it directly tends to suppress whatever is unfavourable to freedom. Without religion, nations may aim at freedom, but they can never attain it; and even although they could, they would be unfit for enjoying it, for, to the end of time will it hold true of communities as of individuals, that 'whom the Son makes free, *they* and they only are free indeed.'

It might even be shewn that religion is fitted to operate favourably in regard to national wealth, by securing industry; by restraining indulgences injurious to health; by hindering all profuse and foolish expenditure of public money; and by preventing to a great extent, and at all events ameliorating, the evils of pauperism which spreads like a leprosy over an immoral population. However despised and overlooked by worldly economists, the statement will be found to rest on a basis of immovable truth, that *godliness is profitable unto all things, having promise of the life that now is, and of that which is to come.**

It requires little penetration to see how religion is subservient to the peace of a nation. It is directly opposed to those false views of national honour, which would associate the glory of a people with the pomp and circumstance of war. Martial music, glittering arms, mustering troops, and far-spreading conquest, have about them a glare by which men are apt to be deceived. It should never be forgotten, however, that war is at the best a necessary evil, and inseparably connected with bloody carnage, fell bereavement, territorial devastation,

---

* Very striking remarks of Canon Birks on the necessity of true religion to sound political economy, are here referred to by the author—pp. 153-160. He called the attention of his students to them, and rejoiced in receiving confirmation of his views from such a quarter. 'To create riches, and in creating to diffuse them so as to ensure the solid well-being of the State, to preserve the people from the double curse of cankered gold and luxurious profligacy—these are tasks which require the knowledge of higher truths, and a heavenly wisdom in those who would indeed fulfil them. . . . Wealth is not measured by gold and silver; for these change their value continually. It does not consist in bales of merchandise; for these ruin the producers when no market can be found for them. It is not measured by the labour bestowed on production; for labour itself may be wasted on useless follies, or on things worse than useless, the fuel and incentive of wickedness and crime . . . Every theory of its nature must be worthless which does not distinguish real from illusive wants, and measure the former by a true standard, derived from the real, solid, and lasting interests of mankind.'

It might have been added, as a matter of history, that each of the great world-empires of antiquity went down under the sheer weight of its precious metals, that is, perished through the effeminacy and moral corruption engendered by fulness. The experiment now being made, under the government of the Mediator, on modern nations, is how far faithful use of the leaven of divine truth will avert from them the same fate. See p. 283 *infra.*—ED.

and a long train of horrible, nay, indescribable miseries. Religion directly tends to promote the blessings of peace. Securing peace with God, it inculcates peace between man and man; it puts a check to those ambitious designs and wicked passions which will be found, on the one side or on the other, or perhaps on both, to originate those wars which prove a scourge and a curse to mankind; while it teaches all to aim at bringing about that happy predicted state of things, when men *shall beat their swords into ploughshares, and their spears into pruning-hooks; nation shall not lift up sword against nation, neither shall they learn war any more.*

Religion can alone secure the true morality of a nation. Its sanctions are powerfully calculated to restrain those outbreakings of injustice and violence which the laws of civil society are designed to repress, and against which mere human enactments and punishments will be found but an ineffectual safeguard. Nor can any thing but true religion present effectual barriers to that torrent of impiety and profligacy, against which no penal laws can be directed, but which powerfully tends to sap the very foundations of national prosperity, and to call down the curse of God upon a people.

In short, without religion no nation can feel itself secure. Ungodliness provokes the anger of the Lord, and, like Israel of old, the nation that neglects religion and gives itself up to iniquity, will not be able to stand before its enemies. It may truly be said of such, *Their defence is departed from them,* for, by so doing, they incur the displeasure of Him who is the only sure *defence and refuge in the day of trouble.* Warriors and statesmen may affect to despise all this, while they put their trust in human wisdom and prowess, but God can soon teach them that it is religion alone that can render a country invincible; that the prayers of the godly are more to be trusted than swords of steel,—the sighs of true penitence a surer safeguard than all the thunders of artillery. Religion is, in truth, 'the cheap defence of nations.'

These remarks, on the connexion between true religion and the welfare of a civil community, are supported alike by Scripture, reason, and history. RIGHTEOUSNESS EXALTETH A NATION, BUT SIN IS A REPROACH TO ANY PEOPLE (Prov. xiv). 34. This sacred maxim is illustrated by all history. The nation of Israel was most prosperous, when it was most religious, under the pious reigns of David and Solomon. And when did it become an abomination, and a hissing, and a destruction, but when it departed from the Lord, and filled up the cup of its iniquity by rejecting the Messiah? The same thing might be said of other nations of antiquity. The period of their greatest prosperity will be found to be that of the greatest prevalence of public virtue. It has been remarked, that, in proportion to the prevalence of truth, justice, benevolence, and industry, were their glory and splendour; while their decline and final overthrow were marked by luxury, voluptuousness, envy, injustice, and vain-glorious ambition. 'The nations which have been hurled down from the supremacy which they formerly possessed, perished not from the want of resources, but of the courage and the skill to use them. God had taken their hearts from them, and they fell into an evil snare. They bowed down under the load of unrepented sin, and submitted their necks to the conqueror. Babylon, Persepolis, Greece, Rome, and Constantinople, were fuller of wealth and arms on the day that they opened their gates to the conqueror than when poor and few in numbers, but resolute in spirit, they first started in the career of victory. Had God restored to them the mind of their forefathers, they would soon have rolled back the battle from their gates, difficulties and dangers which were bringing on their speedy doom would have disappeared as a dream, and with united hearts and hands they would have re-edified to more than their former height their temples and their bulwarks. But sin, with the power of an avenging God, is the ruin of every people. He turns their wisdom into folly, and their strength into weakness. *All these curses shall come upon thee, and shall pursue thee and overtake thee, till thou be destroyed, because thou hearkenest not unto the voice of the Lord thy God, to keep his statutes and his commandments which he commanded thee. Because thou servest not the Lord thy God with joyfulness and gladness of heart for the abundance of all things, therefore shalt thou serve thine enemies which the Lord shall send against thee, in hunger and in thirst, and in nakedness, and in want of all things; and He shall put a yoke of iron upon thy neck until he hath destroyed thee.'* [53]

Such being the close connexion between religion and the best interests of civil society, passing strange were it, indeed, if nations were not at liberty, nay, were not

---

[53] Douglas's Prospects of Britain, pp. 16, 17.

under obligations, to interest themselves about religion. It will be difficult to shew that there is any one thing which can contribute more directly or extensively to the true prosperity of a kingdom than religion ; and yet we are asked to believe that this one thing a kingdom must do nothing to introduce, to support, or to diffuse! Every nation is surely bound to use all lawful means of advancing its prosperity ; and are we to be told that the means which, above all others, tends most powerfully to this end, is one of which it is unlawful for a nation to avail itself? True, the direct and immediate end of civil government is not the maintenance of religion, but the promotion of order, peace, and justice. Yet religion being a means, an eminent means, to the attainment of this end, no government, having the opportunity, can neglect to improve it, without incurring the guilt of neglecting its own true welfare.

As religion can do much for a nation, so a nation has it in its power to do something (may we not say much also?) for religion. It is admitted to be a difficult matter accurately and minutely to define the line and extent of the magistrate's power, *circa sacra*. We have before remarked, that the church of Christ is strictly independent of the state. Civil rulers, we repeat, have no right to dictate to her her creed ; to institute her ordinances ; to appoint her office-bearers ; to control her government or discipline ; in short, to interfere in any one way with either her constitution or her administration. All this we firmly maintain. Yet are there many things which, it appears to us, a Christian nation, through the medium of its rulers, has it in its power to do for the true religion.

The civil magistrate can extend *protection* to the church, in the profession of her creed, in the exercise of her worship, in the administration of her ordinances, in the enjoyment of her privileges, and in the possession of her undoubted rights and liberties. These are all capable of being outwardly assailed; but having in herself no power of defence from external attack, she is entitled to look for this to the collateral ordinance of civil government, which possesses the power required, and is under obligation to exert it for this end. Thus much is unquestionably supposed, in those who are described as 'the shields of the earth' being spoken of also as 'nursing fathers to the church,'—a character which they could ill sustain without throwing the strong arm of protection over their tender charge; as well as in the circumstance of its being specified as one end why Christians should pray for those in authority, 'that they may lead a quiet and peaceable life in all godliness and honesty.' This, we believe, will be readily admitted; but what we contend for, is, not a vague *passive toleration* of the true religion, in common with all manner of false and heretical systems, but an active, formal *authoritative protection* of the true religion, to which the others have no right, and which consequently they ought not to receive.

The nation is capable, also, through its functionaries, of giving a judicial or legal *recognition* to the true religion. The confession of the church's faith may be adopted and ratified by the state, without the state being at all chargeable with the iniquity of dictating to the church what shall be her creed. The authoritative sanction of the magistrate can add nothing, indeed, to the evidence, or weight, or obligation, or authority of the truths to which it is appended. . Nothing of the kind. Nevertheless, such an act of legal recognition or ratification serves the end, not merely of pledging the nation's honour to the defence of these truths, but of constituting an open, public, national profession of the true religion. A nation, being a moral subject of Messiah, is as much bound to make a profession of religion as any private individual whatever. Can that be a Christian nation which makes no profession of the religion of Christ?[*] And how can such a profession be *nationally* made but in some such way as we have supposed, namely, by the functionaries of the nation, in their official capacity, giving their authoritative sanction to the church's creed?

It is vain to plead, here, the difficulty civil rulers must feel in arriving at the knowledge of what is the truth, for this difficulty is not greater on their part than on that of the church or of private individuals, who, it is never once supposed, should be exempted, on this score, from the obligation to profess the truth. The volume of revelation cannot be what its name supposes, if its meaning is incapable of being ascertained; and, if ascertainable at all, it is as much so by one as by another, who possesses the means, and chooses to make use of them for arriving at a knowledge of its contents. Infallible accuracy, it is true,

[*] The author here calls attention to Birks's *Christian State*, chap. v.

is incapable of being attained by the magistrate; but here again he is only on a level with the ecclesiastical functionary and the private Christian, neither of whom can pretend to infallibility any more than the magistrate. Nor is perfect accuracy, in either case, at all necessary; all that is required being that they make a proper use of the means with which they are furnished of arriving at correct views of religion, and that they pronounce according to the best of their judgment. It will be admitted, that the civil magistrate may warrantably legislate on subjects connected with the advancement of the arts and the sciences. Does this suppose him to be accurately acquainted with all these? Or would it be sustained, as a sufficient excuse for his not interfering in such matters, that he is not an artisan or a philosopher? We apprehend not; and why, we ask, should he be precluded from legislating in behalf of religion, on the ground of incompetency to judge in such matters? Has not the magistrate more easy access to the source of information on the subject of religion than to that on the arts and sciences? besides the subject being one in which he must be understood to be far more deeply interested than in the others.

It is quite a mistake to say, that the magistrate's giving his countenance to one set of religious opinions in preference to others, involves the essence of persecution. This arises from supposing that, when the government of a country expresses its approbation of a certain doctrinal creed and form of worship, it must forthwith enjoin on all its subjects conformity in their opinions and practice, and authoritatively require the subjects to believe as the rulers believe. But does this follow? The legislature does not, in any sense, dictate to the subject what his religion shall be. It only determines what system of religious belief shall be taught with the aid and countenance of the state. No means but what are moral are employed to bring the public mind into conformity with that of the rulers. Every man is left, as far as civil authority or legal coercion is concerned, to choose or reject as he sees fit. The conscience of every individual is left free and unfettered; no one has the slightest ground on which to set up the cry of persecution.

The magistrate can, farther, interpose the sanction[*] of the law with regard to the *time* set apart by God to the stated services of religion. We refer here to the institution of the Sabbath. To be sure, on grounds altogether distinct from the sanctions of civil authority, all who have the volume of revelation are bound to 'remember the Sabbath day, to keep it holy;' and there can be no proper sanctification of the Lord's day, in which there is not respect had to the paramount authority of God. But, without the interference of the magistrate, it is impossible that Christians, however well disposed, could, generally at least, have it in their power to obey, in this matter, the law of heaven. And it is surely a duty which nations, as such, owe to Messiah, to take order that there shall be a national observance of the day set apart for celebrating the resurrection from the dead of their Prince, even of Him who 'died for our

---

[*] The author refers here to Birks's *Christian State*, pp. 380-386.

sins, was buried, and rose again the third day, according to the Scriptures.' To the peaceful, orderly, and profitable enjoyment of the Sabbath, by those who are disposed to observe it, it is important that the outward observance be general; and there is no way by which this can be secured, but by the intervention of civil authority enjoining a universal cessation, throughout the land, of the business and amusements of other days. But for such interference, it must be obvious, such is the ungodliness of many and such the spirit of competition among worldly men, that every species of occupation and diversion would go forward on the Lord's day with the same eagerness and publicity as on the other days of the week. There might be some who would suspend their ordinary pursuits, and, retiring into the sanctuary of their dwellings, there pursue their pious meditations and studies; but the bustle that reigned without would effectually prevent their retirement from partaking of the nature of a holy quiet, while their less scrupulous neighbours would, meanwhile, get the advantage of them in the gains of their worldly calling. There might be, and there would be, numbers, who, in spite of the sacrifices they were required to make, and the scoffs with which they were sure to be assailed, would still go up to the house of God, and seek the advantages and the delights of the solemn assembly. But, as they went and as they came, not to speak of the disturbance to which even the acts of public worship should be exposed, how should their pious feelings be hurt, and every serious and edifying reflection be dissipated, by the sounds and the sights of busy secularity, which should everywhere meet their senses!

It is vain to tell us, that the magistrate cannot enforce the spiritual observance of the Sabbath, and that the Sabbath is not kept as it ought, if kept only outwardly. This is a drivelling evasion of our argument. We know that the magistrate cannot enforce the spiritual observance of the Sabbath, and we do not ask him to do so. We know that secular authority can reach only to what is external. We know that it is the prerogative of God to touch, as it is his only to judge, the heart. But does not this hold true in other matters besides the observance of the Sabbath,—matters, too, in which magistratical interference is admitted to be lawful? Might it not as well be pleaded that the magistrate should not make laws for the protection of human life, because he cannot restrain man from cherishing deadly hatred towards his brother man; or laws for the protection of property, because he cannot secure moral honesty; or laws against perjury, because he cannot impart to men a sacred regard to truth; as that he may not legislate on the subject of the Sabbath, because he cannot secure its spiritual observance? Although he cannot do this, we contend that it is still competent for him to interpose the solemn voice of law, and the strong arm of power, in order to secure to the nation a season of rest from public business and public amusements; and that, too, on distinctly religious grounds: and we ask him to do what he can do.

Some who deny to the magistrate all power whatever in matters of religion, nevertheless, admit the propriety of magistratical interference in regard to the Sabbath. But, for consistency's sake, they are compelled to maintain that the civil enactment of a day of weekly rest, proceeds on secular grounds entirely. It is, from the common consent which is understood to be given it by the people of the nation; or, because of its being necessary for the protection of property; or, as a day of mere secular rest;—it is on some such grounds as these that the magistrate is to be understood as warranted to interfere. There must be no respect to the authority of God; no regard to the spiritual ends of the sabbatical institution. It must be brought down entirely from the high and sacred ground of religion, and placed on the low basis of a worldly motive. None of these inferior grounds, however, will be found sufficient to furnish a platform broad enough, even were it firm enough, for the structure of a national Sabbath.

The ground of *common consent* will not serve the purpose, inasmuch as it is preposterous to expect that Jews and infidels would ever agree to an arrangement, which should lay them under a restraint to which they did not feel themselves compelled by their consciences to submit, and their submission to which would consequently tend to involve them in the disgrace of hypocrisy.

Neither will the *protection of property* serve the purpose. For might not the Jew, in this case, complain of being compelled to suspend his lawful employment on the *first* day of the week, in obedience to the law of the land, after having felt constrained to cease from working on the *seventh* day, in obedience to the dictates of his conscience? Nay, if the Sabbath is recognised as property, and only to be protected as such, although no man may *take* another's property, what should hinder a man, as has been acutely argued, from *giving* his property away? 'He who chooses to give up his time to his master may not surely be hindered, nor the master hindered from accepting of it.'[54]

But after all, the low ground of property can only, at the best, secure a cessation from *business*, while it leaves the sanctity of the Lord's holy day open to desecration by every form of amusement, provided only that those who contribute to the entertainment of others, take care to let it be understood they are not pursuing a trade. By day, the streets and avenues of the city, and the places of public resort, may be frequented by crowds, trying their skill in athletic exercises; conducting, in due form, their manly sports; witnessing feats of jugglery; listening, amid shouts of obstreperous merriment, to some low buffoon; or, perhaps, feasting on the deadly combat of noble animals brought together for the purpose of gratifying a *refined* taste, by tearing each other to pieces. And the evening of the day of holy rest may be spent in the fascinating dissipations of the concert, the ball, the assembly, the masquerade, or any other form of fashionable extravagance, which those who are 'lovers of pleasure more than lovers of God' may demand.*

Such are the consequences that must inevitably

---

[54] Willis, p. 48.

* One is reminded of the pathetic language of Richard Baxter, about the state of things which prevailed during his boyhood. He was three years old when the Book of Sports was issued by authority of King James. 'There was no savour of Nonconformity in our family:' yet the sports were carried on, 'not an hundred yards from our door.' 'We could not, on the Lord's spring from maintaining, that civil authority can be interposed on behalf of the Sabbath on no higher ground than that it is the common property of the inhabitants of a nation. . But is it so, that the day of the Lord is to be regarded and spoken of as only a species of human property? 'We absolutely deny,' says Professor Willis with becoming indignation, 'that the fourth commandment is one concerning *property;* no, not even, properly speaking, is it in part so. Except as connected with the end of serving God, the Sabbath is given to no man *as his own.* It is not merely time which no man may exact from another: it is time which no man may alienate to himself. It is neither the servant's nor the master's, except as to be devoted by both to the highest ends of their being. *Property!* why, there is another command for that, whether, in truth, it be money or time that is in question. . . . It will not do:—go where we may to seek our warrant for a law on that principle, let us not go to that sacred statute whose foremost words proclaim its sublimer objects, "Thou shalt remember the Sabbath-day *to keep it holy!*" Such words repel us, as, in a sort, profaning holy ground, as doing a kind of sacrilege, when we would, either in the name of an individual or society, grasp at that part of the com-

day, either read a chapter, or pray, or sing a psalm, or catechise or instruct a servant, but with the noise of the pipe and tabor and the shoutings of the street continually in our ears.' 'When the people, by the *Book,* were allowed to play and dance out of public service-time, they could so hardly break off their sports that many a time the reader was fain to stay till the pipes and players would give over. Sometimes the morris-dancers would come into the church in all their linen and scarfs and antic dresses, with morris bells jingling at their heels; and as soon as the common prayer was read, did haste out presently to their play again.'—*Editor.*

mandment which may more immediately serve our worldly interests; and, separating it from the rest, and calling it our own, would avow that with God's part of it we have nothing to do! We know this right would not be pleaded for the individual; but if *society* can only thus approach the sacred statute, we would say, in the name of religion and of consistency, let the commandment alone! This is desecrating it. It is bringing it down from its lofty altitude. It is erazing from it *His* image and superscription who challenges it as his own. . . . *The time of the labourer is his property!* And so to this it must come in seeking to acquit a nation of the duty of recognising the whole divine law as its rule! You have to set up instead, as supreme, the *will of man!* Man will not obey such a law long, however well he loves to wield such a power. Man armed, even the ruler armed with such a power, will soon wield it either too little or too much. Public sentiment, forming upon such a standard, will speedily manifest the opposition of the natural will of man to the will of his Maker. The pious, the timid, will soon find enough to do to hold on in their veneration of religion and its ordinances, unseduced by the example, or undismayed by the scorn, of others. Farewell to the national Sabbath—farewell, as to most, to the Sabbath itself—when the law shall avow no higher reasons than these! Farewell the holy quiet of that morn which was wont to be disturbed only by the ringing of the church bell, or the tread of the passenger repairing to the house of prayer. First blessing of our country! first friend of the poor! first among our cherished recollections, when in a land of strangers! Instead of the peasant and the labourer conducting their well-ordered households to the sanctuary of God, we shall see the parties of pleasure mustering for their sports;—Jew pursuing his traffic with his brother Jew;—and the company of worshippers crossed in their path by the crowds repairing to the factory; where the offered alternative of working on that day, or another being found to do the work, shall have proved too powerful for the juvenile labourer, and carried it over all the sacredness and authority of a parent's example and precept; or shall have tempted even the willing child against his mind, and for the very parent's sake, not to forfeit the means of dependence, perhaps for both! Nor is it the pious and the timid alone who would have reason, in the issue, to mourn the adoption of such a political theory: the irreligious themselves, brought within the mercy of human covetousness, would exclaim, ere long, Let us fall into the hands of God, but let us not fall into the hands of men!'[55]

If, again, the ground assumed, as that on which legislation is to proceed, is merely that the Sabbath is a day of *secular rest*, of cessation from ordinary worldly employment, it will be found that neither will this ground serve. For, apart from the authority of God and the religious purposes for which he has instituted the Sabbath, what right has any government on earth to interdict its subjects from labour for any length of time whatever, provided they themselves are willing

---

[55] See National Establishments, &c., pp. 54–60. We recommend the whole section from which the above extract is taken, as a masterly exposure of the reasonings of those who take any lower ground for a national Sabbath than the moral law.

to work? Admitting it to have such a right, how is it to fix on a *seventh* part of time, as the due proportion which the season of rest is to bear to that of labour? This difficulty superseded, might not the *second*, the *third*, or any other day of the week, serve the end of secular rest as perfectly as the *first?* Nay, if civil legislation is to have no higher end in view than to secure secular rest, the magistrate can have no higher respect for the interests of his *moral* subjects in this matter than that which he has for *beasts of burden!* Cattle are capable of sharing in all the advantages of secular rest. We are far from thinking it beneath the dignity of a Christian nation to enact laws in favour of the inferior animals: the great Lawgiver himself has not thought it beneath his dignity to do so. But foul scorn do we hold it, to maintain that God's minister for good, when using his authority to enforce the observance of the Sabbath, is to be regarded as having no higher respect to the interests of his moral subjects than to those of the brutal tribes. We enter our solemn protest against this attempt to degrade man, by confounding him with the beasts that perish, by placing him on a level with the ox and the ass.

It thus appears that, if we depart from the high vantage ground of the moral law, if we abandon the authority of God himself, if we lay aside all respect to the religious ends of the divine institution of the Sabbath, and descend to the low motives of political expediency, we shall find that the magistrate must be completely in the dark in attempting to legislate at all on such a subject. There is nothing for him, in short, but to take his stand on the high platform of the FOURTH COMMANDMENT. Let him have respect, in all his enactments on this subject, to the best interests of 'the strangers within his gates.' Let him take, as his model, the lofty patriotism of the governor of old, who, when his heart was grieved at the complicated Sabbath desecration he beheld, contended with the nobles of Judah, and said, *What evil thing is this that ye do, and profane the Sabbath day? If ye do so again, I will lay hands on you.**

The interposition of civil authority may be of service, in the way of restraining many things injurious to religion. This is confessedly a point of great delicacy; and to define the full extent to which the magistrate is entitled or bound to go, in this department, must be acknowledged to be a matter of no ordinary difficulty. On the general point, however, there is no difficulty at all. Because it is not easy, in every case, to describe exactly the limits of magistratical interference in the way of restraint, to conclude that the magistrate should not interfere in this way at all, is no better reasoning than it would be, to maintain that a father should have no manner of discipline in his family, because he may feel at a loss, in certain cases, to determine to what extent he should carry the restraints of parental authority. That restraint of some kind belongs to the civil ruler must be admitted. 'He is a revenger to execute wrath on him that doeth evil.' 'A wise king scattereth the wicked, and bringeth the

---

* The author has here made a reference to Dr. Alexander's Life of Wardlaw; remarks on Wardlaw's Treatise on the Sabbath.

SUPPRESSION OF BLASPHEMY AND IDOLATRY. 299

wheel over them.' 'A king that sitteth in the throne of judgment scattereth away all evil with his eyes.' 'Governors are sent for the punishment of evil doers.' 'Rulers are not a terror to good works, but to the evil.'[56] Now, that the restraint of evils which affect the interests of religion should come within the province of the magistrate, might be inferred from the tendency of religion to benefit civil society, which, of course, supposes a tendency in irreligion to injure it. The Scriptures confirm this view. They furnish us with examples of pious kings, whose authoritative and judicial suppression of blasphemy, idolatry, and Sabbath profanation, are spoken of with manifest commendation, while others, for the neglect of this, are reproved. Take the case of king Asa, for instance. 'And Asa did that which was good and right in the eyes of the Lord his God; for he took away the altars of the strange gods, and the high places, and broke down the images, and cut down the groves; and commanded Judah to seek the Lord God of their fathers, and to do the law and the commandment. Also he took away, out of all the cities of Judah, the high places and the images, and the kingdom was quiet before him.'[57] The well-known words of Job shew the conviction that was entertained by that individual, apart altogether from the judicial institutes of the Jews, that idolatry was a fit object of civil restraint. 'If I beheld the sun when it shined, or the moon walking in brightness, and my heart hath been secretly enticed, or my mouth hath kissed my hand; *this also were an iniquity to be*

---

[56] Rom. xiii. 4; Prov. xx. 26, 28; 1 Pet. ii. 14; Rom. xiii. 3.
[57] 2 Chron. xiv. 2-5.

punished by the judge; for I should have denied the God that is above.'[58] Gross blasphemy, profane swearing, open idolatry, and desecration of the Lord's day, are legitimate objects of magistratical interference; not merely as things hurtful to the commonwealth, and offensive to a majority of the members of society, but as injurious to religion, and highly displeasing to the Almighty. It is altogether out of the question to suppose that 'the minister of God,' in using his influence to put a stop to such iniquities, is to lay aside all regard to the glory of God, and to restrict himself to a low motive of political expediency. The thing is impossible. What is it that renders it politically expedient to restrain such evils, but that they are calculated to bring evil upon the community? And how is it that they bring evil upon the community, but by incurring the displeasure of God, and provoking him to visit them with providential rebukes? It is, as offences against religion, and on religious as well as political grounds, therefore, that the magistrate can alone interpose in cases of this kind. The manner in which the offences are to be met, and the degree of restraint which it may be necessary to exercise in particular cases, are matters in which great prudence and discretion will be required. Whether it may be proper to inflict civil pains, or to interpose only civil disabilities, or perhaps to exercise forbearance, must depend upon the nature and degree of the offences; and the determination of these points must be left to the judgment of the framers and

---

[58] Job xxxi. 26-28.

executors of the constitution and laws. *Wisdom is profitable to direct.*

It is vain to say, in reply to all this, that civil interference cannot promote inward reverence of God's name, or the spirituality of his worship, or the internal sanctification of his holy day. We know that it cannot. But it is not these things we are speaking of. We are speaking of overt acts of profanity, impiety, and immorality. And, although the authority of the civil magistrate cannot promote the former, it is fully within its power to restrain the latter, and, by so doing, to confer no mean benefit both on society at large and on the church. Nor will it do to plead, in opposition to what we have here advanced, that it interferes with liberty of conscience. The conscience has no inherent absolute rights; all the liberty it possesses is conferred upon it by God; and it is utterly absurd to suppose that any man possesses from God a right to blaspheme his name, to worship an idol, or to profane his sacred day. As well might a man claim a right to murder, to commit adultery, or to steal, if only his conscience might permit or prompt him to perpetrate such atrocities. Were civil authority interposed, for the purpose of enforcing on men the profession of certain principles, or the observance of certain forms of worship, or of compelling them to wait on public ordinances on the Sabbath, there might be some ground for complaint on the score of violating the rights of conscience. But the restraint of gross and open acts of irreligion and ungodliness is quite a different thing, and can afford no legitimate ground for such an objection.

A nation may promote the interests of religion by contributing pecuniary support.* For the erection of places of worship, for the maintenance of ministers, and for providing the elements requisite in the administration of at least one of the ordinances, the church must have emoluments. Now, a nation, as such, not only may, but ought to interest itself in providing these supplies. That there was a legal provision for similar purposes, under the Law, will be admitted. In what it consisted we wait not now to inquire. Neither do we wait to discuss, whether a nation ought to interfere in this matter, by direct legal assessment, or only by giving encouragement to voluntary liberality. All that we insist upon is, the obligation of a nation to interfere, some way or other. We observe, that there was once an ample legal provision for religion, which was collected according to law, and could not be withheld by any one, without violating the commandment of God, incurring the divine displeasure, and subjecting to civil coercion.[59] Now, why should not something of the same kind exist in New Testament times? Has God forbidden it? Shew us the prohibition. God has, it is true, ordained that they that preach the Gospel should live of the Gospel, and that he that is taught in the Word should communicate to him that teacheth in all good things. But is the teacher to go forth only among such as are able and willing to pay? Is he not also to go forth, among those who have as yet no relish for his spiritual communications, and who, consequently, cannot be ex-

---

* The author refers to Birks, pp. 404–407.

[59] Num. xviii. 26; 1 Sam. viii. 15; 2 Chron. xxxi. 4, 5; Neh. x. 32; xiii. 10, &c.

pected to contribute for what they have yet to learn to appreciate? How is he to subsist, till his labours have been blessed for the conversion of a number sufficient to support him? And, supposing the teacher supported, how is the place of worship to be provided? By the voluntary contributions, do you say, of such as have already felt the power of divine truth? Not to say that most of these have enough to do with themselves, does not this suppose religion to have been formerly introduced, and to have taken root to some extent in the land? thus shifting the difficulty only a step farther back, where it meets us again with all its force.

It is insisted upon, that it is a *privilege*, as well as a duty, for the people to support religion themselves, and that legal support goes to deprive them of this privilege. Sure we are that the apostle Paul had no such transcendental view of Christian privilege; for, so far from thinking that he had done wrong, in preaching the Gospel freely to the Corinthians, he boldly vindicates his conduct: 'Have I committed an offence in abasing myself that ye might be exalted, because I have preached to you the Gospel of God freely? When I was present with you, and wanted, I was chargeable to no man. In all things I have kept myself from being burdensome unto you, and so I will keep myself.'[60] Is it still contended that the Scripture rule is, that those who receive the benefit of the Gospel shall contribute to the support of the Gospel? Be it so. And does the nation derive no benefit from the existence of religious institutions

[60] 2 Cor. ii. 7, 9.

in a land?—If, after all, taking refuge in a word, it is insisted upon that the support of religion must be *voluntary*, we ask what should hinder it to be both legal and voluntary too? May not a thing be legal and voluntary at the same time? Everything that is *legal* is not necessarily *compulsory*, as everything that is *voluntary* is not necessarily *optional*.* We do many things voluntarily every day, which it is not optional with us, as far as law and obligation are concerned, whether we shall do them or not. A legal assessment for the support of religion, it is easy to see, may be rendered compulsory, by those who ought to pay it voluntarily and cheerfully refusing to do so. But on whom, in this case, is the evil of compulsion to be charged? Why dwell, however, on such points as these? To what object, we ask, can the resources of a nation be, not only more harmlessly, but more profitably applied, than the maintenance and diffusion of that religion which exalteth a nation, and which is at once the glory and safety of a land? Shall countless sums be lavished on wars, and bridewells, and prisons, and penitentiaries, and all the machinery of legal, judicial, and police establishments, for the detection and punishment of crime; and shall not a single farthing be given from the public purse for the support of those religious institutions, the due administration of which is calculated to effect the suppression of crime of every name, and thus, not only to advance the comfort of the community, but to save the expenditure of the national funds? † Nay, do not the pre-

---

* Birks, p. 482.

† In the second edition the author inserts here the following passage from the Hon. and Rev. Baptist Noel's *Letter to Lord Melbourne*, p. 34 :—' A body

dictions which refer to the diffusion of Christ's kingdom in New Testament times, make mention expressly of the pecuniary contributions of persons in authority in their official character? 'The kings of Tarshish and of the isles shall bring *presents*: the kings of Sheba and Seba shall offer *gifts*. He shall live, and to him shall be given of the *gold* of Sheba.—The Gentiles shall come to thy light, and kings to the brightness of thy rising —they shall bring *gold* and incense, and they shall shew forth the praises of the Lord. Surely the isles will wait for me, and the ships of Tarshish first, to bring thy sons from far, their *silver* and their *gold* with them, unto the name of the Lord thy God, and to the Holy One of Israel, because he hath glorified thee.' [61] *

of faithful Christian ministers, whether in the establishment or out of it, are the means of diffusing religion throughout the land. By thus implanting in men's minds the fear and love of God, they dry up the sources of crime, diminish the cost of gaols and hulks, of convict ships and penal settlements, sweeten social life, discountenance fraud, condemn oppression, and lay solidly the foundation of all national prosperity. A grant, therefore, for the erection of new churches by increasing the number of such ministers, would lessen the labours of the police, support the magistracy, uphold the laws, and tend to perpetuate sobriety, good order, industry, wealth, and contentment in the whole nation. That grant refused, the legislature will consign a dense population to religious ignorance,—with the full and certain knowledge that, by the operation of its own laws, by the force of circumstances which it has itself created, they are prevented from being otherwise instructed. It will then doom them to the influence of gin and Sunday newspapers, of vice and ungodliness, of revolutionary orators and furious demagogues. It will provide policemen to apprehend them, gaols to shut them up, ships to transport them, and soldiers to shoot and sabre them when necessary; but it will give them no instructors. It will raise the most costly apparatus to punish them, if criminal, but will not devote a farthing to render them virtuous.'

[61] Ps. lxxii. 10, 15; Isa. lx. 3, 6, 9.

* Those who knew the author could not mistake the reference of this passage to be purely theoretical. For the sake of others, it may be said that no one stood more thoroughly aloof from any gifts of the state which involved compromise of the church's purity and freedom; no one rejoiced

Thus do we see the benefit which a nation, as such, has it in its power to confer on the church. This may be deemed a sufficient answer to those who would represent all national interference with religion as calculated only to injure it. To say that it is capable of being abused, is only what may be said of the very best things that exist. That it has never been abused, we have no design to maintain. But that such interposition of the civil power, as we have supposed, must necessarily tend to secularise and corrupt the religion of Christ we cannot admit. Many, we are firmly persuaded, practise deceit upon themselves here, by confounding the *state* and the *world* with one another. The world of the ungodly, which is the kingdom of Satan, is confounded with civil society, which is the moral ordinance of God: and, because all connexion of the church with the former cannot but injure her, it is concluded that so must all connexion with the latter. But merely to name the distinction between the *state* and the *world*, is all that is necessary to detect the fallacy. Civil society and the church of Christ, being both ordinances of God, can have no *necessary* tendency to corrupt each other, but must be capable of dwelling together in friendly co-operation, and of exerting a mutually beneficial influence. And, as for the case of Constantine, so frequently and so vauntingly brought forward in support of the opposite opinion, who does not

with more enthusiasm in the great Act by which state support was relinquished in 1843; and no one more earnestly and intelligently taught those principles of Christian giving which are embodied in such books as *Gold and the Gospel*. The conclusion of this chapter sufficiently indicates what the author's position was as to any practical connexion with the existing state. —EDITOR.

know that the corruptions which were brought to light at the period in question, had been long before in operation, and that the more flagrant of them proceeded from the excess of that very principle which is contended for, in opposition to all legal recognition of religion?

But, it may be asked, does not such a connexion as that contended for, tend to confound church and state, to blend in confusion things that are essentially distinct? By no means. Our argument, not only is consistent with, but necessarily supposes, an essential distinction between the two. But *distinction* does not necessarily imply *hostility*. Things may be *diverse* without being *adverse*. That civil society and ecclesiastical society differ, we admit;—they differ in their immediate origin, objects, and ends; in their form of administration; in the light in which they regard their subjects; and in the character of the effects they respectively produce. But they are not, on this account, necessarily opposed to each other. On the contrary, there are many things in which they agree;—they agree in their original author, God; in the rule and standard of their administration, the Word of God; in their ultimate end, the glory of God; and in their subjection to the Messiah. They are, therefore, capable of existing in close combination, without being confounded. The church and the state were always distinct; yet we know that once they existed together in perfect harmony, without confusion: so that the objection in question is at variance as much with fact as with the very nature of the respective societies themselves.[62]

[62] 'It is not true, though it has been often recklessly affirmed by the

Fifthly. To say that the church and the state, that national society and true religion, are capable of existing together in harmonious co-operation, and of producing a mutually advantageous effect on each other, is, however, not saying all that may be said on this subject. We may go farther, and affirm that injurious consequences of the most frightful kind, would spring from insisting on their being entirely separated. The amount of pernicious consequences that should, in this way, ensue, it is impossible fully to depict. Society must, of course, in this case, forego all the advantages which, as we before observed, may be derived to it from religion, and religion all the advantages which may be derived to *it* from the countenance, encouragement, and support of the civil power. Not only must religion struggle, unbefriended and unaided, in its benevolent attempts to pervade the great mass of society with its principles,

opponents of establishments, that under the former economy the church and the state were blended together. A most obvious distinction was marked between them. The church was not the nation, nor was the nation the church. Each had its distinct rulers, courts, laws, subjects, penalties, and duration. Moses and his successors were the rulers in the state; Aaron and his successors rulers in the church. The church had her courts of the synagogue and ecclesiastical sanhedrim; the state, those of the gate and the civil sanhedrim. The ceremonial laws were those of the church; the judicial those of the state. Civil and religious privileges were not necessarily extended to the same persons. Proselytes might be members of the church without participating in the privileges of the state; whilst, on the other hand, scandalous offenders against the ceremonial and the moral law, permitted to enjoy civil rights, were nevertheless debarred from the fellowship of the church. A distinction was marked, too, in respect of penalties. Those of the church were purely ecclesiastical, as casting out of the synagogue; those of the state extended to fine, and even to death. In short, the distinction between the Jewish church and state is obviously marked in their respective duration. The latter ended when it became a province of Rome; the former subsisted and retained its ecclesiastical character, down to the destruction of the temple, and the scattering abroad of the Jewish people among all nations.'—*Mackray's Defence of Civil Establishments*, p. 53.

and to diffuse its light among the poor and the illiterate; but civil society must become essentially and avowedly infidel. If the nation must have nothing to do with religion, then, in the constitution of the country, there can be no acknowledgment of God, no recognition of the Bible. Electors may, in this case, feel themselves at full liberty, in the choice of their rulers, to throw aside all respect for religion, and allow themselves to be wholly swayed by the all-powerful influence of party politics. The rulers even must be set free from the trammels of an oath, which is a religious matter, and exempted from all obligation to recognise God in their official enactments. Every allusion to divine Providence may be justly characterised as 'cant and humbug.' There must be no prayers in the national assemblies. There must be no appeal to the divine law in the senate-house. The judge on the bench must be precluded from referring the unhappy culprit whom he condemns, to the solemnities of a judgment to come, or even of recommending him to betake to the blood of atonement for the salvation of his soul. The Sabbath of the Lord may be employed, with impunity, in every kind of business and sport. And the nation, although as we have seen a moral subject of Messiah, must be debarred from ever expressing its allegiance to its King!

Sixthly. But is such a separation as is contended for, practicable, even were it proved to be desirable? We venture to think that it is not. We see not how, in any case, there can be found a basis of national policy at all, where there is an entire disregard of all the sanctions of religion. But the separation is rendered more difficult still wherever Christianity exists. So extensive are the obligations, so powerful the principles of the religion of Jesus, that, where these are felt, it will be found utterly impossible to disregard their influence, even in the ordinary transactions of civil life. The ruler, if a Christian, will not feel himself at liberty to disregard the motives and the interests of religion, in the discharge of his official functions; neither will the subject, either in the choice of his rulers, or in his obedience to the laws. The very existence of the Christian church in a land, must render it impossible to legislate and act in the same way as if it had no existence there. In short, things civil and religious are so closely interwoven, in the circumstances and very constitution of man, that, to effect an entire separation between them, may safely be pronounced chimerical,—impossible if it were attempted, and foolish and wicked in no ordinary degree if it were possible.

It is easy to say, in opposition to the whole argument maintained on this subject, that Christ did not call in the aid of the civil power in support of his church at the commencement; that it flourished notwithstanding, and in spite, too, of bloody persecutions, during the primitive ages; and that, from the time of its alliance with the state, its purity and prosperity began to decline. The case assumed in the latter part of this statement is, as has been often shewn, not matter of fact. The corruptions of the Christian church, as already hinted, were in existence long before the time of Constantine, and the decline of her prosperity can be traced distinctly to other causes than the countenance extended to her by that distinguished individual. And, as to Christianity's having been established at first without the aid of the civil power, this circumstance would form an unanswerable objection to any one who should maintain, that religion could not exist or prosper without the aid of the civil magistrate. But this, be it remembered, is not our opinion. The question is not, whether religion can exist without national support, but what is the duty of nations towards the religion and church of Christ. And, if her primitive prosperity without the countenance of the state is to be pleaded as a valid reason why the church should always remain in the same circumstances, might we not, with equal propriety, contend that there should be no such thing as a course of preparatory education required of ministers; nay, that it is desirable that the civil authorities in a land should, not simply let religion alone, but that they should persecute it with all their might, as it was by means of unlearned men, and amid fire and blood, that the church, in that age, prospered and flourished? What the Head of the church may choose to do for her protection and support, in extraordinary circumstances, and in order to subserve the purpose of setting in a clearer light her spiritual independence and divine vitality, can form no rule of procedure in other circumstances. It is not for us to know the times and the seasons, which the Father hath put in his own power. It is our duty, while we observe with devout adoration the workings of his providence, to take as our guide the dictates of his holy and infallible Word. Nor does it become us to prescribe to God the manner in which the expression of his will, in any case, shall be conveyed to us. The want of a direct precept can form no valid objection, in the matter under consideration, any more than in other cases, such as infant baptism and the Christian Sabbath, for which no direct injunction can be pleaded, and whose obligation is admitted, on much the same sort of grounds as those on which the duty of nations to encourage and aid the true religion is supported.

Such are some of our reasons for maintaining that it is the duty of nations, in virtue of their moral subjection to the Messiah, to have respect to the interests of his church. The grand basis of this obligation, we beg to remind our readers, is the moral supremacy of Christ over the nations. From this, as we have already seen, springs the duty of extending their countenance and support to his church. The other arguments may be regarded as corollaries from this great principle or axiom. Indeed, both the church and the state being placed under the mediatorial dominion,—being, so to speak, only different moral provinces of the same King,—separate departments of one vast moral empire, it is not easy to conceive of them being so irreconcilably opposed as to be incapable of subsisting in close and friendly alliance with one another. The titles, *King of saints*, and *King of kings*, imply nothing contradictory. They are inscribed on the same escutcheon; they sparkle on the same diadem; and, apart from the prejudices engendered by party contentions, one should think that they can call up, on being named, no feeling of incongruity. Let us not, then, be found guilty of attempting to put asunder what God has joined together.

It is impossible, in connexion with the duty of nations toward the church, not to lament that the kingdoms of the world have been so little careful to select the true religion as the object of their fostering care. The continental nations have, for the most part, extended their favour to that church which is the Mystery of iniquity, and which is emphatically antichristian. They have given their power to the Beast. Instead of favouring the chaste Spouse and Bride of Christ, the kings of the earth have taken to their embrace the Mother of Harlots and abominations of the earth; and, by so doing, have furnished the enemies of all alliance between church and state, with a plausible, though ill-founded objection.

By our own nation, it is deeply to be lamented, civil countenance has been extensively given to the same false and pernicious system, both in the colonies and in Ireland. The Protestant establishment of England itself, is, to a considerable extent, an establishment of error, being essentially prelatical, and otherwise loaded with a burdensome mass of unscriptural and superstitious ceremonies. Even the Presbyterian establishment of Scotland, in so far as the creed and government of the church were prescribed by the state at the Revolution Settlement, and ordained because agreeable to the wishes of the people rather than founded on the Word of God, and inasmuch as a decidedly Erastian power is both claimed and exercised over the church, particularly in the appointment of her ministers, is highly objectionable. Both the church and the state, it ought ever to be borne in mind, in entering into alliance for the purpose of securing the mutual advantages which such an alliance is calculated to subserve, are bound, in duty to Christ, to have respect at once to the *character* of the ally with whom they unite, and to the *nature* of the alliance that is formed between them. Both of these are indispensable to a legitimate and useful alliance. Neither must the state, on the one hand, confer support on error and superstition, nor the church, on the other, enter into association with an immoral and antichristian power. And, even supposing the state and the church to be both what they ought to be, care must be taken that the union formed between them, be not such as involves an encroachment of the one on the prerogatives of the other. It must be such as is perfectly consistent with the spiritual independence of the church, such as leaves her in the free and unfettered enjoyment and exercise of all the privileges and immunities that belong to her, by the grant of her glorious and divine Head.

How far this rule has been violated, with regard to the existing establishments of our land, it is not our present object to inquire, or to shew. But it certainly becomes the friends of these institutions to consider, whether much of the opposition with which they are assailed and by which their very existence is threatened, may not arise from this source; and whether, for their stability and security, a thorough searching into every defect, an unsparing reform of every abuse, a complete purgation of every evil, may not be the course which true policy, as well as fidelity to Messiah the Prince, would seem to dictate. It is the existence of these abuses, they may rest assured, that has given weight and influence to the objections of their opponents; and we would, with all possible earnestness, counsel their speedy and complete rectification. It is certainly much to be regretted, that a certain class, in their zeal against great and undeniable evils, have permitted themselves to be carried beyond this legitimate object of assault, and have assailed a glorious and Scriptural *principle.* For this they are undoubtedly to be blamed. But it concerns those of the other class to bear in mind, that the whole blame does not rest with their opponents. Not a little of it is chargeable upon themselves, for countenancing and perpetuating those abuses of a good principle, which have brought the very principle itself into danger and disrepute. And having called upon the one party to attend to an immediate and thorough reform, we would earnestly and respectfully entreat the other to restrict their opposition to the evils in question. They will find here ample employment for all their artillery. In this department, while they conduct the warfare like men breathing the spirit of the Gospel and seeking the interests of truth, let them spare no arrows. But oh! let them beware of pointing a single shaft against the sacred principle of Christ's moral supremacy over the kingdoms of the world. Let them shrink from entertaining a sentiment, or maintaining a theory, which would go to pluck from the head of Emmanuel the crown of the nations, and to blot from his escutcheon the resplendent title, *King of kings and Lord of lords.*

There are those who occupy neutral ground; who are

connected with neither the one party nor the other; who stand aloof from existing establishments, on account of what they conceive to be wrong in them, and who yet feel themselves bound to contend for the principle that nations ought to have some respect for religion. Such we would recommend to keep their ground firmly, and to turn to good account the influence their peculiar position enables them to exercise. They may find it difficult to steer clear of taking a side, in a controversy which is waged with much fierceness. But let them be persuaded that by doing so, they must impair their usefulness. At once their duty and safety are to STAND STILL. Not that we mean that they should stand still in idleness or unconcern,* but that they should continue to occupy the ground to which they believe those who have erred, on the one side and on the other, must ultimately come. Let them contend earnestly for the truth of the great principle, the adoption of which in its purity, is, they are persuaded, to bless, in the end, both the church and the nations, with contentment, peace, holiness, and glory. And let them hold up to the view of all the banner of CHRIST'S CROWN AND COVENANT, that

* At this place the author has added in the margin of his lecture the following clause :—'Not that there should be no negotiating with other churches with a view to union.'

This is interesting and pleasant. The first note of union was sounded in 1863, a year and a half after the author's death, and this significant clause was inserted probably long before. Those much misunderstood both his head and his heart who used his name as that of one who would have been opposed to union. Dr. Symington held the Solemn League and Covenant of the three kingdoms not as an instrument of sectarian isolation, but as a bond of union. He would have deplored as bitterly as his friend Dr. Robert Buchanan did the lamentable interruption of hopeful negotiations in 1873, and would have rejoiced with all his heart in the partial incorporation attained in 1876.—EDITOR.

both civil and ecclesiastical societies may come under its protection, and do homage to the King in whose name it is unfurled. By identifying themselves entirely with the one or with the other class of combatants, they must give up something for which it is important they should strive, and can only subserve, at the best, the interests of a party: but, by holding fast the position they now occupy, they may be of service to the general cause of the Redeemer.

The friends of truth, the subjects of Him who is King in Sion, must stand prepared to surrender the applause of man whose breath is in his nostrils; must value, above everything, the approbation of the Almighty; and aim, at all times, at being able to say in sincerity, *We serve the Lord Christ.* By taking a decided stand on their own proper ground, without being moved from it by the dread of singularity, and without suffering themselves to be swallowed up in the devouring vortex of party strife, or of latitudinarian indifference, their very position of apparent neutrality will carry in it a distinct and palpable testimony for the truth as it is in Jesus. *Prove all things, hold fast that which is good. Wherefore take unto you the whole armour of God, that ye may be able to withstand in the evil day, and having done all to stand. Stand, therefore, having your loins girt about with truth, and having on the breastplate of righteousness, and your feet shod with the preparation of the Gospel of peace. Behold, I come quickly: hold that fast which thou hast, that no man take thy crown!*

CHAPTER X.

PERPETUITY OF THE MEDIATORIAL DOMINION.

The reign of Messiah the Prince is progressive, both as respects the hearts of men and the world at large. Neither his visible nor his invisible kingdom is complete at once. By the use of those special, and also of those common, means which he employs, he carries forward, with irresistible energy, his work of grace and his work of judgment, at once gradually subjugating his enemies and gathering in those given him by the Father. This work embraces a period of several thousands of years, during which his kingdom is making steady advancement. There is to be, even in this present world, a season of unspeakable grandeur, when light, love, liberty, peace, and holiness, shall prevail to an unprecedented extent. But it is in the state of glory that the kingdom of Christ is to receive its grand consummation.

By Christ's mediatorial reign in glory, we do not understand that government merely which he exercises in heaven, extending from the period of his exaltation to the end of the world. Much of his administration, during this period, has respect to his church upon earth, and to other things in subordination to her interests, as well as to the redeemed above. But what we mean by the mediatorial reign in glory, is the dominion which the exalted Mediator exercises, and will continue to exercise, over the redeemed above as such; a dominion which, we conceive, is not to be confined to the period that shall elapse at the final judgment, but shall stretch out into endless ages.

This, it will be readily perceived, is a theme of very great sublimity, and we may reasonably expect to find it involved in considerable mystery. It would argue great presumption, for a weak-sighted mortal to pretend to a complete understanding of such a subject. It is to be approached only with sentiments of profound veneration and humility, and with a fixed resolution to be guided by the light of divine revelation alone, avoiding all vain speculation, and humbly determining not to be wise above what is written.

It is a topic on which, it appears, some diversity of sentiment has existed. From an expression in the writings of the apostle Paul,[1] many have been led to form the idea, that, at the end of all things, the mediatorial reign is to terminate altogether, and the government of the kingdom to devolve, through eternity, on God essentially considered.[*] But there seems to be some confusion of ideas in the minds of those who have expressed themselves to this effect, inasmuch as, in speaking of it, they use language which is inconsistent with the notion itself. The venerable Dr. Owen says, in one place, 'at the end of this dispensation, he shall give up the kingdom to God, even the Father, or *cease from*

---

[1] 1 Cor. xv. 24. 'Then cometh the end, when he shall have delivered up the kingdom to God, even the Father,' &c.

[*] The author here has made a reference to *Christ's Second Coming: will it be pre-millennial?* By Principal Brown. 2nd ed. 1849, pp. 160-166.

the administration of his mediatorial office and power.' And again, 'when this work is perfectly fulfilled and ended, then shall *all the mediatory actings of Christ cease for ever.*' Yet he says, elsewhere, in explanation of his meaning on this subject, 'I would extend this no further than as to what concerneth the exercise of Christ's mediatory office with respect unto the church here below, and the enemies of it;' while he admits, 'that the person of Christ, in and by his human nature, shall be for ever the immediate Head of the whole glorified creation—the means and way of communication between God and his glorified saints for ever—the eternal object of Divine glory, praise, and worship.'[2] From these expressions, it is plain that this distinguished divine was not of opinion that the reign of the Mediator was not to be perpetual, or that it was to be abrogated, properly speaking, at the conclusion of the present state, but, on the contrary, that it was to continue, in some sense or another, for ever. Such being his sentiment, it is to be regretted that he should have allowed himself to speak on the subject without sufficient precision, and to use language which seems to give countenance to the opposite opinion.

Another writer of merited celebrity, in our own day, speaking of what Christ will do at the period in question, says, 'As a faithful ambassador, whose commission is finished, he will honourably *give it back* to Him who appointed him, and will *return to his own personal station, as the divine and eternal Son;* and then will a new order of the moral

[2] Owen's Works, vol. i. pp. 236, 237, 271, Goold's edition.

universe commence, and the unspeakably vast assemblage of holy creatures, delivered and secured from sin and misery, shall possess the IMMEDIATE fruition of the Father.'[3] This language seems to convey the idea, that it was the opinion of this writer, that the reign of Christ as Mediator, even over the church, should come to an end; for he speaks, in the context, of 'the *termination* of the mediatorial reign;'[4] and, elsewhere, ' of the great *parenthesis* of the mediatorial administration.'[5] It is but fair, however, to take notice of certain qualifying clauses which are thrown in, and which illustrate the confusion of ideas of which we have complained. 'When all its designs,' says Dr. Smith, 'are accomplished, the mediatorial system, *as to all these modes of its exercise,* shall cease,' referring to what he had said before, of 'the giving and enforcing of religious laws, the diffusion and success of the Gospel, the heavenly intercession, the operations of divine grace, the vanquishing of all antichristian and other inimical powers, and the adjudication of eternal rewards and punishments.' He also adds, 'Imperfect and obscure as must be our conceptions of the termination of the mediatorial reign, it is self-evident that it can, in no respect, diminish the honours of the Redeemer, or abate the regards of the redeemed. . . . The connexion of Christ and his saints is indissoluble; neither things present nor things to come shall separate them from his love: and the final state of true Christians is expressly called an entering into the ETERNAL kingdom of our Lord and

[3] Dr. P. Smith on the Messiah, iii. 257.   [4] P. 258.
[5] Smith on Sacrifice, p. 92.

Saviour Jesus Christ.' But, after attaching all due weight to this language, as tending to modify what was quoted above, we find it impossible to look upon the expressions in question as otherwise than unguarded and erroneous.

To talk of Christ's *returning* to his own personal station as the Divine and Eternal Son, certainly implies that he must have left his personal station: but is it so? He stooped, indeed, from his personal dignity, but he never laid it aside. The rank of divine and eternal Son was never lost. At the moment of his deepest humiliation, he possessed the personal dignity of the Son of God, and indeed, but for this, his humiliation would have been in vain. This Dr. Smith certainly knows and believes. To speak, as this writer does, of the redeemed in glory possessing the IMMEDIATE fruition of the Father, in the sense of excluding the intervention of the Mediator, is plainly at variance with his own admission, that the connexion of Christ and his saints is *indissoluble*, and that the final state is the *eternal* kingdom of our Lord and Saviour.

The same view of the temporary duration of the mediatorial dominion, is supported in the theological lectures of a late eminent Professor of Divinity, in one of our dissenting churches. This learned author in question speaks of the text at present under consideration as 'confessedly obscure,' and subjoins to his explanation the following modest statement:—'What has now been said, is proposed solely as a probable opinion: it would be presumptuous to speak confidently on a subject so obscure.'[6] The views of this writer will fall to be examined in the sequel.

With all due deference to the distinguished individuals alluded to above, we would venture to submit, whether the saying of the apostle may not, after all, be satisfactorily explained, in full consistency with the proper perpetuity of Christ's dominion as Mediator. The passage, in its connexion, stands thus:—'Then cometh the end, when he shall have delivered up the kingdom to God, even the Father, when he shall have put down all rule, and all authority, and power. For he must reign, till he hath put all enemies under his feet. The last enemy that shall be destroyed is death. . . . And when all things shall be subdued unto him, then shall the Son also himself be subject unto him that put all things under him, that God may be all in all.'[7]

It is necessary to take the whole passage into consideration. The meaning of any one phrase in it, must be consistent with that of others. The apostle cannot contradict himself. It is, of course, requisite that our explanation of one clause agree with that of another. And, if this reasonable principle is closely adhered to in the interpretation of the apostle's language, we apprehend it will be found impossible to explain the delivering up of the kingdom, so as to imply that the mediatorial reign shall ever altogether cease. We remark, then, that such a view appears to be utterly at variance with the expression—'Then shall the Son also be subject

---

[6] See Dr. Dick's Lectures, vol. iii. pp. 239-245.
[7] 1 Cor. xv. 24-28.

unto Him.' In what sense, we ask, but that of Mediator, can any Trinitarian understand the Son to be subject to the Father through eternity? As God, personally considered, the Son is in every respect equal to the Father. Subjection or subordination necessarily implies inferiority of some kind or another; but it is only in an *official* capacity that inferiority, in any sense, can be ascribed to the Son of God. Personally, he 'counts it no robbery to be *equal* with God;' he is 'Jehovah's *fellow.*' One of the writers above spoken of, has been led, by the theory of interpretation which he adopts, to use language on this subject, in our opinion, most unguarded and indefensible. 'The eternal Son of God,' says Dr. Pye Smith, 'is, notwithstanding his Divine nature, subordinate in the order of Deity, and even perfectly obedient to the Father. To have been thus subject to the Father, from all eternity and by the necessity of the Divine personality, is no more incongruous with the proper and essential Divinity of the Son, than it will be, after the consummation of the present system of things, when the great parenthesis of the mediatorial administration shall be completed, and God shall be all in all.'[8] What the writer of these words means by *a necessary and eternal subordination or subjection of the Son to the Father, apart from all respect to the mediatorial economy*, we know not. But, we frankly confess for ourselves, that we can form no idea of any such thing, without adopting the Socinian or the Arian heresy. The slightest degree of such subordination appears to us to be perfectly 'incongruous with the

---

[8] Smith on Sacrifice, pp. 91, 92. See also Treffry on the Sonship, p. 387.

proper and essential Divinity of the Son;' and to speak of such a thing is to us altogether revolting. It is obvious that this respected author has been betrayed into the use of such language, solely by his finding it necessary to reconcile the everlasting subjection of the Son with the preconceived notion that his mediatorial character and reign are to cease at the end of the world. And to us it appears no slight presumption against the correctness of this latter notion altogether, that so able and clear and accurate a supporter of the doctrine of our Lord's divinity, should have found it necessary, in speaking of it, to express himself in language so obscure, contradictory and repulsive. Believing as we do, on the authority of this passage itself, that the Son is to be eternally subject to the Father, we find it impossible to separate this idea from that of the strict perpetuity of his mediatory office. But what, it will be asked, are we, in this case, to make of the *delivering up* of the kingdom?

The term kingdom, does not, in the instance before us, necessarily signify *kingship*, reign, or the possession and exercise of kingly power; but dominion in the sense of territory, or realm,—that, in short, over which the king reigns. The kingdom of Christ, in this sense, is, as we have shewn, most extensive. Besides his church, or spiritual kingdom, it includes all things in the world, in subordination to her interests. And it is the opinion of some excellent and sound theologians, that the kingdom to be delivered up at the end of time is the latter of these—his government over things without the church, and more especially her enemies. It is of his reign over 'enemies,' that the apostle is speaking at the time. This, as we before remarked, is the opinion of Dr. Owen, who expressly says, that the delivering up of the kingdom he would 'extend no farther than as unto what concerneth the exercise of Christ's mediatorial office with respect unto the church *here below*, and the *enemies* of it.' Such also is the view of Dr. Doddridge, who, in a note to his exposition of the passage in question, says, 'To me it appears that the *kingdom* to be given up is the rule of this *lower world*, which is then to be consumed.'* This view of the subject is certainly free from the objection to which that we are combating is exposed. It is also quite agreeable to the context, and perfectly consistent with the perpetuity of the mediatorial reign.

Without, however, taking the word *kingdom* in so restricted a sense; viewing it even as inclusive of the church, the proper realm of the mediatorial King, may not the phrase under review be satisfactorily explained on another principle? It is all along taken for granted, that the words 'deliver up' signify *abandon, surrender, give over;* and so they are understood to import that the divine Mediator shall return into the hands of the Father the *official* commission received from him, and henceforward exercise only a *personal* dominion. But may not the original term, $\pi\alpha\rho\alpha\delta\varphi$, be understood to signify, only bringing the work he was commissioned to perform to a state of completion, and presenting it in that finished state to him from whom the commission was derived, by way of giving account of the trust

---

* See also Urwick on *The Second Advent*, p. 62; and on *The Worship of Christ*, p. 201.

committed to him? Certain it is that the Greek verb here employed, is used in the New Testament in this very sense. 'But when the fruit is brought forth (marg. *ripe*, Gr. παραδῳ) immediately he putteth in the sickle, because the harvest is come.'[9] Here the verb bears the idea of completion or perfection, ripeness or maturity. Now, at the end of the world, the kingdom of the Messiah shall have been brought to perfection; the work given him to do shall have been finished. Those given him by the Father shall have been found out, redeemed, sanctified, saved, and gathered all together into one; their enemies, even death itself, shall have been subdued; and the whole scheme of providence shall have been developed and wound up. The Mediator shall, then, appear and give in to the Father a full account of his mediatorial undertaking; presenting to him the kingdom in that state of consummation to which he shall then have brought it; and receiving from him a clear testimony of his approbation. This is perfectly consonant with the idea that the Son shall retain and exercise his mediatorial authority over his own proper kingdom for ever. 'This kingdom,' says Theophylact, 'he delivers to his Father, by achieving and *accomplishing the purposes* of it. Thus, for instance, if a king commits to his son the management of a war against nations that have rebelled, when the war is finished, and the nations again reduced to subjection, then he is said to deliver up the war to his Father, i.e., *shew that he has accomplished the work committed to him.*'[10]

---

[9] Mark iv. 29. [10] Bloomfield's Recensio Synoptica, vol. vi. p. 681.

It is admitted, on all hands, that there must be, at the period alluded to, an entire change in the mode of administering the kingdom. The mediatorial dominion is conducted at present by means of ordinances and providences. The preaching of the Gospel, the dispensation of sacraments, the services of ministers, and the overruling of the events that fall out in both the natural and the moral worlds, are all made subservient to the interests of the church. At the period alluded to, these shall cease. Christ has given apostles, prophets, evangelists, pastors, and teachers, ' for the *perfecting* of the saints, TILL they come to a *perfect* man, to the measure of the *stature* of the *fulness* of Christ.' By eating bread and drinking wine, believers ' shew forth the Lord's death TILL he come;' but then they are to be introduced to the marriage supper of the Lamb. We have already adverted to the language of Dr. Smith, which accords with this view, when he says that the ' mediatorial system, *as to all these modes of its exercise*, shall cease.' We may add the language of Calvin, who, after quoting the words of the apostle respecting the delivering up of the kingdom unto the Father, says, ' he only intends, that in that perfect glory *the administration of the kingdom will not be the same as it is at present.*'[11] There is thus suggested another principle on which this difficult but interesting text may be interpreted, without supposing a cessation of the mediatorial dominion and character. At present the administration of the kingdom is conducted through the intervention of outward instruments: afterwards it

---

[11] Calv. Inst., Book II. chap. xv. sec. 5.

shall be immediate, direct, personal. According to this interpretation, the phrase, 'that God may be all in all,' means that a new mode of intercourse with the Deity shall then be introduced, to the exclusion, not of the Mediator, but only of those institutions and ordinances which were deemed necessary for the saints in their present state of existence. In the triumphant state, they shall no longer see through a glass darkly, but then face to face; which is, however, perfectly consistent with their receiving the light of the knowledge of the glory of God in the face of Jesus Christ.

In harmony with these views of this difficult passage, especially with the first, is the opinion of an eminent German divine, one of the most triumphant combatants of the system of theology which is unhappily too fashionable in that country. From his dissertation on the meaning of 'the kingdom of heaven,' we give the following extract, for whose length it is presumed no apology is necessary, as the work from which it is taken is not generally circulated.

'The declarations of David (Psalm cx. 1) and of St. Paul (1 Cor. xv. 24, 28),' says Professor Storr, 'ought not to be taken in an opposite sense. Nor does it seem difficult to perceive, that their meaning is far different from this. For, since an *eternal* priesthood is attributed to the Messiah, and this is very closely allied to his *kingdom*, it is evident that they do not intend to deny eternity to the latter. Therefore ἕως in Psalm cx. 1, does not mean, that, when every enemy has been subdued, the government is to be taken away from Christ, but as the general object of this whole psalm is to shew that the designs of his enemies against the divine prince would at length have an ending altogether different from that which they expected, it was in exact conformity with such a design to establish this point, especially, that the divinely appointed Lord should reign, until all his enemies should be subjected to *his own* power. Which does not mean that he to whose government the enemies should be subjected (which circumstance proves of itself the continuance of that government) should then resign his power; but, on the other hand, the result of the whole matter is declared to be this, that they who had refused to acknowledge this prince, and wished to remove him by force from his government, are all *overthrown* and confounded, while he *himself*, on the contrary, *is sitting at the right hand of God*. He shall reign for a considerable time in the midst of enemies, securely expecting an end of the rebellion; but, while he himself is sitting at the right hand of God, it shall at length come to pass that all his adversaries shall be reduced under subjection to *his* authority. Such being the meaning of the psalm, and this sense of it being recognised by St. Paul himself, who has evidently made the dignity of the Messiah, described in the psalm, coequal with his life, which he shews to be eternal, we seem to be going quite in opposition to his design, by supposing that in 1 Cor. xv. any *end* is assigned to the Messiah's kingdom. Therefore, the government, which, it is said in verse 24, he shall restore to God, even the Father, must not be supposed to mean *Christ's* government, but that of *every opposing power*, which is evidently declared to be *destroyed*, that the power may be restored to God. For since those who set themselves against Christ, at the same time resist *God* also; the government is restored to *God* when it is restored to *Christ*, subduing those who are at the same time the enemies of himself and of God, and thus recovering the government for God and for himself, from the enemies who had usurped it. That this is the meaning of the passage under discussion, appears to me to be confirmed also by what immediately follows. For St. Paul clearly shews, in 1 Cor. xv. 27, that verse 25 by no means expresses, in the words *αχρις οὑ*, a limit and end of Christ's government; but that all that we are to understand is, that all things, and therefore all enemies also, are to be subjected to the empire of Christ. According to this interpretation, therefore, the general drift of the apostle will be this; that for all the friends of Christ who, after the example of himself who was the first that rose again, have been recalled from death to a life of blessedness, an end is at hand to which both the expectations of believers are directed, and the divine promises, upon which these expectations rest, all point. For that this is as it were the scope and end of the divine promises, that the empire of Christ will at length so far prevail, that all enemies shall be subjected to him, of whom death must be reckoned the last which will be destroyed by the resurrection of those who have died in faith. For that God has put all things, and therefore all enemies, under him. That, therefore, when Christ shall have destroyed death and also every opposing power, and thus shall have restored the kingdom to the Father, *i.e.*, when he shall have caused it to come to pass that God everywhere prevails and his majesty is universally acknowledged, some rejoicing exceedingly in God their King and deriving their whole pleasure and happiness from this source, from which they see and inwardly feel it to flow, *i.e.*, from the all-powerful and benignant government of God, with never-ceasing reverence,—others, on the contrary, feeling with terror the power of his just government, and not daring to open their mouths against him;—then shall come the end. Nor should it seem strange, that the discourse in verse 24, changed from the government of Christ, who, it was said, should destroy every opposing power, to the Father to whom the kingdom is said to be delivered up by Christ. The reason of this, the apostle adds, in verses 27, 28 : ' When it is written that all things are put under him (by another), it is manifest, that he is to be excepted who put all things under him. Since, moreover, all things are put under him (by the Father), the Son himself also will be subject to him, who has put all things under him, so that God is therefore all in all.' When St. Paul magnificently describes that great power of the *man* Jesus, which is able to overthrow every enemy, and even death itself, this kingdom of Christ, thus august, and delivered from the injury and destruction of every opposing power, he gives to God the Father, not in order to shew that it ceases to be Christ's, but that all things may at last be referred to the glory of God the Father ; especially as the psalms which he had in his mind, when he spoke of that τελος, treated the same subject in a similar manner. But as we read that the Father subjected all enemies to Christ, and that Christ subjected them to himself, so he who is said in 1 Cor. xv. 24, to restore the kingdom to the Father, after the discomfiture of his enemies, may also be said to assert the authority and dignity of *his own* government. In other places, we certainly find it said that, even after the conquest of his enemies, *Christ* shall continue to reign.'[*]

It thus appears, that the passage in question admits of being explained, on various principles, in harmony with the sentiment that the mediatorial character and reign are to continue for ever. We do not take upon us to determine which of these views is the correct one, but we beg it to be remembered that, whether we have hit on the right interpretation or not, in any of the preceding observations, the passage itself asserts the perpetuity in question, and of course must be capable of explanation consistently with this view. The Son is to be *subject to the Father for ever*, which cannot be if he is not to be Mediator for ever. Having thus, we hope, successfully removed this stumbling-block which meets us at the very threshold of our subject, we proceed to submit farther evidence in support of the sentiment that Christ as Mediator is to reign for ever.

1. We go at once to the Scriptures. 'Thy throne, O God, is *for ever and ever.*—His name shall endure *for ever.*—Thy kingdom is an *everlasting* kingdom, and thy dominion endureth *throughout all generations.*—Of the increase of his government and peace there shall be *no end*, upon the throne of David, and upon his king-

[*] Dissertation on the meaning of *the kingdom of heaven*, by Gotlobb Christian Storr, late Professor of Theology in the University of Tübingen.—*Biblical Cabinet*, No. IX., pp. 26-37.

dom to order it, and to establish it with judgment, and with justice, from henceforth, even *for ever*.—In the days of these kings shall the God of heaven set up a kingdom which *shall never be destroyed:* and the kingdom shall not be left to other people, but it shall break in pieces and consume all these kingdoms, and it shall *stand for ever*.—His dominion is an *everlasting* dominion which *shall not pass away* and his kingdom that which *shall not be destroyed*.—He shall reign over the house of Jacob *for ever;* and of his kingdom there shall be *no end*.—An entrance shall be ministered unto you abundantly into the *everlasting* kingdom of our Lord and Saviour Jesus Christ.—The kingdoms of this world are become the kingdoms of our Lord and of his Christ; and he shall reign *for ever and ever*.'[12] All these passages refer to the reign of Christ as Mediator. The language employed is strongly and fully expressive of perpetuity. It is true, the terms in question are not always expressive of absolute eternity; but they are the strongest, be it remarked, that can be found to denote strict perpetuity; and, where they must be understood with any limitation, this arises from the nature of the subject spoken of, and not from the terms themselves. They express in themselves the longest possible duration of which the things spoken of admit. Unless, therefore, it can be proved that there is something about the mediatorial dominion which renders it necessary that it should terminate, the passages quoted must be understood as affirming, without doubt, that it

---

[12] Ps. xlv. 6, lxxii. 17, cxlv. 13; Isa. ix. 7; Dan. ii. 44, vii. 14; Luke i. 33; 2 Pet. i. 11; Rev. xi. 15.

shall endure for ever. Stronger phraseology cannot be found to prove even the eternity of God's existence, or of future rewards and punishments.

The doctrine in question is confirmed and illustrated by the resplendent title, given to Christ, of *King of glory*. In a psalm which is admitted to refer to the ascension of the Redeemer, this designation is applied to him emphatically again and again. Myriads of angelic heralds, as they demand admission for him within the portals of the celestial palace, shout, 'Lift up your heads, O ye gates; and be ye lift up, ye everlasting doors; and the *King of glory* shall come in;' and when the question is propounded, 'Who is this King of glory?' they meet it with the unhesitating response, 'The Lord of Hosts, he is the *King of glory*.'[13] To remove all hesitation about the application of this sublime passage to the Mediator, we have only to advert to the writings of the apostles, where we find him spoken of under the same magnificent appellation. 'Which none of the princes of this world knew,' says Paul, 'for had they known it, they would not have crucified the *Lord of glory*.'[14] 'My brethren,' says James, 'have not the faith of our Lord Jesus Christ, *the Lord of glory*, with respect of persons.'[15] These passages, when compared with another in which Jehovah is spoken of as '*the God of glory*,'[16] cannot fail to leave the impression, on the mind of the humble and candid reader, that the divine Mediator, in his official capacity, is to exercise an undoubted sovereignty over the eternal world, regu-

[13] Ps. xxiv. 7–10.
[14] 1 Cor. ii. 8.
[15] James ii. 1.
[16] Acts vii. 2.

lating and dispensing for ever the communications of celestial bliss. *Glory* is the term peculiarly employed, both by the inspired writers and by others, to denote the state of heavenly felicity, prepared for the people of God, which is to continue for ever; and the title *king* or *lord* denotes government over that state. So far from supposing that this title does not belong to him, or that it belongs to him only for a limited period, it would seem more consonant with Scripture and right reason to conclude, that it is to constitute his most appropriate and enduring designation, and that all his other titles, *King of Sion, King of saints, and King of nations,* are to merge at last in this one, KING OF GLORY.

2. It would seem necessary, to the proper *reward of Christ* for his mediatorial work, that the duration of his reign should extend beyond the period of the consummation of all things. We have before adverted to the claim which he has to reward, and have spoken of the mediatorial dominion itself as partaking of the nature of reward. But, up to the moment of the final judgment, his work itself shall be unfinished. He shall be all the while doing the work for which he is to be rewarded. Till the end of all things, he shall be constantly engaged subduing his enemies; converting them into friends; carrying on the work of grace in their hearts, and carrying forward the scheme of divine dispensations in the world; gathering his people's souls to himself; raising their bodies from the dead; acquitting them from all condemnation; and consigning the wicked to neverending punishment. During all this period, he is, in a sense, making to himself a kingdom. His reward, as

consisting in the full possession of his kingdom, distinguished from his work in preparing it for himself, it thus appears, cannot commence till the time when, according to the supposition of some, his mediatorial character is to cease altogether. No small part of this reward, indeed, is to consist in the perfect salvation of the redeemed; but they will not and cannot be made perfect in soul and body till the last day; not till then can the blessed Redeemer present his church 'holy, unblamable, and unreprovable in his sight—a glorious church, not having spot, or wrinkle, or any such thing.' And are we to suppose that, just when the kingdom is completed, the government of it is to be abandoned? that, just when it has reached the summit of its perfection, he who has brought it to this pitch is to cease to have any connexion with it? that just when he has established his throne, completed his conquest, and secured the privileges and glory of his subjects, that moment the crown is to be plucked from his head, and the sceptre to drop from his hand? How much more natural to think, that then his crown shall beam forth with a brighter lustre, and his sceptre be swayed with more undisputed sovereignty!

It will not do to say, that the glory of having once possessed the kingdom and administered it with wisdom and righteousness will ever remain to him, and will call forth a tribute of praise from the countless myriads of his subjects.'[17] For it cannot be that glory and praise for the work of redemption, are to be ascribed to him in any other character than that of Redeemer. He cannot

[17] Dr. Dick.

be rewarded in one character, for work which he performs in another character. He cannot be rewarded as God, for what he does as Mediator. That he should be rewarded personally, is indeed utterly impossible, on any supposition whatever; but, even supposing it possible, it is contradictory to speak of his being rewarded essentially for work that is official. We need have no hesitation, therefore, in joining in the apostolical doxology, in which everlasting praise is ascribed to him as Mediator:—'To the only wise God *our Saviour*, be glory and majesty, dominion and power, both now and FOR EVER. Amen.'[18]

3. Indeed, that the mediatorial character and dominion should cease, would seem to be *impossible*. The relation subsisting betwixt the Redeemer and the redeemed must be perpetual. If *they* are to retain for ever the character of redeemed, *He* must surely retain that of Redeemer. A redeemer there cannot be without some that are redeemed: no more can there be redeemed without a redeemer. And, unless the Redeemer can forget the redeemed, there must be feelings of delight and complacency, and deep affection, and interest, with which *He* must ever regard *them:* and, unless the redeemed can forget their Redeemer, there are sentiments of gratitude, and love, and high esteem, and regard, with which *they* must ever respect *Him*. But that either Redeemer or redeemed should ever, through eternity, forget one another, is altogether inconceivable. It thus appears to be impossible that the mediatorial character should ever cease. Indeed, so powerfully is this consideration felt by one of the writers quoted above who

[18] Jude 25.

hold the idea of a termination of the mediatorial reign, that, after speaking of it, he adds, 'It is self-evident that it can, in no respect, diminish the honours of the Redeemer, or abate the regards of the redeemed. To suppose this would be to suppose the loss of memory itself in those pure and blessed minds.'[19] We ask nothing more than what is here admitted, as a proof that the mediatorial character and reign shall never terminate.

It is rendered impossible, also, by the inseparable union subsisting betwixt the divine and human natures of Christ. This union, formed at his incarnation, is indissoluble. When his humiliation terminated, his human nature was raised from the dead and taken by him to glory. In the kingdom of glory, it is destined to form a monument of divine condescension and love throughout eternity. Annihilated it cannot be; the very thought is revolting. A separate subsistence it never had, and never can have; the idea of such a thing is scarcely less shocking. There is no alternative, then, but that it shall abide for ever in close and mysterious union with the person of the Son of God. Need we any thing more to convince us, of the absolute perpetuity of the mediatorial character? In what other character can he exist as 'God-man, Emmanuel, God with us'?

But how, admitting it to be possible, are we to suppose that the cessation of the mediatorial dominion shall be brought about? Is it to be understood that he will abdicate the throne himself, voluntarily, and of his own accord? The office and the honour attached to it are too dear to him to admit of his doing so, without

[19] Dr. P. Smith.

some necessity for it which has never yet been shewn to exist. Shall he be dethroned, forcibly deprived of his power, and degraded from the office which he has so honourably and efficiently filled? It is impossible to conjecture by whom this should be done. It cannot be by his own people; for they feel his rule to be at once their safety and their honour. It cannot be by angels; for they also are made subject to him, and delight to do him homage. By devils it cannot be; for they, like his other enemies, shall then be put under his feet. There is but one other supposable source from which such an event can originate, and it is more unreasonable than all the rest—his Father. But He who has given him power, and set on his head a crown of purest gold, has destined that 'upon himself shall his crown flourish, and given him length of days FOR EVER AND EVER.'

4. The *necessities of the redeemed*, not less than the reward of the Redeemer, appear to us to require the continuance for ever of his mediatorial character. This, indeed, is the ground on which the sentiment for which we are contending is opposed. It is supposed that there can be no need for mediatorial administrations after the final judgment, that then the scheme of redemption shall be fully executed, and the official character may be laid aside as no longer required.

> 'Then thou thy regal sceptre shalt lay by,
> For regal sceptre thou no more shalt need;
> God shall be all in all.'
> *Milton.*

'The kingdom will end,' says one of the writers on this subject, 'when its design is accomplished; he will cease to exercise an authority which has no longer an object.' 'Nothing will remain to be done by the power with which our Saviour was invested at his ascension; and, his work being finished, his commission will expire.' 'May we not conceive his mediation to terminate like any other plan, in the execution of which the intention of the contriver has been fulfilled? Why should intercession continue, when there are no sins to be forgiven, and no wants to be supplied, and when the objects of redeeming love are established in a state of perfection beyond the possibility of failure?' However plausible the statements contained in these extracts, we have but to look closely at them to see that they assume the very point to be proved, that they take for granted the very matter in dispute, namely, that through eternity there shall exist no need for the mediatorial administration of our Lord. This we are disposed to question. We freely admit that there will not be need for the same kind of administration; the grounds of necessity will be different from what they were before. The King of glory will have no need to dispense pardon, to subdue rebellious passions, to ward off enemies, or to intercede for the bestowment of the initiatory blessings of redemption. But are there no other things that may call for the exercise of the mediatorial functions? We submit that there are.

May not the continuance of the relations subsisting between Christ and his people render this necessary? In the day of grace, a vital union is formed on the part of the renewed soul to the Lord Jesus Christ, which is essential to the privileges and duties of the Christian life and character. In consequence of this, Christ becomes, to the believer, at once a Head of merit—conferring on him a right to all new covenant benefits, and a Head of influence—communicating to him all needed supplies of strength and enjoyment. It is clearly to him *as Mediator* that this union is formed. Now this union is indissoluble. Christ can never cease to be the Head of merit and of influence to his people. Their right to all the blessings, and their fitness for all the services, and their experience of all the pleasures, of the celestial state, spring from their relation to him. They can spring, neither from themselves, nor from God absolutely considered. Nor are they the mere *effects* of what Christ has done, but effects to the continued existence of which their abiding in him is indispensable. But they could not abide in him as Mediator, unless he continued to be Mediator; and it is the rejoicing of believers' hearts to know that the union between them and their Lord shall never be dissolved. 'Who shall separate us from the love of Christ? I am persuaded that neither *death* nor life, nor angels, nor principalities, nor powers, nor things present, nor *things to come*, nor height, nor depth, nor any other creature, shall be able to separate us from the love of God, which is in Christ Jesus our Lord.' [20]

The redeemed in glory are to be engaged, throughout eternity, in the service of God. 'They serve him day and night in his temple. His servants shall serve him.' [21] While studying the character and works of Jehovah himself, hymning his praises, and performing

---

[20] Rom. viii. 35, 38, 39.   [21] Rev. vii. 15; xxii. 3.

offices of friendship to one another, they shall be actively employed in serving the Lord. And how are these services to find acceptance with God, but through the merits and intercession of the Mediator? As sinners saved, as captives redeemed, they can never claim acceptance on their own merit. Nor does it even appear consonant to the character of the great and holy God, to suppose him holding absolute and immediate intercourse with persons of this description, such as he holds with the angels who have never sinned. Moral fitness or propriety would seem to require, that the fellowship of redeemed men with the Majesty of heaven and of earth, should ever be conducted so as to indicate the peculiarity of their character, and to distinguish them from the unfallen sons of light. And this, we have reason to believe, will be done, by all their communion with God being through a Mediator, without whose intervention they shall not receive one ray of light or one token of divine regard.*

The very nature of the believer's glorious reward, supposes the perpetuity of Christ's mediatorial character. In what is this reward to consist, but in being associated with him in his kingdom? It is abundantly plain, from the following sayings of Holy Writ, that *regal dignity in connexion with Christ* is to constitute a part, at least, of the reward of the redeemed. 'When the Son of man shall sit on the throne of his glory, ye also shall SIT UPON TWELVE THRONES, judging the twelve

---

* The language of John iii. 2, 'We know that when he shall appear we shall be like him, *for we shall see him as he is*,' may be regarded as confirming the reasoning in the text.—ED.

tribes of Israel—They who receive abundance of grace and of the gift of righteousness, shall REIGN IN LIFE by one Jesus Christ—If we suffer we shall also REIGN WITH HIM—They shall REIGN for ever and ever—To him that overcometh will I grant to SIT WITH ME ON MY THRONE.'[22] According to the opinion we are combating, how are these expressions to be interpreted? The saints, agreeably to these Scriptures, are to reign in glory with Christ as Mediator: but, according to the opinion in question, Christ as Mediator is not to reign in glory at all, posterior to the consummation of all things. His reign is to terminate just when theirs is beginning. When theirs commences his ceases. As they ascend *their* throne, he abdicates *his*. When they are made kings to God, he is to be king no more.

Moreover, the perpetuation as well as the nature of the reward of the redeemed, supposes the continuance of the mediatorial dominion. To the continued efficacy of the Saviour's sacrifice, the continued enjoyment of the blessings it procured is to be ascribed. But continued efficacy and application suppose a continued administration, which can only be conducted by the Saviour himself. In the same manner as the suspension of that divine energy by which all things are upheld, would involve the annihilation of all things, so, it appears to us, would the suspension of the mediatorial administration involve the annihilation of all the eternal privileges of redemption. It is the prerogative of a king to reward his subjects; but the King of saints must not only confer, but perpetuate, the reward of his people.

[22] Matt. xix. 28; Rom. v. 17; 2 Tim. ii. 12; Rev. xxii. 5, v. 21.

In whatever this reward may be supposed to consist,—in dignity, honour, exaltation, fellowship, or blissful communications,—it will require to be continued, and this can be secured only by the administration of the King of glory.

To the redeemed before the throne, divine communications shall be constantly dealt out, through eternity. This is no way inconsistent with their being made perfect in glory at the last day. The perfection of creatures must never be identified with infinity. To be made perfect in knowledge, holiness, love, does not suppose the possession of these qualities in an infinite degree. Such a thing is impossible. It only means being free from the imperfections of the present state, while abundant room is left for progressive advancement in every attribute of intellectual and moral being. If angels advance, as we know they do, why may not the redeemed? The infinite character of the sources of eternal bliss admits of endless progression; while the necessary increase of capacity, arising from the exercise of all the faculties, renders progressive communication and advancement as unavoidable in itself as it is essential to the happiness of beings constituted as men are. We have every reason, therefore, to conclude, that there will be everlasting communications of light, life, power, love, and ineffable satisfaction, made to the souls of the redeemed. And through what channel shall these communications flow? Surely through the medium of the King of glory. New covenant blessings can flow only through the Mediator of the covenant. It is not enough that Jesus as Mediator has procured for his people the provisions of the covenant, and brought them in safety to heaven, but he shall administer to them for ever the fulness of his Father's house. 'The Lamb which is in the midst of the throne shall feed them, and shall lead them unto living fountains of waters.' 'The pure river of the water of life' proceeds out of the throne, not merely of God, but '*of the Lamb.*'[23]

It is surely reasonable to suppose that, as the heavenly state is so often spoken of as a kingdom, it must have a ruler. A kingdom necessarily supposes the existence of a king who exercises sovereign rule over it so long as it exists. But the character of the king must bear a relation to the nature of the kingdom. Now, the kingdom of heaven being a mediatorial kingdom, cannot be consistently supposed to be presided over by any but a mediatorial king. Accordingly, we find everlasting dominion ascribed to Christ as Mediator. Jude says, 'To the only wise God our Saviour, be glory, and majesty, and *dominion*, and power, both now and *for ever.*' Of the Prince of the kings of the earth, we find John the divine saying, 'To him be glory and *dominion* for *ever and ever.*' Every creature in heaven and on earth is, also, represented as shouting, 'Blessing, and honour, and glory, and power, be unto him that sitteth upon the throne, and unto the *Lamb for ever and ever.*'[24] It hence appears, that it is part of the regal administration of Christ in glory to bear rule over the whole kingdom of redeemed saints. Nor is there anything in this, incompatible with the dignity of their station, as exalted to the right hand of the majesty on high. They

[23] Rev. vii. 17, xxii. 1.   [24] Jude 25; Rev. i. 5, v. 13.

are still creatures, dependent creatures, whose very nature involves the idea of subjection. So far from its being derogatory to their exalted character to be subject to Messiah the Prince, it is their happiness to be placed under his mild and blissful reign. It is with ineffable delight that they bow before his throne, cast their crowns at his feet, and shout, in full and rapturous chorus, *Alleluia, for the Lord God omnipotent reigneth!* What a glorious reign! A King infinitely wise, holy, powerful, beneficent, divine: an administration righteous, pure, gentle, and unspeakably happy: and subjects, all of whom can appreciate the excellences of their Prince's character and the blessings of his administration, and among whose countless myriads there occurs not a single rebellious action, word, or wish! To do homage to their King is not only the delight, but the ceaseless occupation of the redeemed; and, without the perpetuity of his mediatorial dominion, there would be none to receive their ascriptions of praise, and gratitude, and honour, and glory.

On all these grounds, we may safely conclude that our Redeemer will never lay aside his mediatorial authority, never cease to act in the capacity of King of glory. Indeed all the mediatorial offices, would seem to be exercised in heaven;—the prophetical, in diffusing spiritual illumination; the sacerdotal, in securing the blessing and giving acceptance to the services of his saints; and the regal, in bearing rule, receiving homage, and administering reward to the children of the kingdom. The mediatorial reign is no parenthesis in the plan of God's moral government. It is rather the last and greatest of his works, the climax of his wise and holy administration.

The preceding remarks may help us, in some degree, to form an idea of the nature of the mediatorial administration in glory. Let us lay aside every prejudice that would prevent us from cordially rejoicing in a subject so delightful and animating. It cannot but be honouring to Christ to regard him as reigning for ever and ever; and it cannot but be pleasing, beyond all description, to his saints to think that they are never to lose sight of him as their King, never to cease to be his subjects, never but to yield him their grateful heart-felt homage. It cannot but rejoice them to know that they are to be ever under his rule, and that, even after they are taken to glory, they shall continue to behold him as the Lamb in the midst of the throne for ever and ever. What a prospect! How should it excite us to prepare for its being realised! Happy they who, having submitted themselves to him in time as King of saints, shall be eternally under his sway as King of glory!

CONCLUSION.

Let the children of Zion be joyful in their King! No language can more suitably express the state of emotion, which a proper review of the foregoing chapters would seem calculated to produce, in the breast of a saint. It is only a child of God, indeed, who can feel joyful at the contemplation of any view of the Saviour's character; but every such individual must find, in that which is here presented, abundant cause of grateful and complacent delight. The very place which the regal office of the Mediator holds in the economy of redemption; his glorious and divine qualifications; and the nature, extent, and perpetuity of his dominion, are all fitted to awaken this pious emotion. Authority is thus given to the messages of grace and salvation, by which dignity, force, and efficacy are so secured to them, that the messenger may well be hailed, in the language of entire satisfaction, 'How beautiful on the mountains are the feet of him that bringeth good tidings, that publisheth peace; that bringeth good tidings of good, that publisheth salvation; that saith unto Zion, Thy God reigneth!' The subject we have had under review, is well calculated, also, to furnish us with a criterion by which to test the character, both of churches and individuals. Professing Christian communities are deserving of esteem, in proportion as their principles and usages bring to light the mediatorial dominion of the Messiah; and persons are entitled to our regard, in proportion as they give evidence of taking pleasure in, and yielding obedience to, the Prince of life.

How admirably fitted, too, to yield abundant consolation! Are the children of God in want? It cannot but rejoice them to know, that the spiritual Joseph is ruler over all the land, has under his management the store-houses of nature and grace, and is ready to satisfy every longing soul with ample supplies of wisdom, pardon, holiness, joy, and strength. 'Be glad then, ye children of Zion, and rejoice in the Lord your God; for he hath given you the former rain moderately, and he will cause to come down for you the rain, the former rain, and the latter rain in the first month, and the floors shall be full of wheat, and the fats shall overflow with wine and oil.' Are they placed amid temptations and trials? No consideration, surely, can be more soothing, than that their Lord reigns, and has every circumstance that can occur, every enemy that can arise, completely under his control. 'God is our refuge and our strength, a very present help in trouble: therefore will not we fear, though the earth be removed, and though the mountains be carried into the midst of the sea; though the waters thereof roar and be troubled, though the mountains shake at the swelling thereof. There is a river, the streams whereof shall make glad the city of God, the holy place of the tabernacles of the

Most High. God is in the midst of her; she shall not be moved: God shall help her, and that right early.' Are they led to anticipate a future world? Through faith in the Lord God omnipotent who reigneth, they may confide, in being safely preserved amid the conflict of the present state, being carried successfully forward to full and final victory over every foe, and being introduced at last into all the joys of a never-ending triumph. 'Say ye to the daughter of Zion, Behold thy salvation cometh; behold his reward is with him, and his work before him. She shall be brought unto the King in raiment of needle work: the virgins, her companions that follow her, shall be brought unto thee. With gladness and rejoicing shall they be brought: they shall enter into the King's palace. Come, ye blessed of my Father, inherit the kingdom prepared for you from the foundation of the world!'

Where joy in Messiah the Prince, on such grounds, is felt, the children of Zion can be at no loss to find sufficient opportunities of giving expression to their feelings. By contending for the honours of his regal character; by embracing every opportunity of talking of his qualifications, rights, and acts; by speaking to others, like loyal subjects, of the glory of their Prince; by endeavouring to diffuse correct sentiments, respecting his kingdom and reign, among their friends and fellow-Christians; by standing up, in the midst of enemies, for his crown rights and royal prerogatives; by cherishing the memory, and imitating the example, of those who, in troublous times, contended earnestly for the regal honours of the Mediator, and, rather than forego one iota of his claims, took joyfully the spoiling of their goods, and magnanimously embraced the scaffold and the stake; by cultivating an enlightened zeal for the extension of Messiah's visible kingdom in the world; and, above all, by promptly submitting to his government, conscientiously observing his institutions, dutifully obeying his commands, and looking eagerly forward to being under his eternal reign in glory;—by such means as these, has every one full opportunity of giving decided expression to his complacent and grateful delight in the mediatorial dominion of Messiah the Prince. Let us see to it, that we improve this opportunity.

Nor let us be satisfied with anything short of an entire and implicit surrender of our hearts to King Jesus. It is possible for the subject of an earthly monarch to make a fair show of loyalty, openly to profess allegiance, and loudly to shout attachment, and yet, all the while, to be treating with contempt the institutions of his country, living in daily disobedience to the laws of the land, and perhaps secretly plotting the overthrow of the throne. The subject in profession may be a rebel at heart. In like manner, if we are not complying with the requirements of the Gospel; if we are not having it as our study to believe and repent; if we are not walking worthy of the vocation wherewith we are called; if we are not living holy and obedient lives, in all godliness and honesty; we are unequivocally saying with our actions, what we should perhaps shudder to pronounce with our lips, *We will not have this King to reign over us!* It is, alas! too common for men to shew a willingness to be interested in Christ as a *Priest*, while they obstinately refuse to submit to him as a *King*. They would gladly be *saved* from a coming wrath, but they are utterly indisposed to *obey*. Let them know that these things are inseparable; that the one cannot be had without the other; and that such as will not accept of Christ in *all* his characters, shall never obtain an interest in him in *any*. If we are not the subjects, we are the enemies of this King; and, if his subjects have reason to rejoice, his enemies have reason to tremble. *Thine arrows are sharp in the heart of the King's enemies.* Let us reflect, whose authority it is we despise; whose institutions we contemn; whose laws we disobey. They are his, who has all power in heaven and in earth; who can break us with his rod of iron, and dash us in pieces like a potter's vessel; who can crush us in our impotent rebellion with one stroke of his power, and with one breath of his mouth can bid us away into never-ending ruin. 'He must reign till all his enemies be made his footstool. Those mine enemies which would not that I should reign over them, bring hither and slay them before me.' These are not empty threats. They are the words of him who cannot lie. They shall be fulfilled, to the utter dismay of all who refuse to submit to the sceptre of the Messiah.

O thou benign Prince! enable us to escape this fearful doom; put forth thine efficacious grace in our hearts. Make us a willing people in the day of thy power. May we raise, instead of the shriek of misery, the hymn of triumph, *Alleluia! salvation, and glory, and honour, and power, unto the Lord our God. Alleluia! or the Lord God omnipotent reigneth!* We hail thee, Sovereign of our hearts; we abjure for ever all other lords who have had dominion over us, and declare from the heart, WE HAVE NO KING BUT JESUS!

Μονῳ τῳ Θεῳ δοξα.

www.ingramcontent.com/pod-product-compliance
Lightning Source LLC
Chambersburg PA
CBHW031954300426
44117CB00008B/755